Henry Parry Lidden

Easter in St. Paul's : sermons bearing chiefly on the Resurrection of our Lord

Volume 1

Henry Parry Lidden

Easter in St. Paul's : sermons bearing chiefly on the Resurrection of our Lord
Volume 1

ISBN/EAN: 9783741196065

Manufactured in Europe, USA, Canada, Australia, Japa

Cover: Foto ©Lupo / pixelio.de

Manufactured and distributed by brebook publishing software (www.brebook.com)

Henry Parry Lidden

Easter in St. Paul's : sermons bearing chiefly on the Resurrection of our Lord

Works by the same Author.

Second Edition. Royal 32mo. 2s. 6d.

PRIVATE PRAYERS. By Rev. E. B. PUSEY, D.D. Edited, with a Preface, by H. P. LIDDON, D.D.

Second Edition. Large Type. 24mo. 1s.

PRAYERS FOR A YOUNG SCHOOLBOY. By Rev. E. B. PUSEY, D.D. With a Preface by H. P. LIDDON, D.D.

Crown 8vo. 7s. 6d.

OF THE FIVE WOUNDS OF THE HOLY CHURCH. By ANTONIO ROSMINI. Edited, with an Introduction, by H. P. LIDDON, D.D.

Cheap Edition, Revised. Small 8vo. 2s. 6d.; or in Paper Cover, 1s. 6d.

SOME ELEMENTS OF RELIGION. Lent Lectures.

The Crown 8vo (Fourth) Edition, 5s., may still be had.

Eighth Edition, Revised. Crown 8vo. 5s.

SERMONS PREACHED BEFORE THE UNIVERSITY OF OXFORD. First Series. 1859-1868.

Third Edition. Crown 8vo. 5s.

SERMONS PREACHED BEFORE THE UNIVERSITY OF OXFORD. Second Series. 1868-1882.

Eleventh Edition, Revised. Crown 8vo. 5s.

THE DIVINITY OF OUR LORD AND SAVIOUR JESUS CHRIST. Being the Bampton Lectures for 1866.

DIE GOTTHEIT UNSERES HERRN UND HEILANDES JESU CHRISTI. Acht vorlesungen gehalten von H. P. LIDDON, Domherr und Professor an der Universität Oxford. Autorisirte Uebersetzung der 7. Auflage. Mit einem Vorwort von Ph. Fr. Mader, deutscher Pfarrer in Nizza. Basel Bahnmaier's Verlag (C. Dethoff. 1883).

Second Edition. 8vo. 2s. 6d.

WALTER KERR HAMILTON, BISHOP OF SALISBURY. A Sketch.

Crown 8vo. 3s. 6d.

REPORT OF PROCEEDINGS AT THE REUNION CONFERENCE, held at Bonn, September 1874. With a Preface by H. P. LIDDON, D.D.

WORKS BY THE REV. DR. LIDDON.—*Continued.*

Crown 8vo. 3s. 6d.
REPORT OF PROCEEDINGS AT THE RE-UNION CONFERENCE OF 1875, with Preface by H. P. LIDDON. [London: B. M. PICKERING.]

Fourth Edition. With Portrait. Large Type. 24mo. 2s. 6d.
A MANUAL FOR THE SICK; with other Devotions.
By LANCELOT ANDREWES, D.D., sometime Lord Bishop of Winchester.

A Father in Christ: A Sermon preached in St. Paul's Cathedral, at the Consecration of the Right Reverend Edward King, D.D., Lord Bishop of Lincoln, and of the Right Reverend Edward Henry Bickersteth, D.D., Lord Bishop of Exeter, on the Feast of St. Mark the Evangelist, 1885. With a Notice of the Rev. Dr. Hatch's Paper in the *Contemporary Review*, June 1885. Third Edition. 8vo. 1s.

Edward Bouverie Pusey: A Sermon preached in St. Margaret's Church, Prince's Road, Liverpool, in Aid of the Pusey Memorial Fund, on Sunday, January 20, 1884. Second Edition. 8vo. 1s.

The Recovery of St. Thomas: A Sermon preached in St. Paul's Cathedral on the Second Sunday after Easter, April 23, 1882. With a Prefatory Note on the late Mr. Darwin. Second Edition. 8vo. 1s.

Phœbe in London: A Sermon preached at the Parish Church of Kensington on the Second Sunday after Trinity, June 10, 1877, for the Parochial Mission Women Association. 8vo. 1s.

Bishop Wilberforce: A Sermon preached at the Parish Church of Graffham, Sussex, on its Re-opening after Restoration, Nov. 2, 1875. 8vo. 1s.

Love and Knowledge: A Sermon preached in King's College Chapel, at its Inauguration, on the Twenty-second Sunday after Trinity, 1873. 8vo. 1s.

The One Salvation: A Sermon preached in St. Paul's Cathedral on the Fifth Sunday after Easter, 1873, at the Anniversary Service of the Bishop of London's Fund. 8vo. 1s.

The Moral Groundwork of Clerical Training: A Sermon preached at the Anniversary Festival of Cuddesden College on Tuesday, June 10, 1873. 8vo. 1s.

St. Paul's and London: A Sermon preached at St. Paul's Cathedral on the Fourth Sunday after Epiphany, 1871. 8vo. 6d.

The Day of Work: A Sermon preached in St. Paul's Cathedral on Sunday, August 6, 1871, being the Morrow of the Funeral of the Very Rev. H. L. Mansel, D.D., Dean of St. Paul's. 8vo. 1s.

The Purchas Judgment: A Letter of Acknowledgment to the Right Hon. Sir J. D. Coleridge, one of the Lords of Her Majesty's Most Honourable Privy Council; together with a Letter to the Writer by the Rev. E. B. Pusey, D.D., Eastertide, 1871. 8vo. 1s.

The Purchas Judgment: A Letter to the Right Hon. and Right Rev. the Lord Bishop of London by the two Senior Canons of St. Paul's Cathedral, June 1, 1871. 8vo. 1s.

Easter in St. Paul's

Easter in St. Paul's

SERMONS
BEARING CHIEFLY ON THE RESURRECTION OF
OUR LORD

IN TWO VOLUMES
VOL. I

By H. P. LIDDON, D.D., D.C.L.
CANON OF ST. PAUL'S

Surrexit Dominus verè.   Alleluia

RIVINGTONS
WATERLOO PLACE, LONDON
MDCCCLXXXV

THE VERY REVEREND

RICHARD WILLIAM CHURCH, D.C.L.

DEAN OF ST. PAUL'S

WHOSE TENURE OF HIS HIGH OFFICE HAS BEEN

NOT LESS A BLESSING TO LONDON

THAN A CONSTANT SOURCE OF THE TRUEST HAPPINESS

TO THOSE OVER WHOM HE MORE

IMMEDIATELY PRESIDES.

PREFACE.

THESE Sermons are published in deference to the wishes of many persons to whom from time to time they have been useful. As here arranged, they can make very little pretence to system; and, from the nature of the case, they often repeat each other, in substance if not in words. Some of them, however, are bound up with the formation or recovery of religious convictions in a manner and degree which exert a first claim on the author's consideration; and this has made him unwilling to omit passages, or even entire discourses, which a true literary judgment would have proscribed.

It ought perhaps to be added that the 35th Sermon was preached in St. Paul's, at the invitation of the late Dean Milman, and at a date when the preacher had not become a member of the Chapter.

If this volume should prove to be at all generally acceptable, the author might hereafter publish other Sermons preached during his Residences at St. Paul's, since February 1870, in the months of August and December. Of these, the latter would relate, for the most part, to our Lord's First and Second Coming. The former would deal with a wider range of subjects, although generally such as are suggested, however incidentally, by the Services of the Church.

3 AMEN COURT, ST. PAUL'S,
  St. James's Day, 1885.

CONTENTS.

SERMON I.

THE IMPORTANCE OF THE RESURRECTION.

1 COR. xv. 19.

If in this life only we have hope in Christ, we are of all men most miserable. 1

Preached at St. Paul's on Low Sunday, April 1, 1883.

SERMON II.

THE EMPTY TOMB.

ST. JOHN xx. 13.

And they say unto her, Woman, why weepest thou? She saith unto them, Because they have taken away my Lord, and I know not where they have laid Him. 16

Preached at St. Paul's on Easter Day, April 1, 1877.

SERMON III.

CHRISTIANITY WITHOUT THE RESURRECTION.

1 COR. xv. 14.

If Christ be not risen, then is our preaching vain, and your faith is also vain. 34

Preached at St. Paul's on Low Sunday, April 8, 1877.

SERMON IV.

CHRISTIANITY WITHOUT THE RESURRECTION.

1 Cor. xv. 14.

If Christ be not risen, then is our preaching vain, and your faith is also vain. 51

Preached at St. Paul's on Easter Day, April 13, 1879.

SERMON V.

GROUNDS OF FAITH IN THE RESURRECTION.

1 St. John v. 6.

It is the Spirit That beareth witness. . . . 67

Preached at St. Paul's on Low Sunday, April 20, 1879.

SERMON VI.

THE RESURRECTION INEVITABLE.

Acts ii. 24.

Whom God hath raised up, having loosed the pains of death: because it was not possible that He should be holden of it. . 83

Preached at St. Paul's on Easter Day, April 16, 1876.

SERMON VII.

THE REALITY OF THE RESURRECTION.

St. Luke xxiv. 39.

Behold My Hands and My Feet, that it is I Myself: handle Me, and see; for a spirit hath not flesh and bones, as ye see Me have. 103

Preached at St. Paul's on Low Sunday, April 12, 1885.

SERMON VIII.
OUR LORD'S RESUMPTION OF LIFE.
St. John x. 18.

I have power to take it again. 120

Preached at St. Paul's on Easter Day, April 17, 1881.

SERMON IX.
THE POWER OF RECOVERY.
Psalm cxviii. 17.

I shall not die, but live, and declare the works of the Lord. 134

Preached at St. Paul's on Easter Day, April 13, 1884.

SERMON X.
THE LIVING NOT AMONG THE DEAD.
St. Luke xxiv. 5, 6.

Why seek ye the living among the dead? He is not here, but is risen. 152

Preached at St. Paul's on Easter Day, April 13, 1873.

SERMON XI.
THE POWER OF THE RESURRECTION.
Phil. iii. 10.

That I may know Him, and the power of His Resurrection. . 163

Preached at St. Paul's on Easter Day, April 5, 1885.

SERMON XII.

EASTER HOPES.

1 St. Peter i. 3.

Blessed be the God and Father of our Lord Jesus Christ, Which according to His abundant mercy hath begotten us again unto a lively hope by the Resurrection of Jesus Christ from the dead. . 180

Preached at St. Paul's on Low Sunday, April 7, 1872.

SERMON XIII.

EASTER JOY.

Psalm xxx. 12.

Thou hast turned my heaviness into joy: Thou hast put off my sackcloth, and girded me with gladness. . . . 196

Preached at St. Paul's on Easter Day, April 9, 1882.

SERMON XIV.

THE UNDYING ONE.

Rom. vi. 9.

Christ being raised from the dead dieth no more. . . . 208

Preached at St. Paul's on Easter Day, April 5, 1874.

SERMON XV.

THE DAY OF DAYS.

Psalm cxviii. 24.

This is the day which the Lord hath made: we will rejoice and be glad in it. 226

Preached at St. Paul's on Easter Day, April 21, 1878.

SERMON XVI.
EASTER CONSOLATIONS.
St. Luke xxiv. 17.

And He said unto them, What manner of communications are these that ye have one to another, as ye walk, and are sad? . . 241

Preached at St. Paul's on Low Sunday, April 24, 1881.

SERMON XVII.
THE EMMAUS ROAD.
St. Luke xxiv. 32.

Did not our heart burn within us, while He talked with us by the way, and while He opened to us the scriptures? . . . 256

Preached at St. Paul's on Low Sunday, April 20, 1884.

SERMON XVIII.
JESUS ON THE EVENING OF EASTER DAY.
St. Luke xxiv. 39.

Behold My Hands and My Feet, that it is I Myself: handle Me, and see; for a spirit hath not flesh and bones, as ye see Me have. 271

Preached at St. Paul's on Low Sunday, April 4, 1875.

SERMON I.

THE IMPORTANCE OF THE RESURRECTION.

1 Cor. xv. 19.

If in this life only we have hope in Christ, we are of all men most miserable.

ST. PAUL, in this great passage, makes Christianity answer with its life for the truth of our Lord's Resurrection from the dead. "If Christ be not risen, then is our preaching vain, your faith is also vain."[a] He would not write in this way unless he had in view a temper of mind which made a statement thus explicit and startling not less than necessary.

The Greek converts at Corinth entertained objections to the Resurrection which were suggested by the philosophical habits of thought of their earlier, unconverted life. They could not make out to themselves a satisfactory physical theory of the Resurrection. "But some man will say, How are the dead raised up? and with what body do they come?"[b] St. Paul answers these questions so far as the occasion required; and he then goes on to a point of even graver importance. For these Greeks, in their airy, light-hearted, careless manner, would seem

[a] 1 Cor. xv. 14. [b] 1 Cor. xv. 35.

to have suggested that it did not matter very much whether the Resurrection were true or not; that the Resurrection, however interesting, was not the central feature in the Christian creed; that even if man is not to rise hereafter, and if Christ did not rise on the third day from the dead, Christianity has already done, and will yet do, very much for man in this life to subdue and chasten his passions, to sweeten his temper, to make duty welcome and sorrow bearable, and the relations of men with each other kindly and unselfish. These Greek converts, who had as yet so much to learn about Christianity, would suggest that the Resurrection was a matter of merely intellectual interest, lying outside the real, beneficent and moral action of Christianity: so that even if the Apostle who preached it was wrong, and if they who questioned it were right, there was no reason for discomfort as to the claims or worth of Christianity as a whole. Christianity was really, they thought, independent of the question, and would survive it.

This is the position upon which St. Paul is making war;—with which, in fact, he will make no terms whatever. He will not allow that the question of our Lord's Resurrection, and of the general Resurrection, which is attested by it, is for Christianity anything less than vital. It is not that he himself is, after all, only a Jew in Christian guise, who cannot enter into the subtle and delicate analysis, to which Greek thought must fain submit all subjects which come before it. It is not that as a keen dialectician he enjoys the intellectual pleasure of forcing men to look their premises in the face; of making them accept unforeseen and possibly unwelcome conclusions, to which they had by implication committed themselves. It is that, for him, Christianity is bound up with the Resurrection as with a fact inseparable from its existence.

He cannot detach Christianity from this truth, after the fashion of those off-hand Corinthians; if the Resurrection goes, Christianity goes too; it vanishes in its essence, and as a whole. A Christ who did not rise is not the Illuminator, or the Redeemer of men, and the world is still without deliverance from its darkness and its sin.[a] And a reason for this is that Christianity, as St. Paul thinks of it, is a great venture.[b] It is a venture staked upon the eternal future. It bids men lay out their time, and dispose of their lives, and order their daily action[c] on the supposition,—the tremendous supposition, which it treats as certain,—that this life is but a preface, and a very short preface, to another, and an endless life, that will follow. And the warrant for doing this is that Christ has risen from the dead,[d] and has thus shown us by a demonstration addressed to sense not only or chiefly that Death is not the end, but that He is Lord of the world beyond the grave;[e] that He has the keys of hell and of death.[f] But if this warrant is unsubstantial; if this venture is unwarranted; if in this life only we have hope in Christ; we have indeed made a capital mistake, and are of all men most miserable.

I.

What then is the hope respecting a future which we owe to our Risen Lord?

Is it the hope that we shall exist for ever? Is our continuous existence hereafter altogether dependent upon faith in and communion with the Risen Christ? Shall we be annihilated, if we die out of His grace, and hear His sentence of condemnation passed upon us?

[a] 1 Cor. xv. 14, 17.
[b] 1 Cor. xv. 30-32.
[c] 1 Cor. xv. 32-34.
[d] 1 Cor. xv. 20.
[e] 1 Cor. xv. 25, 26.
[f] Rev. i. 18.

No, brethren, this is not what the Apostle meant. Our immortality is not a gift of the Redeemer; it is the gift of the Creator. It is just as much part of our being as are any of the limbs of our bodies, or as is reason, imagination, or any other of the natural endowments of our minds.

Observe that belief in a future state does not begin with Christianity. It is as deeply rooted in the human soul as belief in God. It is found among mankind, here in considerable strength, there faint and indistinct. But, in some sense, it is wellnigh universal. The honour so widely paid to the graves of ancestors is a natural expression of belief in their survival after death. Those tombs in Etruria, upon which the earliest art of Italy lavished its best, did not merely mean that the dead lived on in the memory of survivors; but that in the belief of survivors, they were actually living in another world, and had, according to the rude notions of the time, to be honoured and provided for. It was this belief which made an ancient Egyptian deem the due embalming and preparation of his mummy the most important thing that could happen to him: it was this belief which built the Pyramids, and which conferred its strange power on the ancient Egyptian priesthood, who were less active as ministers to the living than as the accredited guardians of the dead: it was faith in immortality which rendered the Greek mysteries of Eleusis so welcome to those upon whom the old popular religion had lost its power, and which made great thinkers, such as Plato, at least in their higher moods, capable of thoughts and aspirations which Christians, in all ages, have welcomed as almost anticipating their own.

For without a Revelation, man suspects, if he does not certainly know, himself to be an immortal being. He has this idea of immortality in his mind: whence did he get it?

He sees around him the incessant energy of death: he knows that he is on the road to die; he calls himself in nearly all the known languages of the race, a mortal; as if this predestination to death were his governing characteristic. And yet he has within him a consciousness of which he cannot divest himself, that he is also something that will not die with the death of his body. My brethren, human reason can satisfy itself that the soul is a distinct thing from the body. The human body is made up of a number of organs, and each of these organs of an indefinite number of particles physically distinct from each other; and as we gaze on the decomposition of a body after death, we see before our eyes the separation between these always separable particles gradually establishing itself. Whereas that in us which thinks, which loves, which resolves, is certainly and absolutely one and the same indivisible thing. The spiritual force in us which wills, is also that which feels, and that which thinks; there are not in us three beings, thinking, feeling, and resolving, but one being or person conscious of its indestructible unity while performing these several operations. Thus the soul knows itself to be distinct from the body, by this consciousness of being indivisibly one; but it also knows this by its consciousness of possessing permanent identity. The material of the body is always changing; each day it is losing some particles, it is assimilating others; the elements of which it is composed are constantly disappearing and as constantly being renewed, like the volume of water which fills the bed of a great river. They say that in seven years, every particle of a single body will have changed. And although the form, the stature, the countenance remain, yet, with time, these also are modified; man loses the outward semblance of his former self. But how different is it with the soul! Whatever may be the vicissitudes of its secret history, whatever its sorrows or its aspirations, whatever its intolerable burdens, or its buoyant hopes; whether it be contemplating the present, or recalling the past, or endeavouring to pierce the veil of the future, it knows itself to be ever the same; nay, this persistent sameness of which it is thus conscious in the midst of change, is the very basis of its idea of time. Thus it is clear that the causes which bring about the dissolution of a divisible and ever-changing organism like the human body would not touch the existence of an indivisible and permanently identical being like the soul: and that, although, as Kant remarks, the soul might conceivably perish by a gradual languor or extinction of its vital force, or as others have suggested by a fiat of the Almighty Creator, there is no producible reason for thinking that it will do so. On the other hand, since the death of the body cannot be presumed to affect it, there are strong reasons for anticipating its enduring life. In nothing do we more nearly touch the consciousness of immortality than in our sense of carrying within us much that never attains completeness here. The more we reflect upon the capacity of the different gifts and powers of the mind, and upon their imperfect satisfaction in this present state; the more we become interested in adding to what we know, and in trying to discover a purpose in it; the more we make efforts to attain moral excellence, and find, in doing so, that we have become conscious of entering upon new spheres of existence which before were hidden from us,—the more certain we are that we must live hereafter. In short, we have within us an appetite for or sense of the Infinite; and it never can be satisfied within the narrow bounds of our earthly existence. Above all, deeply implanted in our nature is the idea of justice and of duty in relation to it. Justice is wholly unsatisfied within the limits of this earthly existence; and as we acquire a stronger sense of its certainty and its imperativeness as a law of the universe, and of the Being Who made and Who rules us, so do we become increasingly certain that there must be a future state in which the demands of justice will be satisfied.

II.

We look forward then, as reasonable beings, to immortality. But to what sort of immortality does this anticipation point?

Is it the immortality of the race? Does the individual really perish at death, and ought he, if he be humble and unselfish, to be satisfied with knowing that humanity survives? No; this is not the immortality to which we men look forward. The immortality of the race! Is it anything more than a phrase? What does it mean? It means the succession, indefinitely prolonged, of a countless number of totally distinct beings of a single type. Each single being dies: but the type, the resemblance between them, survives. How is this shadowy survival entitled to the name of immortality? A race of beings does not live, apart from the individuals which compose it; and therefore when we talk of its immortality we are the victims of a phrase of rhetoric. Only a person,—the reflecting and resolving centre of individual life,—can be properly immortal; the indefectibility of the type of animal to which he belongs is no more to him than would be the imperishableness of the earth or the sky, or the indestructibility of matter, if indeed these expressions could represent anything real.

Is it then an immortality of fame? Is the yearning of a human soul to be satisfied by the knowledge that after death its virtues will live in the memory of posterity?

But how many in each generation can hope to share in such an immortality as this? How many of us are called to positions, to actions, to sacrifices, of such importance that they command the attention of more than a handful of men? How many of us will have a place in the public memory and, as the phrase goes, live in history? For most of us life is made up of little duties,—very necessary to be performed, often performed with effort and suffering,—but of so humble a kind that they hardly have a place in our own memories from day to day, much less in those of others. The Gospel indeed says that these duties are the scene of our probation no less truly than are the historical actions of kings and statesmen. But if there is no life after death, and the only immortality is that of fame, what is to become of them, that is, what is to become of this kind of immortality in the case of the greater part of the human race? Is not this immortality only a perpetuation of inequalities which disfigure our earthly life, and of which a future of absolute truth and justice would know nothing? Does it not consecrate all the successful ambitions, all the unworthy or hypocritical careers which have made a noise in the world, while it condemns virtues whose only crime is that they have been secret? Have we not here a reversal of that saying of our Lord's, which pierces so deep into the conscience of mankind, that one day "the last shall be first, and the first last"?[a]

Is it then an immortality of our good deeds? To say that a man lives in his good actions may be Christian language: it is said, we know, of the dead who die in the Lord, that "their works do follow them."[b] To this day the saints of the Bible history live in the works which are recorded of them. Even the smallest act when in-

[a] St. Matt. xx. 16.   [b] Rev. xiv. 13.

stinct with noble motive may, like Magdalene's anointing the Feet of the Redeemer, endure after the lapse of intervening ages, as a power in human life. But there are actions in all true and saintly lives which are known only to God, and which, so far as we can see, have no certain consequences here on earth. There are lives of unwitnessed, unmentioned, patient suffering; there are good deeds, carefully disguised even from the suspicion of those who benefit by them. Christians know that these are not lost; that they leave indelible traces on the soul of the agent; that they are recorded before God. But if the soul perishes at death what becomes of them? in what sense are they immortal?

And are our good deeds our only deeds? Have not our evil deeds—some of them—consequences; and do these consequences punish the agent, if he really perishes at death? What shall we say of writings which destroy faith in virtue and reverence for truth? or of acts, which make the lives of others miserable, or which cannot be recalled without the contagion which is inseparable even from their memory? The writer, the agent, has ceased to exist, so we are told, at death. To say that he is punished by the actions which thus survive him is to toy with language. Others than he are punished: the innocent whom he has defamed; the believing whom he has robbed of their hope; the relations whom he has condemned to an association with infamy; the young or the unprotected whom he has first introduced to the knowledge of evil. No; the immortality of our actions is not an immortality which satisfies the yearnings of the heart of man,—since this yearning is based always and especially on its sense of justice.

There are many well-intentioned people who think to honour our Lord and Saviour by referring altogether to

Him both the belief in and the gift of immortality. May God bless them for their motive, and save them from their error! The truth of immortality is taught us, at least indistinctly, by our natural reason: the fact of our immortality is part of the natural endowment with which we issue, each one of us, from the hands of the Creator. Do not let us think to honour the teaching of Revelation by depreciating that of reason; or to exalt the blessings of Redemption at the expense of God's love and bounty as displayed in creating us. Our knowledge of immortality is older than the Gospel; and our possession of it is independent of the work of Jesus Christ.

What then is the hope in Christ, which redeems Christian life from the failure and misery alluded to in the text? It is the hope, that through His precious Death and His glorious Resurrection, our inevitable immortality will be an immortality of bliss.

Of course, it is not denied that He has "brought life and immortality to light."[a] For multitudes before He came it was a vague and dreary anticipation: He has made it a blessed and welcome certainty. He has familiarised us with the idea, that all live unto God; that belief in God, as the God of the ancient dead, carries with it belief in their permanent individual existence;[b] and He has further taught the future resurrection of the Body, as completing the life beyond the grave.[c] He thus has altogether removed the question of life after death from the region of speculation into that of certainty, founded upon experience; since when He rose from death and presented Himself to the senses of those who saw Him, He was Himself but the first-fruits from the dead.[d] But the hope

[a] 2 Tim. i. 10.　　　[b] St. Luke xx. 37, 38.
[c] St. John vi. 40.　　　[d] 1 Cor. xv. 20.

in Christ is something more than this conviction; it is the hope of a *blessed* immortality. This He has won for us by His one Perfect and Sufficient Sacrifice on the Cross, whereby our sins are blotted out, and the grace of His Spirit and His New Nature is secured to us in His Church, so as to fit us, by sanctification, for His eternal presence. That His Cross has this virtue is proved to us by His Resurrection from the dead; that He lives in order that we may live also,[a] is the basis of our hope in Him.[b] Apart from this conviction, Christianity is indeed a worthless dream; the efforts and sacrifices of the Christian life are wasted; we are the victims of a great delusion; we are of all men most miserable.

III.

There are signs in our day that faith in a future after death is less taken for granted than was the case a generation ago.

One of these signs is the increased number of suicides all over Europe. As to the fact, I fear, there can be no question. There are not merely the pathetic suicides of the very wretched, who in a paroxysm of suffering close their eyes to the desperate nature of their attempt to escape from it: there are the suicides of votaries of pleasure, who having exhausted all the faculties of enjoyment, are, as one has said, sated with life, and would throw it away like a toy which has ceased to please. Suicides like these are the crimes of old civilisations: they are almost unknown in the young fresh life of a nation or a race. They mean, that the opportunities for enjoyment have in certain classes outrun the power to enjoy; that wealth, luxury, splendour, which seem so enviable to those who do not share them, only make the

[a] St. John xiv. 19.   [b] Rom. viii. 10, 11.

sense of moral lassitude and fatigue more intolerable, when they no longer please; only augment the desire to escape from life,—with as little pain as may be,—into an existence with new sensations, or, if it might be, into annihilation. Suicides are only possible, when through continuous enervation of the moral nature, the awful realities of immortality have been lost sight of: and their increase is a serious symptom of what must be passing in large classes of minds.

While the hours of last year, 1882, were running out, an event of European importance, as we now know, was taking place. The most powerful man in France was dying. And one of the first events in this present year upon which the eyes of Europe were fixed was Gambetta's funeral. Everything was done that could be done by a grateful country to give it political importance. The State paid the expenses, and nothing on the same scale of splendour and publicity had been seen in Paris since Morny was buried. And, among other noticeable circumstances in connection with it, *this* was especially noticeable;—that throughout the proceedings, nothing was said or done to imply that man lives after death, or that God, or the religion which binds us to Him, are entitled to notice.

It could not be but that such a circumstance would command much and anxious attention, from Christians as well as from the opponents of Christianity. The latter, in this country as elsewhere, insisted upon its significance. It was the first instance, they said, of a total disregard of profession of faith in a future at the funeral of a European politician of the first rank. Even Robespierre had been eager to proclaim his belief in immortality: and many a man in high position who, like Talleyrand, during life might have repudiated the claims of religion, had welcomed its ministers when on the bed of death, and had been interred amid the words of hope, the prayers, the benedictions, which are so dear to Christians. Of the religious worth of this tardy or posthumous honour to religion, I am not now speaking:—Gambetta's funeral may have been, in a terrible sense, sincere. But the significant thing is that such an event should have been possible. It meant a great deal first and immediately for France, and then, more remotely, for Europe. It showed that, in our day, on an occasion of national importance, a great people in the heart of Christendom could officially look death in the face, and ignore everything that follows it.

Much seems to show that in the modern world two entirely different beliefs about man are confounded with each other.

According to one of these, man is really only the highest of the beasts that perish. He is much more accomplished than any of the other beasts; he has somehow developed qualities and capacities which enable him to master them; he occupies a position in Nature, and makes her subserve his purposes, after a fashion to which they can lay no pretension. But in the end it is much the same with him as with them. If they vanish utterly with the decay and death of their bodies, so does he; and his case only differs from theirs in that extinction is more pathetic when there is so much more to lose and to deplore. As the old sceptic in Ecclesiastes says: "That which befalleth the sons of men befalleth beasts; as the one dieth, so dieth the other; yea, they have all one breath; so that a man hath no preeminence above a beast: for all is vanity. All go unto one place; for all are of the dust, and all turn to dust again."[a]

[a] Eccles. iii. 19, 20.

Opposed to this idea of man, as an accomplished animal which perishes outright at death, is the Christian belief that man differs from the lower creatures altogether, except in the fact, that he owns a body, which is governed, chemically and physiologically, by the same laws as theirs. For man, his body, instead of being the substantive and central part of his being, is an appendage. Man is really a spirit with a body attached to it; a body in which he works out his probation here, and which, after parting with it at death, he will receive in a spiritualised form hereafter. The soul of man no more dies when it leaves the body, than the musical genius which makes that organ do so much to aid the devotion of God's people in this Cathedral forfeits its knowledge and its skill when it ceases to touch the key-board. In man the central or substantive feature is the soul; and of the life of the soul, this earthly life in the body is but a very small portion indeed. It is related to what follows, as is a brief preface to a very voluminous book: it throws light on what is to come; it is relatively insignificant. "The things which are seen are temporal: the things which are not seen are eternal."[a]

And Easter is the season at which Christians should rekindle in themselves, and if it may be, through intercourse, in others, this sense of immortality. If man is not immortal, human life is a very poor thing indeed. But Christian life is more than a misfortune; it is a signal mistake. It was the rule of an excellent person now with Christ, before he left his room every morning to say this, among other prayers: "Grant, O Lord, that in all my works and words this day, I may never forget eternity." Let us also endeavour to cherish and extend the thoughts and resolutions which befit beings who must exist for

[a] 2 Cor. iv. 18.

ever. What are our prayers but the language of immortal spirits addressed to One Who has neither beginning nor end? What are our friends, our acquaintances, our enemies, if unhappily we have any, but beings, who like ourselves have before them an endless existence, and in whose destiny He Who has redeemed us by His Blood has an interest not less than in our own? What are our actions—be they, according to human standards, great or insignificant—but steps which our wills are taking, daily, hourly, in whatever direction, towards a future which ought to be for Christians the subject of all their best hopes? "The hope which is laid up for us in heaven"[*]— let us think well of it. Let us have the courage—I had almost said, the logic—of our faith. Let us remember that time is short, and that eternity is long.

[*] Col. i. 5.

SERMON II.

THE EMPTY TOMB.

ST. JOHN XX. 13.

And they say unto her, Woman, why weepest thou? She saith unto them, Because they have taken away my Lord, and I know not where they have laid Him.

THE tears of St. Mary Magdalene before the empty sepulchre of Jesus Christ are at first sight out of keeping with the exulting joy of the Easter festival. Doubtless, as the wise man says, there is a time for everything.[a] By common consent, mirth is unseemly at a funeral, and mourning at a wedding. No good Christian would think of giving an entertainment on Good Friday; and Easter Day, if it be anything, is a day of joy. It is the brightest, happiest day in the whole Christian year, for every sincere worshipper of Jesus Christ. This day reminds the Christian of the foundation fact which proves that his creed is true—the Resurrection of Jesus Christ. This day proclaims that the future life, for which Christians live, is a solemn and certified reality, warranted by the risen life of their Lord and Saviour. Above all, this is the day of Christ's triumph over His enemies, over the enemies of man, over sin and death.

[a] Eccles. iii. 1.

As the Christian has sympathised with the mental and bodily sufferings of his Lord, so now he rejoices in his Lord's victory; he rejoices because it is Jesus Christ Who triumphs. The song of Moses is also his song. "I will sing unto the Lord, for He hath triumphed gloriously."[a] On such a day as this, if ever, "the voice of joy and health is in the dwellings of the righteous;" because "the Right hand of the Lord bringeth mighty things to pass: the Right hand of the Lord hath the pre-eminence: the Right hand of the Lord bringeth mighty things to pass."[b]

Thus it is that on Easter Day the tears of Mary Magdalene are at first sight inappropriate—almost intrusive. They seem to traverse and check the free flow of joy which is the prerogative grace and privilege of the festival. They recall the sadness of the Passion, of the Burial; the bewildering uncertainties and keen anguish of Good Friday. And yet let us be sure that they do not appear here in the inspired accounts of the Resurrection, and in the Easter services of the Church, without good reason. Probably in our present state of existence it is impossible to surrender ourselves unreservedly to one mood of feeling. No earthly sorrow is unrelieved by some ray of brightness, no joy is without the shadow of some threatening or attendant grief. It might seem that we require the foil if we are to do justice to the positive feeling of the moment; just as a landscape which is relieved by the alternate play of light and shadow, is more welcome to our natural eyesight than that which lies under the uniformly splendid but oppressive glare of a southern sun.

Tears, they say, are wont to be unreasonable. They may be, sometimes. But Mary Magdalene knew quite well why she wept before the sepulchre. The angels "say

---

[a] Exod. xv. 1.   [b] Ps. cxviii. 15, 16.

unto her, Woman, why weepest thou? She saith unto them, Because they have taken away my Lord, and I know not where they have laid Him." There is reason in the tears of Mary: they show her strong and tender love. The most reasonable of all possible forms of love was the love which she had for the perfect moral Being, our Lord Jesus Christ. Her tears express her bitter disappointment. She had come to find Him, and He was gone. "They have taken away my Lord." Moreover they imply her longing for more knowledge about Him than she has as yet; they are the earnest of her perseverance. "I know not where they have laid Him." Let us take these points in order.

I.

The affection of Mary Magdalene for Jesus Christ was not of yesterday. He had rescued her from sin and shame; He had cast out of her seven devils.[a] His love had not fallen, this time, upon an ungrateful heart. While He sat in the house of the Pharisee, who had forgotten the ordinary duties of Eastern hospitality, the poor penitent pressed into His presence, that she might anoint His feet with her choicest and her best, and wipe them with the hair on which in the days of her vanity she had most prided herself.[b] When He hung dying on Calvary, she was there, between the desolated mother and the beloved disciple; she had bent down in love and sorrow at the foot of the cross.[c] And now early on the day of the Resurrection she is first at the sepulchre; "her eyes prevent the night-watches, that she may be occupied"[d] in her service of love; her hands are

[a] St. Mark xvi. 9.   [b] St. Luke vii. 38.
[c] St. John xix. 25.   [d] Ps. cxix. 148.

laden with spices and ointments, that she may do the last sad honours to Him Who still had the first place in her heart.

Let us remark, that according to the most probable explanation of the Evangelical narratives, Mary Magdalene arrived at the sepulchre, alone and first of all. As you would know, there is some difficulty at first sight in harmonising St. John's account of the first occurrences on Easter morning with that of the three other Evangelists. St. John, in to-day's Gospel,[a] describes Mary Magdalene as coming alone to the sepulchre, finding it empty, and then going to fetch St. Peter and himself. Whereas the other three Evangelists speak of a group of women, of whom Mary Magdalene was one—St. Matthew names two, St. Mark three,—as visiting the sepulchre, finding it empty, conversing with the angels who guarded it, and then going away to inform the disciples. Now the best way of accounting for this divergence, is to make what in the circumstances and with the persons concerned would be a very natural assumption. We may assume, without doing violence to the text of the Gospels, that this entire company of women, of whom Mary Magdalene was one, set out together from the city long before daybreak to visit the tomb of Jesus, which, as you will remember, was outside the walls; but that Mary Magdalene, under the impulse of her strong and tender love, gradually moved away from the rest, and hastened on before them. Just as an hour or two later, on that same morning, St. Peter and St. John ran together to the sepulchre, but "that other disciple did outrun Peter, and came first to the sepulchre,"[b] so there is reason to think it had been with Mary Magdalene. Her more ardent love was impatient of the measured pace of others, who indeed

[a] Easter Day: St. John xx. 1.   [b] St. John xx. 4.

loved Jesus well, but assuredly loved Him less than she. Thus in the Gospel narratives, taken together, we have two visits of women to the sepulchre before the scene described in the text; and also two embassies of women to disciples or Apostles; and two Appearances of Jesus to women in the early morning. First Mary Magdalene reaches the sepulchre, and finds the stone rolled away. She does not look within; she sees no angel; she returns to the city, by some other and shorter path than that along which her companions were advancing, to share her anxieties with St. Peter and St. John. Then the other women reach the sepulchre: they too find the stone rolled away; unlike Mary they enter the sepulchre, and are bidden by an angel to return to Jerusalem and inform Peter and the disciples that Christ had risen. Meanwhile Mary Magdalene is on her way back to the sepulchre to pay it a second visit; this time she is in company with St. Peter and St. John. These Apostles first examine all that met the eye, and then return to the city, leaving Mary alone before the empty grave. There she stands, as the lesson which has just been read describes her, weeping in the bitterness of her grief. This time she stoops down and looks in and sees the traces of the Body of Jesus; then she enters, almost without intending it, into conversation with the angel. Jesus is the one thought that fills her soul; and when she is asked, why she weeps, she answers, "Because they have taken away my Lord out of the sepulchre, and I know not where they have laid Him."

Mary Magdalene then, during the first hours of Easter Day, must not be merged in the company of devout women who visited the sepulchre of Jesus Christ. Her relation to the Resurrection is all her own; it is unique. She, the frail woman, the crushed broken-hearted peni-

tent, makes the first visit to our Saviour's Tomb. To her
He appears alive, before He appears either to Peter or
to John. And the secret of this her high distinction
among the first and greatest of the servants of Christ, is
her love. "She loved much;"[a] this had been the reason
for her full and free forgiveness. "She loved much;"
this was the motive power which associates her, more
than any other human being, with Christ's Resurrection
glory. And in this surely there is reason. For what is
rightly-regulated love but moral power of the highest
order? As St. Paul puts it, "The love of Christ con-
straineth us."[b] Few men have ever explored the heights
and depths of our human nature more thoroughly than
did St. Augustine, and St. Augustine has a saying which
shows how highly he valued the invigorating and trans-
forming power of love. "Only love," he said, "and then
do what thou wilt."[c] Love is indeed the very muscle and
fibre of moral force. If the condition of mankind is
bettered, this is effected by those who love their fellow-
men. If goodness is embodied in life and character,
this is by those who begin by seeing, however imperfectly, the beauty of goodness. They are enamoured of it,
before they try to make it their own. If truth is sought
and found, amid and across difficulties which have
seemed insuperable, this is not seldom by intellects to
which truth has presented itself as an object in itself so
beautiful as to win the love of their hearts. And if Mary
rose in the dark night to visit the grave of her slain
Master, and to pay Him such honours as her poverty
could yield, this was because her soul was on fire with
the moral power of a strong and pure affection, which was
to be rewarded presently by the attainment of its object.

[a] St. Luke vii. 47.   [b] 2 Cor. v. 14.
[c] "Dilige et quod vis fac."—*In Epp. Johann.*, Tr. vii. sect. 8.

All this might well seem commonplace truth: but it requires to be reasserted from time to time, and not less in our own day than in past years. The moral power of love; of love for goodness, of love for humankind, of love for right as against wrong, of love for truth as against error, is sometimes discredited among us, by being labelled with a new name. "Beware," men say, "of being led by emotion. Emotion is for women, for the unthinking, for the young; it deserves no recognition in the life and conduct of a well-instructed thoughtful man; since he should be swayed only and entirely by reason, or by what he conceives to be rational. He has as little to do with emotional motives as with the toys of his childhood or with the toilette of his wife."

Here observe, first of all, an assumption which is by no means warrantable, namely, that emotion is always another name for love. True, all love is emotion of a certain kind: but all emotions are by no means love. Emotion may be vulgar passion; it may be violent hate; ay, passion and hate, which, for the moment, pose in the garb of the most unimpassioned philosophy. And emotion is by no means always power. It may be the expenditure and forfeiture of power; it may be as unfruitful as any speculation respecting the unknowable that ever haunted the brain of a pedant. But love is power. Love, the concentration of purified desire upon an infinitely noble object, does move and constrain all the resources and faculties of man; love summons man to make the utmost of his manhood, whether by work or by endurance. And, therefore, love, so far from being the monopoly of women or children, is the very grace of the strongest and noblest manliness; it kindles reason itself into activity; it gives nerve and impulse to will. Woe to the man who is without love, without enthusiasm; woe to him, above all, if he glories in his moral poverty; if the glow in others of a strong love for goodness or for truth only provokes in him a smile or a sneer. Little as he may suspect it, his intellect, or common sense, when divorced from love, is a poor and awkward instrument, for all practical purposes. Little as he may suspect it, his manhood is enfeebled; he has parted with the secret of its strength. He has done his utmost when he has raised a laugh at the cost of men who pursue what they believe to be good with steady enthusiasm. But, be he who he may, he will himself never achieve anything solid or great, for the good of his fellow-creatures, or for the glory of his God. It is love,—now as in the days of Mary Magdalene,—which conquers difficulty and outlives disappointment.

II.

For Mary's words do breathe cruel disappointment. Mere curiosity would have been tranquil where Mary is in an agony: Mary is so bitterly disappointed because she loves. "They have taken away my Lord out of the sepulchre, and I know not where they have laid Him." It may be thought that Mary expected too much: that she hoped to find her Lord and Friend living and risen. But this is to reflect back upon her thoughts in that dark sad hour our own knowledge of the finished Resurrection. There is no reason for thinking that she believed more, hoped for more, saw further and deeper, than did the Apostles. At that time they expected to find Jesus in His grave; and so did she. They must have then interpreted His saying about rising again the third day in a figurative sense; and so must she. They then thought that in the great conflict with the Jewish people, He had finally succumbed; so did she. The past was beyond recall; the past was failure—tragic, irretrievable failure; so she thought. But in His dear Body, laid honourably and tenderly in the rich man's grave, there was an object, a centre-point for love. Nothing else was left. The voice, the manner, the living presence, the strong and tender words, the works of charity and of wonder; all this was of the past. So she thought. It was gone irrevocably and for ever. But there was the mangled Form, lying out of sight, lying in the grave. This she would honour, this she would love and worship, upon this she would lavish her costliest and her best. She did not care to look forward. For the moment this was enough; it was her all. And then she came, early in the morning, and found Him gone. It was dreadful. She could bear the Way of Sorrows,—the Crucifixion,—the last hour—the last cry—better than this. For the moment it was the ruin of the little that was left to love. It was the sacrifice of her all. Thus it was that she stood without at the sepulchre, weeping. Thus it was that she answered the inquiry about her sorrow—" They have taken away my Lord out of the sepulchre, and I know not where they have laid Him."

But here it may be observed that if Mary only expected to find the Body, the cold dead Body of her Master, her passionate sorrow at missing It is unreasonable. For Mary, of course, did not know, what we who believe in the Incarnation of our Lord Jesus Christ do know,—that the Body of Jesus, as It lay in the tomb, as well as the Soul of Jesus, as It descended to the spirits of the dead,[a] were alike uninterruptedly united to His Divine Person, although Body and Soul were for the time separated by death. To her His Body was only that of a human friend, which must in time mingle with the parent earth.

[a] 1 St. Pet. iii. 19.

And thus it may be thought that Mary was spending her sorrow upon what was after all transient and accidental.

Ah! you who think thus know little of true affection. Certainly love seeks its object; but if its object be out of reach then it seeks anything which suggests that object. The picture of an absent child, the handwriting of a friend who has passed away, the bit of old furniture, the flower, the animal, the dress, the gait or habit, the recurrence of a season of the year which is entwined with a memory, the repetition of a phase or mood of Nature, nay, the marked absence of something which has been customary, and which is therefore recalled by a subtle sense of contrast,—almost anything—is enough for love. The objects upon which it fixes are, to other states of feeling, matters of indifference, or matters of repulsion, or, at best, matters for wonderment. But to love they are everything. They feed and stimulate a glow of tenderness which resolutely transfigures them, and makes them what in other eyes than those of love they never could be. So it was with Mary Magdalene, weeping before the dawn of day, at the door of the sepulchre. We can imagine what comment her tears would have provoked from some well-to-do Scribe or Pharisee, learned in the law, holding a high place or a commission of some sort in the administration of public justice in Jerusalem. We can conceive the wondering, pitying scorn, too amused to be indignant, yet too annoyed to be thoroughly pleased, with which these traces of passionate attachment to the memory of a criminal condemned by the highest Court in Jerusalem, would have been regarded. Why should a Jewish girl thus care to haunt the precincts of the dead, in the early hours of the morning, when as yet the world was not about? Why should she trouble herself, if the masonry had been disturbed, if the grave had been rifled, if the supreme disgrace of crucifixion had been followed by the more tolerable insult of disentombment? Surely there were objects in the world, nearer her home, with greater claims upon her sympathies! Let her rid herself of this distorted mawkish sentimentalism as soon as may be. This is what would have been felt by such a personage as I am imagining; but what would it have mattered, did she know it, to Mary Magdalene? Love is, as a rule, supremely indifferent to criticism. It has ears and eyes for one object only; it moves straight forward to that on which its heart is fixed; it passes by all other objects—not with pride or disdain,—not even with effort: it heeds not their existence. Mary was at that very time gazing on an angelic form, so splendid and so unearthly, "that for fear of him" the soldier-keepers of the grave "did shake and became as dead men."[a] To Mary, in that moment of supreme sorrow, this glorious angel was as nothing. All that she cared for, and hoped for, all her purest feeling, all her loftiest thought, had been buried some thirty-five hours ago in that rocky tomb along with the mangled Body Which they bore away in the evening from the hill of Calvary. Do not talk to her of misplaced sentiment, or of attachment to the trifling or the accidental. Do not try to measure the movements of a soul on fire by the stilted rules of your artificial society, which can create and understand anything better than an unselfish love. Let her cry on bitterly, as she stands there; for she heeds you not. Have the grace to let her cry a while, and then consider if her tears and her love have not that in them from which you may learn something.

[a] St. Matt. xxviii. 4.

III.

Yes! in Mary before the Holy Grave we find something beyond love and disappointment; we find persevering resolution. "I know not where they have laid Him." She does not mean to sit down, there in the garden, and wring her hands, and beat her breast, and cease to inquire and to hope. No; He must be somewhere; perhaps she has a dim hope of the glorious reality, that He has not been taken away by human hands after all. Anyhow she will persevere: she will cross-question any one that she meets, whether it be an angel or a gardener, till she knows the truth. The disappointment does not overmaster her love: her love is still the motive power of her soul: she has her grief, so to say, well in hand, and does not mean to despair, because she has hitherto met with failure. When, afterwards, she supposed herself to be talking with a gardener, who had come at daybreak to set about his work, "Sir," she said, "if thou have borne Him hence, tell me where thou hast laid Him, and I will take Him away."[a] Here there is no trace of despair; here is perseverance, energy, resolution, readiness for any emergency, strong and patient expectation that, after all, something will happen to relieve her anxieties. It was said of English soldiers by a great foreign commander—half in eulogy, half querulously, when recalling his own experience,—that they did not know when they were beaten. And so Christian hope refuses to believe that it is ever beaten. It is imperturbably buoyant; it makes the best of disaster; it is sure that the darkest night will be followed by morning.

Brethren, it is to tempers of this kind that Jesus ever reveals Himself: it is the hopeful who in fact succeed.

[a] St. John xx. 15.

In Mary Magdalene that old promise was made good: "They that seek Me early shall find Me."[a] He Whom she sought was not in His grave; not because human hands had rifled it, but because He was alive for evermore.[b] He Whom she sought was not lying before her eyes, cold and motionless; because He was already close to her, bending over her, did she but know it, with a love for her greater far than was hers for Him. "She turned herself back, and saw Jesus standing, and knew not that it was Jesus. Jesus saith unto her, Woman, why weepest thou? whom seekest thou? She, supposing Him to be the gardener, saith unto Him, Sir, if thou have borne Him hence, tell me where thou hast laid Him, and I will take Him away. Jesus saith unto her, Mary. She turned herself, and saith unto Him, Rabboni; which is to say, Master."[c] She had recognised the voice, and it was enough. He Whom she had sought in the tomb was alive before her eyes; and her joy was fulfilled.

IV.

Mary Magdalene, weeping before the empty tomb of Jesus, reappears in each generation of Christians; it is not hard, at least for some of us, to recognise her among ourselves. She is the type of those who have a genuine love of religion, but who from whatever cause, and in various ways, are for a time, at any rate, disappointed. And religious disappointment is difficult to bear, in proportion to the genuineness and sincerity of a man's character: because it is felt that much is imperilled, while such disappointment lasts. For religion invites a larger stake—a bolder investment of thought and feeling and purpose than any other subject, corresponding to its

[a] Prov. viii. 17.   [b] Rev. i. 18.   [c] St. John xx. 14-16.

transcendent importance. And when those who have given up all else that they may win this, think that they have missed what they hoped to have; when those who like the merchant in the parable have sold their all to buy the pearl of great price, and suppose, though it be without reason, and only for a short while, that they have bought a flint after all; the recoil of baffled hope is even terrible.

Take the not uncommon case of a person who has for some years, for whatever reason, paid scant attention to religious matters. He may not have broken God's law in any very flagrant way: he may not have been exactly the Prodigal Son of the parable. He may only have been a very eager man of business; or a very accomplished man of letters; or a great favourite in society; or a dreamer of unpractical but absorbing dreams. But he has lost sight of God. God has not merely had something less than His true place in the man's thoughts, but scarcely any place at all. Still he remembers something of what he learned from his mother; something of his early prayers; something of his Bible; something, it may be, of the glow and happiness of a Confirmation and a First Communion. And as he knows that the years are passing quickly, and that he must die, he trusts himself to the guidance of these memories of the past. He sets out—it is a painful and a creditable effort,—he sets out to visit the sepulchre of his early life as a Christian. There he trusts to find again the reality of religious faith; there he seeks the Body of the Lord Jesus. He sets out with Mary Magdalene, that he may pay as of old his homage to the Person of his Lord;—but like Mary, perchance, he finds that the mouth of the sepulchre is open, and the Body of Jesus gone. He remembers how he used to think about sacred subjects; but somehow his old thoughts will not recur to him. He cannot recognise the accustomed haunts of his spirit; the old phrases of thirty years ago are no longer to him what they were. There is something in the air which has changed the aspect of what was once for him so full of grace and life; and he gazes on it as on the shell of an extinct creature, as on the ruined castle of a noble race. He opens his Bible: but alas! it is interesting to him only as literature; it is no more to him than Shakespeare or any other work of human genius: it does not speak to his immortal spirit: for him the Body of Jesus is not there. He tries to pray; and prayer is to him only like poetry, an exercise which warms the soul, but which is not felt to be actual conversation with an Unseen Person: the Body of Jesus is not there. He will do his best; he approaches the Holy Communion. But, here, again he finds only a symbolical ceremony which recalls the dead past; there is no sense of contact with the Lord of Life: the Body of Jesus—so far as his experience goes,—of course he knows nothing of the Reality —the Body of Jesus is not there. Everywhere he sees traces of the old presence which haunts his memory. He counts the napkin, and the linen clothes; he measures the chamber in which, as memory reports, his Lord had lain. But now there are voices that tell him how things have changed since those days of which he is thinking. They say that much which of old kept out light and air has been rolled away; that many a scheme for setting a watch over the grave of some crucified Truth has been defeated; that many a Truth, buried out of sight by the ignorance or the scorn of men, has risen to a new and glorious life; and that all is not really lost, as it seems to him. He listens to these voices, perplexed, half incredulous, yet not altogether without hope; but he still murmurs sadly that criticism, or controversy, or the spirit of the time, or religious movements of this kind or of that, have taken away the Lord out of the sepulchre. And he knows not where they have laid Him.

Is it not possible that he is repeating the mistake, the very intelligible mistake, of Mary Magdalene? Is he not forgetting the meaning of the lapse of time? Mary assumed that she would find on Easter morning all that had been left, as it was left, on the late evening of Good Friday. She knew not that there are hours, in the life of souls, which may count for centuries; and that she had been living through such hours as these. She did not bethink herself that her Saviour might be preserved to her, not in the tomb where they laid Him, but under new conditions; in the freedom of the glorious Body, Which passed the sealed doors, and Which ascended to the heavens. Had Mary remained at the sepulchre, from the Burial onwards, watching—as did Rizpah the daughter of Aiah, in her tragic sorrow, before the corpses of her slain sons,[a]—had she sat continuously over against the sepulchre even throughout the second night after the Death of the Lord, she must have witnessed the Resurrection. She would have beheld the Body, re-animated with the Holy Soul of Jesus, flash forth from the tomb into the dark night. She would have seen the stone rolled away. As it was, she had been absent. She had lost the thread of continuity which linked the present to the past. She was perplexed. In time she found that her Lord was there, as before. But He was in the garden, not in the grave; a living Source of life, not a dead body to be covered with spices and ointments.

Nor need it be otherwise with such a case as I am considering. Believe it, my friend, the old Truth is what it was. But time has done its work; and under the guidance of God's providence the minds of

[a] 2 Sam. xxi. 10.

men have been active around and about it. A generation has passed since you were a boy; and a generation counts for much in a busy age like this. What wonder if some of those associations of a boyish mind have been disturbed; if some misapprehensions have been corrected; if some questionable prejudices have to be abandoned; if the relations which should exist between different fields of thought and knowledge have been made clearer—during the interval? What wonder if some of this activity has resulted in what looks like dislocation or destruction; or if it have at least caused intelligible perplexity? Depend on it, the Body of Jesus is not lost. Do not despair because you find It no longer amid the old conditions, the grave-clothes, the napkin, the sepulchre, of a bygone time. Distinguish between the Unchanging, Indestructible Object of the religious life of the soul of man, and the ever-shifting moods of human thought and feeling that circle around Him, as the ages pass. Be patient, as Mary was patient, hopeful as Mary was hopeful; and your share in Mary's tears will surely be followed by Mary's joy. You will recover for your Bible, for your prayers, for your Communions, all, or rather much more than, their old meaning. You will have exchanged Jesus in the tomb for Jesus in the garden; the religious thoughts and resolves of a boy for the religious horizons and aspirations of a ripened manhood.

Perhaps on this, as on every Easter Day, there are certain characters who always need the lesson of the text. Easter, so full of joy, in earth and in heaven; Easter, the queen of festivals; Easter Day, the Day which the Lord hath made, that His Redeemed may rejoice and be glad in it, comes to them not without a shadow of disappointment. They have been looking forward to it, through Lent. They have been preparing for it, as Christians should, who would find in it a blessing. And now it is upon them. And if they are to say the truth, it is without that illumination from above, that sense of the Divine and the Eternal, on which they think they had a special right to reckon. They are standing with Mary Magdalene, but throughout the day, outside the sepulchre. They complain that the Lord has been taken away from them and laid they know not where.

True enough this may be, but—patience. Be earnest in seeking your Lord; and you will find Him. If not on the festival itself, yet afterwards: if not in the public services of the Church, yet privately: if not in human words, yet in the sanctuary of your spirit's life: if not in warm and elevated feeling, yet in a sober and wholesome awe. Do not despair because for a moment the spiritual sepulchre seems to be empty. Rely on His love, on His goodness, on His interest in you personally, on His chartered kindness to those who seek Him. Mary was so bitterly disappointed because she loved. Yet it was her love which, in the end, forbade despair and conquered disappointment. And eighteen centuries have not emptied of its power that great promise of our Divine Lord—" If any man love Me, he will keep My words; and My Father will love him; and We will come unto him, and make Our abode with him."[a]

[a] St. John xiv. 23.

SERMON III.

CHRISTIANITY WITHOUT THE RESURRECTION.

1 COR. XV. 14.

If Christ be not risen, then is our preaching vain, and your faith is also vain.

LAST Sunday we were looking at the Resurrection from the garden of the Sepulchre, and with the eyes of St. Mary Magdalene. The second lesson of the Morning Service of to-day carries us at a bound over a quarter of a century to listen to discussions about the Resurrection in one of the active centres of Greek life and thought. The text takes us to the Christian schools of Corinth, and St. Paul is pointing out to some ready but not very far-sighted disputants the consequences of their denying the Christian doctrine of the Resurrection of the dead. "How say some among you that there is no Resurrection of the dead?" To deny this doctrine in the block—so the Apostle argues—is to deny that Christ Himself has risen. If He has really risen from His grave, it is impossible to say absolutely that there is no such thing as a Resurrection of the dead, since here we have a representative instance of it.

There were, it seems, some at Corinth who did not

* 1 Cor. xv. 12.

shrink from encountering this argument by denying that even He, our Lord Jesus Christ, had really risen. To these persons the Apostle points out, that, however unconsciously, they are in point of fact giving up Christianity altogether. If Christ was still in His tomb, the errand of the Apostles to the world, and the obedience of the faithful to the doctrine which they preached, were equally based upon a vast illusion. "If Christ be not risen, our preaching is vain, your faith is also vain."

I.

It is pretty certain that the persons with whom St. Paul is arguing this matter were not converts from Judaism to the faith of Jesus Christ. Whatever may be said of those Jewish freethinkers, the Sadducees; a religious Jew, or a Pharisee, had no difficulty whatever in professing his belief that the dead would rise. He had always believed it. How strong and clear this Jewish faith was, in an age before the coming of our Divine Lord, we see from the account of the martyrdoms in the Book of Maccabees: those pious Jews died, under the hand of the persecutor, firmly believing that they would rise again.[a] And when St. Paul was arrested in Jerusalem and placed before the Sanhedrim, he knew how to strike a chord which would at once enlist the sympathies of the majority of his hearers: "Men and brethren," he cried, "I am a Pharisee, the son of a Pharisee: of the hope and resurrection of the dead I am called in question."[b] The appeal was successful. "The scribes that were of the Pharisees' part arose, and strove, saying, We find no evil in this man: but if a spirit or an angel hath spoken to him, let us not fight against God."[c]

[a] 2 Mac. vii. 9, 11, 14, 23.   [b] Acts xxiii. 6.   [c] Acts xxiii. 9.

On the other hand, to the Pagan Greek the idea of a coming resurrection of the dead was not merely novel; it was unwelcome. It was opposed to current Greek conceptions about the condition and destiny of the dead. To an ordinary Greek it would have seemed a materialistic way of stating the very shadowy possibilities of a future existence which alone presented themselves to his mind. So palpable and literal an assertion, that man would live once more an unmutilated life, in his body as well as his spirit, would have repelled the Greek. For the immortality of the soul itself, although an original truth of natural religion, appears in Greek literature only as a fugitive speculation; elegant and pathetic as its rendering at times undoubtedly is. Indeed the resurrection of man's body lay altogether beyond the frontier of customary Greek habits of thinking. When St. Paul began to preach the Resurrection at Athens, his hearers missed his true meaning so entirely, as to suppose that the word which expressed it was the name of a new deity. "He seemeth to be a setter forth of strange gods," they said, and this "because he preached unto them Jesus and the Resurrection."[a] And when these deeply-rooted prejudices were carried by converts from Greek Paganism into the Church of Christ, they contributed largely to form the systems of fantastic error which took definite forms in the second century after Christ, and are collectively described as Gnostic. Ten years after writing to the Corinthians St. Paul mentions to his pupil and legate, Timothy, two Greek teachers at Ephesus, Hymenæus and Philetus, "who concerning the truth have erred, saying that the Resurrection is past already."[b] These persons would seem to have wished on the one hand to keep to the language of the Apostolic Church, but on the other to get rid of its

[a] Acts xvii. 18. [b] 2 Tim. ii. 17, 18.

meaning and substance. They accepted a Resurrection; but it was a past Resurrection, not a Resurrection in the future; a moral resurrection of the soul, not a literal resurrection of the body. This, you observe, was the Greek feeling, in secret rebellion against the faith, but not wishing to come to an open rupture, and so attempting an explanation which might hold to the terms of a Christian profession, and at the same time reject the realities which those terms were meant to convey.

At Corinth we see the same feeling at work; but the Corinthians were recent converts, and they did not all of them know what a Revelation from God meant and involved. They thought that it was much like one of their own philosophies, something to be reviewed, discussed, partly accepted, partly rejected, at their pleasure. There was much in Christianity that they liked and accepted, without difficulty, nay, with enthusiasm. But "the Resurrection of the dead" some of them at any rate could not tolerate. They asked, in contemptuous scorn, "How are the dead raised up? and with what body do they come?"[a]—as if such questions had only to be raised in order to show all sensible people how absurd it was to expect an answer. Their difficulties about it arose out of their physical speculations, their theories about the Universe, their ideas of the nature and destiny of beings. But they did not imagine that in denying the Resurrection of the dead they were trifling with essential Christianity, or doing anything more or worse than rejecting a coarse dogma of Jewish origin.

This was the state of mind with which St. Paul is dealing in the text: and his first object is to oblige his readers to understand what their words really came to. In all matters to some extent, in religious matters espe-

[a] 1 Cor. xv. 35.

cially, people use language without weighing its meaning; without asking themselves how much it involves and whither it will carry them. The Corinthians who denied "a Resurrection of the dead" would like to have confined themselves to discussing a presumed physical impossibility of anything of the sort. St. Paul cuts them short by saying, 'If you mean what you say, you mean that Christ Himself never really rose.' If any of the Corinthians were prepared to accept this consequence, they probably did not see why they could not deny even the Resurrection of Christ, and yet somehow continue to be Christians. They did not wish in terms to give up Christianity. They may have flattered themselves that they still retained a firm hold upon all that was really essential in it; that they had only given up legendary additions to the simple story of the life of Christ; additions which their Greek science had pronounced impossible. They were still willing to believe in a Christ Who displayed before the eyes of men a perfect example; Who did many works of wonder and of love; Who taught a heavenly doctrine; Who died a cruel and shameful death. But the assertion that, being dead and buried, "He rose again the third day, according to the scriptures," was, they thought, a superstitious, although an Apostolical, addition to the simple truth. It was no part of the fragment of Christianity which approved itself to their order of intelligence as being really fundamental; and they dismissed it as unimportant, if not untrue.

It is to these persons that St. Paul says solemnly, "If Christ be not risen, our preaching is vain, your faith is also vain." St. Paul will not allow that this faith in a Christ Who has not risen from His grave is any Christianity at all. According to him, if it is a religion at all, it is another religion; it has nothing really to do with the

Faith preached by the Apostles. These Corinthians might still talk about our Lord Jesus Christ. They might still claim the honours and the risks of the Christian Name. They might even imagine that they only differed from the Apostles in being more clear-sighted and better informed, without being less tender-hearted and devout. But St. Paul will allow nothing of the kind. Do not let them deceive themselves in a matter of such momentous import. To deny or ignore Christ's Resurrection is to abandon Christianity. It is to give up the very core and heart of the Faith. The beliefs that remain may have an interest of their own; but it is the sort of interest which belongs to a corpse. It may remind us of the past. But it has no longer any place in the land of the living.

II.

Why, it may be asked, should this be the case? Why cannot a man be a true Christian believer who rejects the Resurrection of Christ? How is it that the rejection of this truth can make the faith which still clings to much else, but denies this particular doctrine, vain or empty?

The answer is, Because the Resurrection of Christ is the foundation-fact on which the Christian creed rests, in a believing soul. If any one of the Apostles had been asked, how it was that they knew that Jesus was the promised Messiah, the Eternal Son of God, the Saviour of the world, by Whose teaching and example men were to be enlightened; by Whose Blood men were to be redeemed; to Whom all the children of men were bound to pay the homage of their obedience and their love,—the answer would have been, Because the Lord Jesus rose from the dead. When you go home, read through their sermons as reported at the beginning of the Acts of the Apostles.ᵃ And observe how they base the claims of Jesus Christ upon the fact of His Resurrection, the fact to which they themselves bore a personal witness. In their eyes the Resurrection of Jesus was God's visible interference with the order of nature in order to certify the true mission and claims of Jesus. Our Lord Jesus Christ indeed had appealed beforehand to this very certificate: the sign which He had given to an unbelieving generation, in proof that He came from God, was that He would raise the temple of His Body from the dead in three days.ᵇ And therefore the Apostles began by preaching this fact of the Resurrection. They virtually said, 'He has been as good as His word; He has risen from the dead; therefore let us believe Him.' Thus, as St. Paul observed, "He was declared to be the Son of God with power, according to His Holy and Higher Nature, by the Resurrection from dead." ᶜ

But the Resurrection does not merely light up the past: it is an earnest of the future. It is the warrant that Christ will come to judge us. When St. Paul has told the Athenians that God has "appointed a day in which He will judge the world in righteousness by that Man Whom He hath ordained," he naturally reflects that a critical and sceptical audience will ask what proof there is to allege in favour of so startling an announcement. Accordingly he adds, "Of this God has given assurance unto all men, in that He has raised Jesus from the dead." ᵈ The Apostles, when preaching the Faith, were like those

---

ᵃ Acts ii. 22-36; iii. 12-16; iv. 10-12, 33; v. 29-32; x. 34-43; xiii. 16-41.

ᵇ St. John ii. 19.

ᶜ Rom. i. 4: τοῦ ὁρισθέντος υἱοῦ Θεοῦ ἐν δυνάμει, κατὰ Πνεῦμα ἁγιωσύνης ἐξ ἀναστάσεως νεκρῶν.   ᵈ Acts xvii. 31.

architects who make a stone roof of wide area depend for its support on a central pillar. They know that the pillar is strong enough for its work. They were themselves appointed to be witnesses of the Resurrection; and they never met the world without bearing their testimony. They knew that if the Resurrection were sincerely believed all else in the Christian Creed would hold good. They knew also that if the Resurrection of Christ was rejected, nothing else could be, in the long-run, received at all.

Suppose for instance that one of these Corinthian rejecters of the Resurrection had said, 'I am not a man to believe in Christ's Resurrection, but I do not wish to reject the benefits of His Death.' The Apostle would have asked, 'What benefits do you mean?' What becomes of the Death of Christ if it was not followed by His Resurrection? It at once descends to the rank of a purely human event. It does not differ in character from the death of any other high-minded and disinterested man for a cause to which he is attached. It may still have—it undoubtedly still has—the importance of a great moral example; of devotion to truth, to charity, to justice. But the language which the Apostles use about it, and which Christendom has ever believed, becomes at once unmeaning. Why should the death of a mere man, whose body has mouldered in his grave, be a power in earth and heaven, mighty to cleanse from guilt, and to win for the sinner pardon from God? St. Paul's bones rest somewhere in or near the great city where they slew him, some thirty-five years after his Master's death. But who could speak of Paul as dying for his followers, or for "the ungodly,"[a] or as "bearing their sins in his own body,"[b] or as being set forth as "a propitiation through

[a] Rom. v. 6. [b] 1 St. Pet. ii. 24.

faith in his blood"?ᵃ Who would dare to say that Christians are "reconciled to God by the death"ᵇ of St. Paul, or that, by him, they had "received the Atonement,"ᶜ or that Paul is a "propitiation for their sins, and not for theirs only, but also for the sins of the whole world,"ᵈ or that Paul "gave himself a ransom for all'"?ᵉ Every believer in Christ feels the shocking profanity of applying this language to any other than the Divine Redeemer. But why is it so profane? Because it is the Divine Person of Him, Who died on Calvary, Which gives such meaning to His Atoning Death. "Ye were not redeemed," exclaims St. Peter, "with corruptible things, as silver and gold," or indeed as the blood of a merely human victim, "but with the precious Blood of Christ, as of a Lamb without blemish and immaculate."ᶠ "If God," argues St. Paul, "spared not His Own Son, but freely gave Him up for us all, how shall He not with Him also"—it is the inevitable Christian inference,—"freely give us all things?"ᵍ But then how do we know that the Sufferer on Calvary was God's Own Son? The answer is, By the Resurrection. The Resurrection, if I may dare so to speak, put the death of Jesus Christ before the world in its true light. It was an immense reversal of *primâ facie* appearances. What had looked like a defeat was seen to be a triumph. What seemed the execution of a condemned criminal was recognised as an awful transaction, having immense results on earth and in heaven, throughout all time. If Christ "was crucified through weakness, yet He liveth by the power of God."ʰ This was the keynote of Apostolic teaching: the Resurrection had lifted His death to a higher or rather altogether

ᵃ Rom. iii. 25.   ᵇ Rom. v. 10.   ᶜ Rom. v. 11.
ᵈ 1 St. John ii. 2.   ᵉ 1 Tim. ii. 6.   ᶠ 1 St. Pet. i. 18, 19.
ᵍ Rom. viii. 32.   ʰ 2 Cor. xiii. 4.

different level from that of any human sufferer. But then if the Resurrection is denied, all the Apostolic language about the Atonement becomes a tissue of mystical exaggerations, which as applied to the death of a mere man, are worse than unintelligible. This consequence the Corinthians might not have seen at once. But at any rate their faith in the Atonement was already undermined by their disbelief in the Resurrection of the Crucified Christ.

But suppose the Corinthians to say, 'Very well, we will give up the Atonement, but we will continue to believe in the beauty of Christ's language and example. This, after all, is in our opinion the essential thing in Christianity. The rest may go; and we shall not, perhaps, be the worse for losing it.'

Here St. Paul would have explained that in order to recognise the beauty of Christ's language and example there was no necessity for faith, properly so called, at all. Faith is the acceptance of the unseen upon sufficient testimony. It is a venture, warranted indeed, but not by experience. Its proper object is something which does not lie within the range of our experience. You and I do no need faith, or anything but ordinary judgment and common moral sense, in order to do justice to the good sayings and good actions of any one of the many excellent people who may be named as having died some twenty or thirty years ago. We know enough about them, on very good evidence, to enable us to give full play to our admiration, and we admire them accordingly. It would be absurd to call them objects of faith.

Certainly St. Paul would have said, that faith, by which the soul takes possession of the Invisible, is not wanted for any such purpose as these. Corinthians might have pleaded. But might he not, would he not, have gone a step further? Must he not have pointed out that to deny the Resurrection, and at the same time to profess to admire the words of Christ, or the example of Christ, is really impossible? Did not our Lord more than once, when challenged for a sign or warrant of His claims, say that He would be put to death and rise again the third day?[a] Remark how He insists on "the third day;" there is a precision in the announcement which forbids figurative interpretation of this language, as if, forsooth, it could be satisfied by the remote triumph of His Name or doctrine, while His Body mouldered in the grave. No, it is impossible to admire some of His best-attested words if His Resurrection be denied. Let me add, that it is impossible to admire His example. Upon what kind of ground can we explain or justify His inviting the love and trust and homage of all those pious souls who thronged around Him, if in reality He was not more than one of themselves; if He had not in Himself some sources and supplies of strength which were more than human? "We preach not ourselves,"[b] says His Apostle. But He, the Master, says, "I am the Way, the Truth, and the Life;"[c] "Come unto Me, all ye that are weary, and heavy laden;"[d] "I am the Light of the world;"[e] "I am the True Vine;"[f] "I am the good Shepherd; all that ever came before Me are thieves and robbers."[g] The constant, reiterated self-assertion of Jesus Christ,—in the face of His Own precepts about the beauty of being humble, and self-forgetting, and retiring,—is to be explained by the inward necessity laid upon Him by His Divine Personality, of which His Resurrection was a visible witness to the world. Deny His Resurrection, and His character, as we have it in the Gospels, requires "reconstruction" if it is not to be met by the moral sense

---

[a] St. John ii. 18, 19; St. Matt. xii. 38-40.
[b] 2 Cor. iv. 5.   [c] St. John xiv. 6.   [d] St. Matt. xi. 28.
[e] St. John viii. 12.   [f] St. John xv. 1.   [g] St. John x. 11, 8.

of man with a judgment very different indeed from that of sympathy and admiration.

III.

These are some of the grounds on which St. Paul would have maintained that "if Christ be not risen, the faith of Christians is vain." But observe the character of his argument; it is an argument from the consequences of rejecting the Resurrection. Elsewhere he proves the Resurrection directly. It may be inferred from the words of Jesus, from the language of prophecy, above all, from the actual experiences of actual eye-witnesses to be counted by hundreds, and many of whom were living when St. Paul wrote. Here St. Paul says, 'See what will happen, if you reject Christ's Resurrection. You will have to give up your Christianity altogether. If Christ be not risen, our preaching is vain, your faith is also vain. You Corinthians are in a dilemma. You must go forward or you must go back. You must either believe with us Apostles, in the Resurrection of Christ, and in the Resurrection of the dead which is its consequence, or you must fall back into the darkness from which you emerged at your conversion.'

This is a kind of argument which—if it were not being handled by an inspired Apostle—we should describe as trenchant. Plainly it is meant to cut discussion short, and to bring matters to an issue by a short and easy method. St. Paul feels that something must be said which will not be forgotten. He feels as when he told the Galatians—"If ye be circumcised, Christ shall profit you nothing,"[a] or "If we, or an angel from heaven, preach any other gospel unto you than that which we have preached

[a] Gal. v. 2.

unto you, let him be accursed,"ᵃ or the Corinthians, " If any man love not the Lord Jesus Christ, let him be Anathema Maranatha."ᵇ It was in this same state of mind, with this same general intention, that, namely, of rousing dull minds by some vivid statements to see how matters really stood, that he wrote, " If Christ be not raised, our preaching is vain, your faith is also vain."

It may be urged that arguments of this kind are inconsiderate and unsuccessful. Do they not crush out, with their relentless logic, the still surviving faith of weak but inconsequent believers; do they not forget Him Who would not quench the smoking flax, or bruise the broken reed?ᶜ And secondly, do they always succeed? Do they not rouse opposition, almost resentment, among persons of independence of character, who are not therefore hostile to religion? May they not entirely defeat the object with which they are used: when of the alternatives presented the one is taken which was really designed to make the other inevitable? The lever breaks in the workman's hand, just as it is being applied.

This, it must be granted, is true enough of the employment of such arguments in a great many cases among ourselves. No doubt there are writers and talkers who take pleasure in forcing people, as they say, to be consistent; whatever may be the kind of consistency that is enforced. These writers and talkers are like a reckless man who rides at full tilt down a street full of children at play. They are thinking only of their own feat and prowess, nothing of the consequences. Often, indeed, as we must know, the employment of such intellectual weapons is very cruel: they leave wounds and doubts in tender minds which are healed only slowly or never at all. They may be very fine feats of reasoning. But like the sports of

ᵃ Gal. i. 8.   ᵇ 1 Cor. xvi. 22.   ᶜ St. Matt. xii. 20.

ancient kings, they are indulged at the cost of the defenceless and the weak. Too seldom indeed do many speakers and writers, in private and in public, track out the effect of their inconsiderateness in the shattered hopes, and the distressed consciences, and the weakened resolves, which are really due to it ! But, granting this, it does not by any means follow that arguments like that of St. Paul—'You must believe more than you do, or you will cease to be a Christian'—are not sometimes necessary and charitable. They are like critical operations in surgery ; which no one would undertake or undergo without adequate necessity, but which are sometimes necessary to saving life.

Everything depends upon the spirit *in* which, upon the purpose *with* which, an argument like this is used. It may be used as a vain display of personal power, as a means of achieving intellectual victory. In this case nothing can well be more criminal. It may be used in a spirit of true charity; in order to save a soul which has wandered into dreamland, and mistakes the pictured forms of its own fancy for the Eternal Truths. In this case nothing can be more charitable. The knife may be employed by a scientific surgeon to save a patient's life by a timely operation: or by a bungler, who is only thinking of his professional reputation : or by a burglar, to cut a man's throat. St. Paul, who watched with such tender solicitude over the weak brethren in Rome and at Corinth, would never have forced his hearers or readers to choose between the acceptance of one particular doctrine and the rejection of the Christian faith, unless under the pressure of a stern necessity. He had fully reckoned on the risks. He knew what the effect would be on those whom he addressed. He would never have placed them in the dilemma, unless he had been satisfied that they loved their faith better than their speculations; and that they would accept the Resurrection of our Lord Jesus Christ when they found that to reject it was to reject Christianity. A serious logical operation was needed. But the Apostle knew that the patient could bear it.

There are two practical considerations which present themselves.

First, reflect how dangerous it is to pick and choose in the things of God. It is not too much to say that some persons who would be distressed at the idea that they were bad Christians, have no idea at all of the truth that the Christian Revelation, if accepted at all, must be accepted as a whole. They speak and think as if, in approaching the truths which God has set before us through His Beloved Son, they were like intending purchasers entering a shop, perfectly at liberty to select whatever might strike their taste or fancy, and to reject the rest. The question of believing or rejecting belief, appears to them a matter to be decided by personal bias or inclination; although of course in reality this is as unreasonable as it is irreverent. Unreasonable, because all really revealed truth rests on exactly the same grounds, and recommends itself equally to a perfectly balanced mind; and irreverent, because, to reject any part of Revelation is virtually to tell the Divine Revealer that He has set before the mind of His creature that which is either unnecessary or incredible. At the same time, it is true that some truths may be rejected with less ruin to the entire fabric of faith than others: just as certain limbs of the human body may be amputated without destroying life, although they impair its perfectness, while others,—the head for example, —cannot be parted with, without instant death. Thus too, mistakes may be made about the doctrines of grace, or the meaning of large portions of Scripture, without necessarily leading to fatal consequences. But to reject the Resurrection is to cut at the root of Christian belief; it is to cease, as far as thought and faith go, to be a Christian at all. A Christ who never rose from his grave is not the Christ of the Bible or of Christendom. Such a Christ has nothing in common with our living and adorable Saviour except the name.

Secondly, and lastly, ask yourselves, each one, What does the Resurrection of Christ mean to me? How much of my life, of my thought, of my resolve, is influenced by it? Put to yourselves the supposition,—for a Christian the impossible supposition,—that it was untrue. What would you have lost? Try to estimate the difference in your thoughts and lives, which the absence of this truth would involve. We know what the loss of a near relation would mean to us. We can calculate the effect, by thinking over our habits throughout the day. We know what the reduction of our income to such or such a sum would involve, in the loss of comforts, or in our means of doing good. What then would be the effect upon us of the withdrawal, if we could conceive it possible, of the doctrine of the Resurrection of Jesus Christ from the Creed and from the Bible? How would it affect our hold of other Christian truths? How would it change our thoughts about the future; about the World Unseen, about death, about all that is to follow after death? How would it touch our thoughts and feelings throughout each day, as they move around the Person of an Unseen but Present Lord and Saviour? If we get this question honestly answered, we may form a tolerably fair estimate of the value of our faith in Christ's Resurrection at this moment. If we do indeed believe that He is risen, that stupendous faith does and must mould thought, feeling, resolve, in very various ways. If we do believe that He is risen and living, then we know, that to part with this faith would affect the life of our spirits, just as the extinction of the sun's light and warmth in the heavens would affect all beings that live and grow on this earth. If Jesus Risen is indeed the Object of our faith, then our religion is not merely the critical study of an ancient literature, but a vitally distinct thing; it is the communion of our spirits with a living and Divine Being. It is faith in the Resurrection which marks our present relations to Jesus Christ as altogether different from those which we have to the famous dead who have in past years filled the thoughts and governed the history of mankind. At the beginning of this century,—as it is natural to reflect within these walls,—Nelson and Wellington were names second to none among the men who claimed the attention of the world. Where are they now? Their ashes moulder beneath our feet. Where are they now? Their disembodied spirits are waiting, we know not exactly where, for the hour of the Judgment. But where is Jesus Christ? He, risen from His grave, arrayed in His Glorified Manhood, is seated on the Throne of Heaven; He is the meeting-point and centre of the vast empire of living souls; He is in communication, constant and intimate, with millions of beings, to Whom, by His Death and His triumph over Death, by His persistent and exhaustless Life, He is made Wisdom and Righteousness and Sanctification and Redemption.[a] Yes! To believe in the Risen Jesus is to live under a sky which is ever bright. It is to believe that He is "alive for evermore, and has the keys of hell and of death." [b]

[a] 1 Cor. i. 30.   [b] Rev. i. 18.

SERMON IV.

CHRISTIANITY WITHOUT THE RESURRECTION.

1 COR. XV. 14.

If Christ be not risen, then is our preaching vain, and your faith is also vain.

THIS is St. Paul's way of saying, as strongly as he can, that there is no doubt whatever about the fact of our Lord's Resurrection from the dead. He tells his readers that Christ is risen, because if He is not risen consequences must follow which he knows they will treat as plainly absurd. ".If Christ be not risen, then is our preaching vain, your faith is also vain." Certain members of the Corinthian Church, converts, we cannot doubt, from Greek heathenism, had brought with them into the Church of Christ some of the habits of thought as to the evil nature of matter, which they had learnt from the Greek philosophers. This led them to regard such a doctrine as that of the Resurrection of the dead as too gross and material a conception for a spiritual religion like Christianity; and they thought that Christianity would do better without it. Accordingly they said, in so many words, that there was no Resurrection of the dead.

Many people are always to be met with who commit themselves, especially on religious subjects, to general and sweeping statements without thinking out what these statements mean, what they lead to, or what they take for granted. St. Paul will not allow such a very serious matter as the Resurrection to be dealt with after this fashion. He says in effect to the Corinthians: 'Measure your words. You say that there is no Resurrection from the dead. Very well, if this is the case, Christ our Lord Himself did not rise from the dead. If you mean your general assertion, it commits you in this particular instance. It forces you to this dreadful and appalling conclusion. You must deny the Resurrection of Christ. And to do that,' he proceeds, 'is in fact to deny the truth of Christianity. For if Christ never rose from His grave, the teaching of the Apostles was mere rhetoric, to which nothing corresponded in the world of fact. If Christ never rose from His grave, you yourselves, Corinthian Christians, who still call yourselves believers, yet hold a faith which has no ground to rest upon. Its very heart has been taken out of it. "If Christ be not risen, then is our preaching vain, your faith is also vain."'

There is no reason to suppose that the Corinthian Christians who are in question denied in terms that Christ rose from the dead. They were thinking chiefly of the general Resurrection at the last day, as taught by the Apostolic Church; and they held generally that there was no Resurrection. They may not have thought of the bearing of this general opinion on the Resurrection of Christ. But St. Paul is determined that they shall think of it. He wishes to oblige them to give up their error about the general Resurrection by reducing the principle of this error to a profane absurdity, which, once presented to a Christian believer, would be indignantly set aside. "If there be no Resurrection of the dead, then is Christ not risen: and if Christ be not risen, then is our preaching vain, your faith is also vain."ᵃ

I.

"If Christ be not risen, then is our preaching vain." *Our* preaching! St. Paul associates himself with the older Apostles who had seen the Lord Jesus on earth, and especially after His Resurrection. He and they had alike been preaching a message to the world, which, if Christ had not really risen from His grave, was vain. It was "empty;" a mere assortment of words and phrases, without substance or soul. It was a doctrine, if it could still be called a doctrine, devoid of all that entitled it to command the attention of human beings. Now the Corinthians who denied the general Resurrection had no intention of casting any slur upon the teaching of the Apostles, much less of bringing it to such utter discredit. They probably, as did other Greeks, thought themselves able to criticise it freely, and in some respects even to improve upon it. As yet they did not understand that a Revelation, if accepted as such, must be accepted as a whole, as coming from the Author of all truth; and as being, from the nature of the case, beyond the reach of human judgments. But, whatever their inconsistencies, they had no idea that they were by implication proclaiming to the world that the teaching of the Apostles was in reality an unsubstantial dream.

It was St. Paul's duty to undeceive them. As their denial of any resurrection involved that of the Resurrection of Christ, so the denial of Christ's Resurrection was fatal to the claim of the Apostles to be serious teachers of Religion. For if there was any one truth upon which

---
ᵃ 1 Cor. xv. 13, 14.

the Apostles had staked their credit, as messengers of God, it was the truth that Christ had risen from the dead. His Resurrection was the instrument by which they forced their way to popular attention. His Resurrection was the proof of the truth of what they had to say. His Resurrection was the most important part of what they had to say. Two months had not passed since it occurred when they first began to preach it, and with the confidence of men who knew that they would not be contradicted, and that their assertion had everything to gain by inquiry. The first, it might almost have seemed the only, duty of an Apostle was to proclaim the Resurrection. When St. Matthias was chosen into the vacant chair of Judas, St. Peter thus defined an Apostle's work—"a man ordained to be a witness with us of" Christ's "Resurrection."[a]

Now observe how the reported preaching of each of the great Apostles St. Peter and St. Paul corresponds with this. What was the first sermon ever preached in the Church of Christ, by St. Peter, surrounded by the eleven Apostles, on the Day of Pentecost? Its point is to show that the Resurrection, to which he and his brother Apostles could bear witness, had been prophesied by David in Psalm xvi.[b] Again, how does he explain the miracle of healing the lame man at the Beautiful gate of the Temple, in the two addresses which he delivered, first to the assembled spectators, and next after his arrest before the Sanhedrin? In both he refers the miracle to the power of Jesus Christ; living because risen, and risen, although crucified and dead.[c] The Resurrection of Jesus is the clue to the mystery which so oppressed the imagination of the Jews and their rulers, that poor unlettered men should be working such miracles and winning such influence. Again, when numerous conversions had taken place, and

[a] Acts i. 22. [b] Acts ii. 22-36. [c] Acts iii. 12-16; iv. 8-12.

the Apostles were a second time arrested and charged with having filled Jerusalem with their doctrine, what is St. Peter's apology? He says that, in fact, the Apostles cannot help it; the Resurrection is a fact which lays a necessity upon them. "Peter and the other Apostles answered and said, We ought to obey God rather than men. The God of our fathers raised up Jesus, Whom ye slew."[a] Once more, when St. Peter is instructing the heathen soldier Cornelius and other inquirers, in the grounds of Christian doctrine, at Cæsarea, what is his main argument? "The Jews," he says, "slew Jesus, and hanged Him on a tree; Him God raised up the third day, and showed Him openly; not to all the people, but unto witnesses chosen before of God, even to us, who did eat and drink with Him after He rose from the dead."[b] Nor is it otherwise in the reported sermons of St. Paul. St. Paul had not seen the Risen Jesus before the Ascension. But he knew what other Apostles had seen. And he himself had had sensible proofs that Jesus was alive. Consider then the great discourse which he pronounced in the synagogue of Antioch in Pisidia.[c] Everything in it leads up to Christ's Resurrection. Christ was slain by the pressure put upon Pilate by the Jews; Christ was raised by God the Father from the dead, and seen many days by those who came up with Him from Galilee to Jerusalem. And then this is shown to agree with prophecy, as the Jews understood it, in the Psalter and in Jeremiah. Or read the speech which he made on the Areopagus at Athens.[d] All God's previous dealings with mankind, so he contends, had led up to the Apostolic preaching of repentance. And repentance was necessary because judgment was coming; and the Judge was to be a Man ordained

[a] Acts v. 29, 30.
[b] Acts x. 39-41.
[c] Acts xiii. 16-41.
[d] Acts xvii. 22-31.

by God: "whereof," he adds, "God hath given assurance unto all men, in that He hath raised Him from the dead." Or read his speech at Cæsarea before Agrippa.[a] He defends himself against his Jewish accusers by saying that he taught "none other things than those which the Prophets and Moses had foretold; namely, that the Christ should suffer, and that He should be the first that should rise from the dead."[b] That is St. Paul's own account, when put upon his defence, of his general teaching.

In fact, it is impossible to read the reports of the early teaching of the Apostles without seeing that their teaching centred in, and rested on, the Resurrection. The Resurrection was their reason for teaching at all; it was also the main substance of what they taught. If they were deceived as to its reality, their teaching had neither basis nor substance; their exhortations, their apologies, their appeals, their entreaties, their interpretations of prophecy, their account of the facts before them, their anticipations as to the future, all become forthwith a confused and irrational array of phrases; and the world might well regret that such teaching had not already died away upon the breeze and been forgotten. Nay, St. Paul uses sterner language. If Christ be not raised, "we are found false witnesses of God; because we have testified of God that He raised up Christ."[c] Full well might he exclaim—"If Christ be not risen, . . . our preaching is vain."

II.

But St. Paul adds, "If Christ be not risen;—your faith is also vain." He supposes some Corinthian to say: 'After all, the Resurrection of Christ is only one article of the Christian faith: if we give it up, we can still believe the

[a] Acts xxvi. 2-23.   [b] Acts xxvi. 22, 23.   [c] 1 Cor. xv. 15.

rest. The Apostles may be discredited by promulgating the Resurrection; but much of the Apostolic teaching will survive their discomfiture. Christ may never have risen; yet portions of the faith which bears His Name may well have other grounds to rest on, and may still be the strength and solace of human souls.'

This is what a Corinthian might have said. But St. Paul will not allow it. He maintains that as it is with the preaching of Apostles, so it is with the faith of Christians. Both are alike vain, if Christ never rose from the dead.

Let us try in some degree to follow him, if we can. And, with a view to this, let us ask ourselves what are the leading features of the state of mind which Christian faith creates in the soul, and how these are likely to be affected by the denial of Christ's Resurrection from the dead.

1. The most characteristic trait in the habitual thoughts of a believing Christian is the conviction, never absent from his consciousness altogether, often present with an urgent and constraining power, that, although most unworthy, he is a redeemed man; that by the perfect Obedience, the atoning Passion and Death of Jesus Christ, and the graces and gifts which flow from it, he has been bought out of bondage to sin and death, and placed in a new relation towards God; a relation of freedom and of sonship, begun in this world and to be perfected hereafter.

This consciousness of Redemption, this buoyant, thankful, exulting sense of living beneath the smile of the Author of his existence, through the reconciliation which has been so generously effected by Christ, enters into all the recesses of the Christian's soul. It regulates thought, it inspires prayer, it impels to action. It determines the course of feeling towards and intercourse with others, it leaves no district of mental or moral action altogether unaffected by its pervading influence. St. Paul's words, "He loved me, and gave Himself for me,"[a] are emblazoned everywhere within the chambers of the soul. They reappear in each district of thought and feeling; and all the soul's faculties conspire to sing the hymn of the redeemed, "Worthy is the Lamb that was slain, to receive power, and riches, and wisdom, and strength, and honour, and glory, and blessing."[b]

But, if Christ has not risen from His grave after all, where is the justification of all this? Is it not all an illusion? How can a fellow-mortal, as little the final conqueror of sin and death as any one of us, be the author of a new life? How could a Christ who was laid in his grave to see corruption and to mingle his body with the dust, be the Redeemer of Christendom? Pay such a Christ what compliments you will on the score of this or that portion of his teaching of which you happen to approve, or of such and such a trait in his character which wins your admiration. These eulogies do not make him the Lord of life and death, nor do they invest his death with atoning power. Why was it that in dying Jesus wrought out such vast and unimaginable blessings for our fallen race? Because His Person gave to His Death an infinite value: because each pang of His Soul, each drop of His Blood, was charged with all the virtue of His Godhead. But "in the sight of our eyes He seemed to die, and His departure was taken for misery."[c] How were men to know that an event so exceptional had taken place; that a superhuman Person had been crucified? The Apostle replies that He was "declared to be the Son of God with power, in respect of His Holy and

[a] Gal. ii. 20.   [b] Rev. v. 12.   [c] Wisdom iii. 2.

Higher Nature, by the Resurrection from the dead."ᵃ The Resurrection pours a flood of light upon the Passion. The Resurrection shows what it was that made Calvary the scene not merely of a public execution, but of a world-redeeming Sacrifice. And if Christ be not risen, then there is no proof that He Who suffered on Calvary was more than the feeble victim of an enormous wrong; powerless, as His enemies said, to save Himself, and much more powerless to achieve the salvation of others. To quote St. Paul once more: "If Christ be not raised, your faith is vain; ye are yet in your sins."ᵇ

2. A second ruling feature of a Christian's habitual state of mind is that he is constantly looking forward to another life. A Christian does not speculate on another life as a possibility; he takes it for granted as an ascertained fact. He looks forward to it, as he looks forward to the changes of Nature, to the setting of the sun, to the succession of the seasons. He knows that death will come to him as to everybody else; that each day of his life brings it nearer; that it means a momentous, and an unimaginable change. But he knows something too of what will follow it. Christ our Lord has converted what was, before He came, at best a splendid guess, into an absolute certainty. He has explored that unknown world. If He has unveiled its terrors He has enhanced its beauties. He has told all who will trust Him as a Guide, how to secure in it a blessed Immortality. And therefore, as I have said, a Christian looks forward. He treats this life as a preface to that which will follow it. He gives it up, if need be, to secure the life beyond. He does not pretend to be particularly heroic, or other than a prudent man who acts upon the knowledge which has been put in

---

ᵃ Rom. i. 4.   ᵇ 1 Cor. xv. 17.

his way. But he looks forward to the time when "mortality will be swallowed up of life,"ᵃ and meanwhile he "rejoices in the hope of the glory of God."ᵇ

Suppose, however, that Christ has not really risen from His grave, what then becomes of these bright anticipations? Is there any real warrant for them? There remain, you say, the Words of Christ. Granted. But what is their authority? If Christ never rose from His grave, how do His words about the future life of man differ from the words of Plato? They are more positive, no doubt. But do they represent any sources of knowledge altogether distinct in kind from those which Plato had at command? No; if Christ died, and did not burst the fetters of death; if His dust in very deed still mingles with the soil of Palestine; then it is trifling with language and with the hopes and anxieties of the soul of man to tell us that He has "brought life and immortality to light through the Gospel,"ᶜ or that He has "opened the kingdom of heaven to all believers." If He be indeed not risen, He has only added a few more positive assertions on the subject of immortality to the stock of speculations which mankind already possessed. But we do not really know more about immortality than we did before He came. Unless Christ have risen from His grave, your faith, Christian brethren, in a future life, so far as it is based on His additions to our natural anticipations, is undoubtedly vain.

3. A third feature of the state of mind created in the soul by Christian faith is belief in the possible perfection of man. It is difficult to exaggerate the value of this particular conviction. Our average experience of human character, in ourselves if not in others, is so disheartening, that a strong faith in man's capacity for perfection is a

---

ᵃ 2 Cor. v. 4.   ᵇ Rom. v. 2.   ᶜ 2 Tim. i. 10.

necessary ingredient of all earnest moral effort. And this is afforded us by our Lord Jesus Christ. Whatever must be said of mankind in general; whatever abatements must be made from the character even of those who have lived lives the highest and the nearest to God,—One Life, we Christians know, there has been, which has been unstained by any taint of sin; One absolutely true and unclouded intellect; One heart whose affections were perfectly pure; One Will of which the rectitude and the vigour was never for an instant impaired. He could challenge a jealous world to convict Him of sin, if it could, He could dare to say of His actions, "I do always such things as please the Father."[a] In the judgment of those who watched Him most closely, He "did no sin, neither was guile found in His mouth."[b] And indeed "such an High Priest became us, holy, harmless, undefiled, separate from sinners."[c] We needed Him as our Priestly Representative in Heaven. We needed Him no less as our Standard of true human Excellence on earth.

But if Christ be not risen, is He still a perfect character? If the event to which He solemnly referred as the ratification of His mission never occurred at all, can He be acquitted, I will not say, of levity, but of trifling with the confidence and hopes of His followers? What would be said of a modern teacher or leader who had encouraged men to give up all their prospects in life upon the strength of promises which were never realised, and which he must have known never could be realised; and who had done this with so much solemnity and detail, as to preclude any possibility of their misapprehending him? We should use severe language in describing his offence. If he could be acquitted of an intention to deceive, it would only be by admitting that he was himself the victim

[a] St. John viii. 29.   [b] 1 St. Pet. ii. 22.   [c] Heb. vii. 26.

of a delusion, so serious, as to disqualify him altogether for undertaking the guidance of others. No, my Christian friends, if Christ be not risen, it may be possible to save something out of the wreck of His character;—we will not discuss further what must be for a Christian so intolerable a discussion. But your faith in His perfection must perish irretrievably. It is also vain.

4. A last characteristic of the state of mind produced by Christian faith is confidence in the ultimate victory of good over evil. Here again is a truth, over which much in the world at large, and in the lives of single men, may well cast a shadow. "The righteous perisheth and no man layeth it to heart:"[a] the "ungodly are in no peril of death, but are lusty and strong; they come in no misfortune like other folk, neither are they plagued like other men."[b] This is the appearance which human life wears from age to age. Here and there, we see notorious exceptions to the rule. But upon the whole evil seems to be in possession, and, as far as experience goes, it is likely to hold its own. When a Christian is haunted by this impression, which strikes at persistent faith in the moral supremacy of God, he turns his thoughts to the Resurrection. Never did evil obtain such a triumph over pure goodness as when it nailed Jesus Christ our Lord to the Cross of shame. Never was the ultimate victory of goodness so clearly vindicated as on the morning of the Resurrection. Of this supreme event, Joseph's exaltation to be the ruler of Egypt, David's triumph over Saul, Israel's deliverance, in one age, from the Egyptian bondage, in another from that of Babylon, were but faint adumbrations. The greatest proof that ever was given that the world is governed by a moral God, was given when Jesus, the sinless Victim of

[a] Isa. lvii. 1.   [b] Ps. lxxiii. 4, 5.

triumphant evil, was rescued by the Resurrection from the clutches of death.

But if Christ be not raised; what then? Then it must be admitted that the greatest of all injustices on record has never yet been redressed, and that God has given us no visible pledge that it ever will be redressed. Then it must be owned that the claims of evil and darkness to rule the world are not really shaken by a dead Christ; that all which Christianity,—so to call the tenets of any who, while denying a Risen Saviour, yet care for the name —all that Christianity has to offer is fair words, precarious hopes, but no new facts whatever, to enable the sinking heart of man to maintain its struggle with predominant evil. If Christ be not risen, your faith in the ultimate victory of good, so far as it rests on what He experienced, is only too surely vain.

III.

It has been a matter of complaint against St. Paul, and against others who have followed him, that recourse should be had to arguments of this kind; arguments which are said to kill or cure, and to cure less frequently than they kill; arguments which show more care for logical consistency than for our Lord's example, Who would not " break the bruised reed or quench the smoking flax."[a] For the Corinthians, it is said, might have replied to St. Paul's challenge, by accepting the consequences with which he hoped to frighten them. They might have said to him: 'Very well; if we have to choose between abandoning our objection to the resurrection of the dead generally and the denial of Christ's Resurrection, we will deny Christ's Resurrection. And if you tell us that this means the

[a] 1 Cor. i. 30.   [b] St. Matt. xii. 20.

rejection of Christianity, to all intents and purposes; we shall not shrink from rejecting it.'

Had this been the state of mind of the Corinthians, St. Paul, we may be sure, would have dealt with them differently. He knows his ground, as is plain from other passages in this very Epistle; he sees clearly the malady with which he has to deal, and he chooses his instruments accordingly. The Corinthians are inconsequent. They do not see what results from their premises. But they are inconsequent believers; they are not inconsequent sceptics. Their creed is mutilated and erroneous; but they do not wish to be in error. They may err, as the saying goes, but they have no mind to be heretics. Devotion is not always logical, and so far as they go, they are, in intention, devout. Their hearts are in the right place. And therefore the Apostle, anxious to do the best he can for them, subjects them to the strain and pressure of this trenchant argument. For he knows that they can bear it. He knows that they will end, not by proclaiming the vanity of Apostolic preaching and of Christian faith, but by confessing the Resurrection as he himself believes it. If he were living among us now, and read all that is written by some who profess the faith for which he worked and died, is it impossible that he might think some argument of the same kind not less necessary than it was in Corinth?

St. Paul, I have said, could wield this bold argument because he knew who they were to whom it was addressed. But he knows more than this; he knows that, in affirming that Jesus has risen, he has behind, beneath him, solid, irreversible fact. No dim suspicion haunts his soul that this faith in a Risen Saviour for Whom he would gladly die, rests, in the last analysis, on the dreams of an hallucinated woman, or on some cunningly-devised fable, the product of a bitter disappointment, or on some fond popular anticipation, which hope, in a mood more eager than discerning, has twisted into the semblance of history. St. Paul knows that while he writes there are still more than two hundred and fifty persons living who saw Jesus Christ Risen on one occasion;[a] he knows that Apostles saw Him,[b] one and another; that they ate with Him,[c] that they conversed with Him,[d] that they were blessed by Him again and again.[e] "Now," he exclaims exultingly, "is Christ risen from the dead, and become the first-fruits of them that slept."[f] We must not follow him to-day any further into the grounds on which this vital conviction rests. It is enough to have seen what he thinks about the consequences of rejecting it.

But it is because Christ's Resurrection from the grave is at once so vital and so certain, that on this great Festival the Church throughout the world abandons herself to such ecstatic transports of joy and praise. This, and nothing less, is the meaning of her Alleluias; she knows the foundation of the faith of Christians to be a reality. At the empty tomb of Jesus, faith plants her foot firmly on the soil of earth, and then presently she raises her head to the heights of heaven. If Christ have indeed risen, then the Redemption on Calvary, then the life beyond the grave, then the unassailable sanctity of the Perfect Man, then the coming triumph of goodness over evil, are certain and indisputable. If Christ be risen indeed, then neither is the Apostolic teaching vain, nor is the faith of Christians

---

[a] 1 Cor. xv. 6.
[b] St. Matt. xxviii. 16, 17; St. Mark xvi. 1, 14; St. Luke xxiv. 31, 36; St. John xx. 21, 26-29; 1 Cor. xv. 7, 8.
[c] St. Luke xxiv. 30, 43; St. John xxi. 12, 13; Acts x. 41.
[d] St. Matt. xxviii. 9, 10, 18-20; St. Mark xvi. 14-18; St. Luke xxiv. 17-51; St. John xx. 19-23, 26-29; xxi. 1-22; Acts i. 3-8; ix. 5, 6.
[e] St. Luke xxiv. 36, 50; St. John xx. 19, 21, 26.
[f] 1 Cor. xv. 20.

vain. "The Lord is risen indeed." And therefore, to the end of time the Apostolic message will sway successive generations of men with a conviction of its truth and power; and the faith of Christendom will be, as it has been, the strength and the consolation of millions, as they pass through this world into the life beyond the grave.

SERMON V.

GROUNDS OF FAITH IN THE RESURRECTION.

1 St. John v. 6.

It is the Spirit That beareth witness.

ON Easter Day we were considering St. Paul's argument, that without faith in the Resurrection of Jesus Christ serious Christianity is impossible; that, when the Resurrection is denied, Apostolic doctrine and Christian faith are alike emptied of all vital force. A Christ who died, and who never rose from death, is not the Christ of the New Testament, or the Christ of Christendom. Such a Christ as this never would have converted the world, and a Christianity, so to call it, which centres in such a Christ, will not long even interest it. A Christ who died, but who never has conquered death, is plainly an intellectual makeshift; the creation and the toy of souls, who are passing, whether consciously or not, from the faith of their fathers to infidelity. If it can be shown that Christ did not really rise from His grave, Christianity sinks at once to the level of a purely human theory of life and conduct, whose author failed altogether to make good his language about himself. Certainly Christ's Religion has played too great a part in human affairs to be forgotten by history;

but it would, in the event contemplated, have forfeited all right to obtrude itself any longer on the attention of mankind, as God's great revelation of Himself to His rational creatures.

It is natural to ask a question, the answer to which was only glanced at last Sunday,[a] namely, What is the evidence that Christ did really rise from the dead ? And here, as St. John says in to-day's Epistle, "it is the Spirit That beareth witness."[b] St. John, indeed, is speaking immediately of that faith in our Lord's Eternal Sonship which overcomes the world. But since the Resurrection is the main proof of our Lord's Divinity; since He "was declared to be the Son of God with power, as regards His Holy Higher Nature, by the resurrection from the dead;"[c] it follows that the Spirit must also bear witness to the Resurrection. And He does this in two ways. It is His work, that those historical proofs of the Resurrection which have come down to us, and which address themselves to our natural reasoning faculties, have been marshalled, recognised, preserved, transmitted in the Church of Christ. The Spirit, as we Christians believe, bears witness in the sacred pages of the New Testament to the Resurrection of Jesus. But He bears another witness, as we shall presently see, by His action, not so much on the intelligence, as on the will of the believing Christian. Let us ask ourselves, first of all, What is the evidence with which we are supplied on the subject of the Resurrection? what is there to be said on the subject to a person who believed, I will not now say, in the supernatural inspiration, but in the general trustworthiness of the writings of the first Christians?

[a] Cf. Sermon IV. [b] 1 St. John v. 6. [c] Rom. i. 4.

I.

In order to know that our Lord did really rise from the dead, we have to satisfy ourselves that three distinct questions can be answered.

Of these, the first is whether Jesus Christ did really die upon the Cross. For if He merely fainted or swooned away, then there was no resurrection from death. Then He merely recovered consciousness, after whatever interval. But each one of the four Evangelists says expressly that He did die. The wonder is not that He died when He did, after hanging for three hours in agony, but that, after all His sufferings at the hands of the soldiers and the populace, before His crucifixion, He should have lived so long. Yet suppose that what looked like death on the Cross was only a fainting-fit. Would He have survived the wound in His side, inflicted by the soldier's lance, through which the blood yet remaining in His heart and the water of the pericardium escaped? We are expressly told that the soldiers did not break His legs, because He was already dead:[a] and before Pilate would allow the Body to be taken down from the Cross he ascertained from the centurion in command that death had already taken place.[b] But suppose, against all this evidence, that when Jesus was taken down from the Cross, He was still living. Then He must have been suffocated by Joseph of Arimathæa and Nicodemus when they embalmed Him. They rubbed one hundred pounds weight of myrrh and aloes over the surface of His Body; and then they wound linen bandages round each of His limbs, His Head and His Body, before they laid Him in the grave. The Jews carefully inspected and

[a] St. John xix. 33.   [b] St. Mark xv. 44, 45.

sealed His tomb: they had sentinels placed there; and were satisfied that the work was thoroughly done. To do them justice, the Jews have never denied the reality of our Lord's death; it is impossible to do so, without paradox.

A second question is whether the disciples did not take our Lord's dead Body out of His sepulchre.

They would not have wished to do it. Why should they? What would have been their motive? Put yourselves in the position of the disciples, when convinced of the reality of our Lord's death. They either believed that He would rise from the dead, or they did not. If they did believe it, they would have shrunk from disturbing His grave, as from an act not less unnecessary than profane. If they did not believe in it, and instead of abandoning themselves to unreflecting grief, allowed themselves to think steadily, what must have been their estimate of their dead Master? They must now have thought of Him as of one Who had deceived them, or Who was Himself deceived. If He was not a clever impostor who had failed, He was a sincere but feeble character, Who had been the victim of a religious delusion. On either supposition, why should they rouse the anger of the Jews, and incur the danger of swift and heavy punishment? What would have been gained, for good and simple men, by persuading the Jews that He had risen, or that He was the Messiah, or that His anticipations had come to pass, if, all the while, they themselves knew that He was dead, and that His dead body had only been shifted by themselves from one resting-place to another? If they were mere religious adventurers, they could not have hoped to succeed: the trick would have been not less fruitless than absurd. The world, after all, is not converted by sleight-of-hand. And in order to believe that the Apostles would not have wished to remove our Lord's Body from the sepulchre, it is only necessary to credit them with ordinary common sense.

But had they desired, they surely would not have dared it. Until Pentecost, they were, by their own account, very timid men. When Jesus was arrested, all the disciples forsook Him and fled.[a] St. Peter denied Him.[b] Only St. John ventured to follow Him to Calvary, and to stand near His Cross.[c] For some days afterwards the disciples did not presume to show themselves in public, for fear of the Jews.[d] When our Lord stood in the midst of the closed chamber, they took Him for a phantom, and were seized with terror.[e] Were these the men to risk a desperate struggle with a guard of soldiers, and to take a dead body from its tomb at the dead of the night? Even if one or two of the disciples could have ventured on such an enterprise, could they have counted on the co-operation of the others? Would they not have dreaded betrayal by some of their companions, who, whether from motives of honesty or of rivalry, might have denounced the plot to the Jewish authorities?

And, once more, had they desired and dared to remove our Lord's Body from its grave, such a feat was obviously beyond their power. The tomb was guarded by soldiers. Every precaution had been taken by the Jews to make it secure.[f] The great stone at the entrance could not have been rolled away without much disturbance, even if the Body could have been removed without attracting attention. The character of the guards was at stake; had they countenanced or promoted any such crime their almost

---

[a] St. Matt. xxvi. 56; St. Mark xiv. 50.
[b] St. Matt. xxvi. 69-75; St. Mark xiv. 66-72.
[c] St. John xix. 26.   [d] St. John xx. 19.
[e] St. Luke xxiv. 37.   [f] St. Matt. xxvii. 66.

inevitable detection would have been followed by severe punishment. In after years St. Peter was released from prison by an angel,[a] but the sentries were punished by Herod with death. Certainly the guard at the sepulchre was largely bribed by the leading Jews to say that the Body of Jesus had been taken away by the disciples while they slept.[b] Whatever the eagerness of the soldiers to touch the money, they would have been unwilling to circulate such a report as this. And the Jews never ventured to treat it as practically true. When they imprisoned and scourged St. Peter and the other Apostles; when they persecuted first St. Stephen, and many another servant of Christ, they did not accuse their victims of having stolen Christ's Body from the grave, and then of having spread a false report of His Resurrection. The charge was simply that the Apostles and others had preached the Resurrection after being ordered to be silent.

A third question may be raised, as to the amount of positive testimony which goes to show that Jesus Christ did rise from the dead.

There is, first of all, the witness of all the Apostles. They affirmed publicly that during forty days they saw Jesus Christ alive; that they held converse with Him; that they ate and drank with Him; that they touched Him.[c] They gave their lives in attestation of this fact. Their conduct after the day of Pentecost is throughout that of men whose trustworthiness and sincerity of purpose are beyond dispute. You and I, unless strengthened by Divine grace, might too probably hesitate to give our lives for what we know to be undoubted truth. But, at least,

[a] Acts xii. 7-11.   [b] St. Matt. xxviii. 13-15.
[c] St. Luke xxiv. 39, 40; St. John xx. 25, 27.

we should not—I will not say—die, but even make any considerable sacrifice, for the sake of impressing the world with the truth of an occurrence which we believe to be in any degree doubtful.

Next, there is the testimony of a large number of persons besides the Apostles. Take the case of the three thousand converts on the day of Pentecost.[a] Here were three thousand people professing belief in the Resurrection fifty days after the date of its occurrence. They had every means of verifying its truth or falsehood. They were on the spot. They could visit the tomb. They could collect and investigate the current stories. They could discuss matters with the Jews. They could cross-question the guards. They could compare, balance, analyse the conflicting opinions around them. They had unrivalled opportunities for satisfying themselves of its being a reality or a fiction. Yet at the risk of comfort, position, nay life, they publicly professed their belief in its truth. They could not be Christians without making this profession. And they had no hesitation about making it.

Or consider the case of the two hundred and fifty and more persons still living when St. Paul wrote the First Epistle to the Corinthians, who had seen the Risen Jesus on one occasion during the forty days. "After that He was seen of five hundred brethren at once, of whom the greater part remain until this present, but some are fallen asleep."[b] There is no doubt about the document which contains this assertion. The most destructive of the negative schools of modern criticism ranks this First Epistle to the Corinthians among the four books of the New Testament whose genuineness and authenticity it holds to be beyond dispute. There is no reason for questioning the accuracy of the Apostle's information; and the significance

[a] Acts ii. 41. [b] 1 Cor. xv. 6.

of the statement can hardly be exaggerated. Five hundred persons could not be simultaneously deluded. Their testimony would be considered decisive as to any ordinary occurrence, where men wished only to ascertain the simple truth.

II.

And the force of this body of testimony is not really weakened by objections which do not directly challenge it, and which turn on accessory or subordinate points.

For instance, it is said that the Evangelical accounts of the Resurrection itself, and of our Lord's subsequent appearances, are difficult to reconcile with each other. At first sight they are; but only at first sight. In order to reconcile them two things are necessary: first, patience, and secondly, a determination to exclude everything from the narrative which does not lie in the text of the Gospels. Two-thirds of the supposed difficulties are created by the riotous imagination of the negative commentators. Left to themselves, the Evangelists do not indeed tell us a great deal that we should like to know. But they do not contradict each other. If they had forged the whole story, and had written with any degree of concert, they would have been at once more explicit and less careless about appearances than they are. They would have described Jesus Christ bursting forth from His grave in a blaze of splendour; terrifying His guards; welcoming His faithful followers, who would have been collected on the spot. They would have written as painters have painted; without any admission of ignorance, without any reserve, without permitting any suspicion of differences. As it is, the differences are just what might be expected in four narratives of the same event, composed at different periods, by different authors, who had distinct sources of information at command. Each says what he has to say with blunt and simple directness; without an eye to the statements of the others, or to the possible comments of hostile critics. To show their agreement in detail would carry us beyond our limits. Suffice it to say, that in describing the Resurrection, as elsewhere, Holy Scripture takes no precautions against adverse judgments. It speaks as might a perfectly truthful child in a court of justice, conscious only of its integrity, and leaving the task, whether of criticism or apology, wholly to others. It proceeds on the strong conviction, that in the end, here as in other matters, "Wisdom is justified of all her children." [a]

It is, further, objected that the Resurrection was not sufficiently public. Jesus Christ ought to have left His grave, so it is urged, in the sight of a crowd of lookers-on; and, when risen, He ought to have hastened to show Himself to the persons least likely to believe in His Resurrection,—to the Jews at large, to the High Priests, to Pilate, to His executioners, even, it is of late hinted, to a scientific commission of some kind which, after careful investigation, might have drawn up a report upon the subject.

Here it is obvious, first of all, that the guards may very well have seen Jesus leave His tomb. Scripture says nothing on the point. But they were terrified, almost to death, at the sight of the angel of the sepulchre.[b] Any number of witnesses who had been present would have been as much frightened as were the guards. Our Lord's object was not to strike terror; but to convince, to reassure, to console. It was not easy to do this, when the disciples first saw Him after He was risen. But nothing would have been gained by their

[a] St. Luke vii. 35. [b] St. Matt. xxviii. 2-4.

seeing Him leave the tomb. They knew that He had been laid in it dead. They saw Him alive before their eyes. And they put the two facts together.

Nor is the old objection of Celsus, that Jesus Christ ought to have shown Himself to the Jews and to His judges in order to rebuke their unbelief, more reasonable. Had He appeared to the Chief Priests, would they have believed in Him? Would they not have denied His identity, or argued that a devil had taken His form before their eyes, just as, of old, they had ascribed His miracles to Beelzebub? There was no greater reason for our Lord's showing Himself to the unbelievers of that day than to the unbelievers of each succeeding century, from then till now. God gives evidence enough to make faith easy and reasonable. But He does not give that particular kind of evidence which captious unbelief may from time to time demand, possibly for no better reason than because it thinks that such evidence will not be given. They who cried on the day of Calvary, "Let Him now come down from the Cross, and we will believe Him,"[a] would not really have believed Him, if He had taken them at their word. Unbelief is the product of a particular state of heart and mind, much more than of the absence of some one kind of evidence. The Jews had ample opportunities of ascertaining that the Resurrection was a fact, if they had desired to do so. But, as it was, they were not in a mood to be convinced, even by the evidence of their senses. It was with them, as with the brethren of the Rich Man in the Parable: "If they hear not Moses and the prophets, neither will they be persuaded, though one rose from the dead."[b] If the testimony of the Apostles, and of so many other persons, was insufficient, the appearance of our Risen Lord Himself would not have done more than add to the

[a] St. Matt. xxvii. 42.   [b] St. Luke xvi. 31.

list of their rejected opportunities, and to the sentence of their condemnation.

Far deeper than these objections is that which really lies against all miracles whatever, as being at variance with that conception of a rigid uniformity in the processes of Nature, which is one of the intellectual fashions of our day. Suffice it to say, that any idea of natural law which is held to make a miracle impossible, is also inconsistent with belief in the existence of God. When a believer in God talks of a law of Nature, he can never mean more than God's uniform mode of working. He cannot mean anything independent of God, any force or impact which, if originally due to Him, has now acquired a right to maintain itself in spite of Him, or is at any rate out of His reach. To hold this idea of law is to hold that God is not Master of the Universe; in other words, that He is not Himself. That He works uniformly is a matter of observation, and is only what we should anticipate from that Law of Order which is an attribute of His Being. And this uniformity is the foil to the miracle, which purposely innovates on it. Without such general uniformity in the background there would be nothing striking in the miracle. But if God is Omnipotent, so that His eternal moral attributes alone limit His powers of action, then it cannot be denied that miracle is always possible. And if God be a Moral Being, Who as such deems the interests of His moral creatures higher than those of the inanimate and irrational beings around, then miracle, at certain crises in human history, is even to be expected. The only real question for a serious believer in God is whether the producible evidence for any alleged miracle is sufficient.

From the nature of the case, it is impossible to give more than a scanty and imperfect outline of a great subject like the evidence for the Resurrection, within the compass of a sermon. But it is to be wished, in these days especially, that Christians would make themselves better acquainted with the grounds of their faith than they often are. Such old-fashioned but useful books as Sherlock's *Trial of the Witnesses*, in which the evidence for the Resurrection is discussed conformably with the rules of the English Bar, would do a great deal of good, if they were better known. Undoubtedly, new points have been raised since Sherlock's time; and to a certain extent the controversy has shifted its ground. But, in the main, his presentation of the case is of lasting value, and is better suited to our national tastes and temper than the works of some more recent apologists.

III.

Here then we are coming round to the point from which we started. For it is natural to ask, Why, if the Resurrection can be proved by evidence so generally sufficient, it was at the time, and is still, rejected by a great many intelligent men? The answer to this natural and legitimate question is of practical importance to all of us.

There can, I apprehend, be no sort of doubt that if an ordinary historical occurrence, such as the death of Julius Cæsar, were attested as clearly as the Resurrection of our Lord—not more clearly, nor less,—as having taken place nineteen centuries ago, all the world would believe it as a matter of course. Nay more, if an extraordinary occurrence, traversing the usual operations of God in Nature, were similarly attested, it would be easily believed, if only it stood alone, as an isolated wonder, connected with no religious claim, implying no religious duties, appealing only to the understanding, and having no bearing, however remote, upon the will.

The reason why the Resurrection was not always believed upon the evidence of those who witnessed to it is, because to believe it means, for a consistent and thoughtful man, to believe in and to accept a great deal else. To believe the Resurrection is to believe, implicitly, in the Christian Faith. The Divine Person of our Lord, the atoning work of our Lord, the teaching authority of our Lord, the efficacy of His Intercession in Heaven, and of the great means of grace which He has given us on earth, depend on and are bound up with His Resurrection. It is no mere speculative question, whether Jesus Christ did or did not rise from the dead; it is an eminently practical one. The intellect is not more interested in it, than the will; perhaps it is even less interested. If the intellect alone could have the decision of the question in its keeping, the number of unbelievers would be comparatively small. The real difficulties of belief lie, generally speaking, with the will. And nothing is more certain, I may add, more alarming, than the power of the will to shape, check, promote, control conviction. The will too has a reasoning power of its own; the will is, in a sense, another reason within us. It looks ahead; it watches the proceedings of the understanding with a jealous scrutiny; it watches, and, if need be, it interferes. It sees the understanding on the point of embracing a conviction, which means much more than speculative assent; which means action or suffering, that is to say, something entirely within its own province—the province of the will. It sees the conviction, all but accepted; it sees the understanding stretching out its arms to welcome the advancing truth; and it mutters to itself,—" This must not be, or I shall be compromised. I shall have to do or to endure what I do not like." And such is the power of the will that it can give effect to this decision. It can baulk and thwart the action of the intellect; give it a perverse twist, and even set it scheming how best to discredit or refute the truth which but now it was on the point of accepting. This is what happened to the Jews of the Pentecostal period. They had no prejudices against miracles. On the contrary, they expected miracles to occur from time to time. They entirely believed in astonishing miracles in their own past history; although many of these miracles rested upon evidence far less cogent than the Resurrection of Jesus Christ. Had it been for them only a speculative question, they would have believed in this too; but so far from being a speculative question only, it was charged with practical consequences. The will of the Jew instinctively suggested to him: 'If Jesus of Nazareth rose from His grave, then a great deal else follows for which I am not prepared: then He is the Messiah, and the present order of things will be seriously changed; and new duties, new sacrifices, will be expected of me and mine. I must inquire, if His Resurrection be so very certain; if there be not a natural explanation of it; if it be not due to a trick, or to an hallucination. Anyhow it must not, it cannot, be accepted as true. It may triumph at the bar of probable evidence. But common sense, as I understand common sense, is against it.'

This, or something like this, is what the Jew would have thought to himself. And his will would have carried the day against his understanding. And thus we may understand what it is that the Spirit does to produce faith. He does not set aside or extinguish the operations of the natural reason; reason too is a guide to truth which God has given us. But He does change the temper, or the direction of the will. And thus He sets the reason free to do justice to the evidence before it. It is thus that, within us, the Spirit beareth witness. The evidence for the Resurrection is of such a character that an unspiritual man, with no more than average powers, who understands the value of a probable as distinct from a mathematical argument, can see its strength and force. But this perception is useless, unless the will be ready to do its part, or at least not to interfere with the verdict of the intellect. And it is the Spirit who secures this: He

> Bends the stubborn heart and will,
> Melts the frozen, warms the chill,
> Guides the steps that go astray.

The evidence for the Resurrection was not stronger on the Day of Pentecost than it was on the day before. But the Descent of the Spirit made it morally possible for three thousand converts to do that evidence something like justice.

And now we can see why St. Paul makes so much of faith,—especially in a Risen Christ,—in his great Epistles. Faith is not merely the assent of the understanding: it is also the assent of the will. It is even less an intellectual than a moral act. And thus it is a test and criterion not only or chiefly of the worth of a man's head-piece, but pre-eminently, of the rectitude of his dispositions, of the goodness of his heart. This is one reason why it justifies; in an act of faith the whole moral nature concurs in the justifying assent to revealed truth. If the understanding were alone concerned there would be no more reason for our being justified by faith in a Crucified and Risen Christ than for our being justified by our assent to the conclusion of a problem in Euclid. It is because the will must indorse the verdict of the understanding, and so must mean obedience as well as assent, that "by grace are ye saved through faith; and that not of yourselves: it is the gift of God."ᵃ

At the close of Easter Week, let us endeavour to remember this. Pray for that Divine Spirit Who witnesses to the Resurrection, as in the sacred Books of Scripture, so by His action upon the hearts and wills of men. Remember that as no man can say that Jesus is the Lord but by the Holy Ghost,ᵇ so no man can profess to any purpose faith in Christ's Resurrection but by the Holy Ghost. It is the Spirit that beareth witness, now as nineteen centuries ago, by that influence on the will of man, which leaves the intellect at liberty to do justice to the evidence before it. Pray that most Blessed Spirit so to touch your heart and will that you may have no reason for wishing the Resurrection to be untrue. Pray for this His gracious assistance; that you may recover or strengthen the great grace of faith, and have your part in that Apostolical Promise —"If thou shalt confess with thy mouth the Lord Jesus, and shalt believe in thine heart that God hath raised Him from the dead, thou shalt be saved."ᶜ

ᵃ Eph. ii. 8.   ᵇ 1 Cor. xii. 3.   ᶜ Rom. x. 9.

SERMON VI.

THE RESURRECTION INEVITABLE.

ACTS II. 24.

Whom God hath raised up, having loosed the pains of death: because it was not possible that He should be holden of it.

THIS is the language of the first Christian Apostle, in the first sermon that was ever preached in the Church of Christ. St. Peter is accounting for the miraculous gift of languages on the Day of Pentecost. After observing that it was, after all, only a fulfilment of the prophecy of Joel* about the outpouring of the Spirit in the last days, he proceeds to trace it to its cause. It was the work, he says, of Jesus Christ, now ascended into heaven;—"He hath shed forth this which ye now see and hear." But Jesus Christ, he argues, had really ascended into heaven, because He had first really risen from the grave; and it is to St. Peter's way of accounting for Christ's Resurrection that I invite your attention to-day—as being the first Apostolic statement on the subject that was given to the world. And certainly, even if the point were only one of antiquarian interest, it would be full of attraction for every intelligent man to know how the first Christians thought about the chief truths of their

* Joel ii. 28, 29.

Faith; considering the influence which that Faith has had and still has on the development of the human race. But for us, Christians, concern in this matter is more exacting and urgent. Our hopes and fears, our depressions and our enthusiasms, our improvement or our deterioration, are bound up with it. "If Christ be not risen, our preaching is vain, your faith is also vain." Let us then listen to what the Apostle St. Peter says about a subject upon which his opportunities, to say nothing of higher credentials, qualified him to speak so authoritatively.

I.

First of all, then, St. Peter states the fact that Christ had risen from the dead. "Whom God hath raised up, having loosed the pains of death." Let us remember that he is preaching in Jerusalem, the scene of the Death and Resurrection of Christ, and, as his sermon shows, to some [a] who had taken part in the scenes of the Crucifixion. Not more than seven weeks have passed since these events,—about the time that has passed since the Sunday before Ash Wednesday. And in Jerusalem, we may be sure, men did not live as fast as they do in an European capital, in this age of telegraphs and railroads. An event like the Crucifixion, in a town of that size, far removed from the greater centres of human life, would have occupied general attention for a considerable period. It would have been discussed and re-discussed in all its bearings. All that happened at the time, and immediately afterwards, the supposed disappointment of the disciples and ruin of the cause, as well as the agony and humiliation of the Master, would have been still ordinary topics of conversation in most circles of Jewish society.

[a] Acts ii. 23.

It was then to persons keenly interested in the subject, and who had opportunities of testing the truth of what he said, that St. Peter states so calmly and unhesitatingly the fact of the Resurrection. He states it as just as much a fact of history as the Crucifixion, in which his hearers had taken part. " Ye men of Israel, hear these words; Jesus of Nazareth, a Man approved of God among you by miracles and wonders and signs, which God did by Him in the midst of you, as ye yourselves also know : Him, being delivered by the determinate counsel and foreknowledge of God, ye have taken, and by wicked hands have crucified and slain :" and then he adds, " Whom God hath raised up, having loosed the pains of death."[a] " This Jesus," he adds a little afterwards, " hath God raised up, whereof we all are witnesses." [b] Not one or two favoured disciples ; but all, even the doubter, all had seen their beloved Master. They had heard the tones of that familiar voice ; they had seen the wounds of the Passion; they had recognised in repeated conversations the continuity of heart, of thought, of purpose. It was the Jesus of old days, only invested with a new and awful glory. On the very day that He rose, He had been seen five times. And "He showed Himself alive after His Passion by many infallible proofs, being seen of His disciples forty days, and speaking of the things pertaining to the kingdom of God." [c]

Some twenty-six years later, when St. Paul wrote his first Apostolical Letter to the Church of Corinth, there were, he says, more than two hundred and fifty persons still alive who had seen Jesus Christ after His Resurrection on a single occasion.[d] The number of witnesses to the fact of the Resurrection, to whom St. Peter could appeal, and whom his hearers might cross-question if they liked, will account for the simplicity and confidence of his assertion.

[a] Acts ii. 22-24.   [b] Acts ii. 32.   [c] Acts i. 3.   [d] 1 Cor. xv. 6.

In those days men had not learnt to think more of abstract theories than of well-attested facts. The world had not yet heard of that singular state of mind which holds that an *a priori* doctrine about the nature of things, or, stranger still, an existing temper or mood of human thought, is a sufficient reason for refusing to listen to the evidence which may be produced in favour of a fact. Nobody, it may be added, who professed to believe in an Almighty God, thought it reverent or reasonable to say that He could not for sufficient reasons modify His ordinary rules of working, if He chose to do so.

St. Peter then preached the Resurrection as a fact, and, as we know, with great and immediate results. But how did he account for the Resurrection? what was the reason which he gave for its having happened at all? This is the second point, to which I invite your attention; and it will detain us somewhat longer than the first.

II.

St. Peter, then, says that Christ was raised from the dead, "because it was not possible that He should be holden of" death. Thus St. Peter's first thought about this matter is the very opposite to that of many persons in our day. They say that no evidence will convince them that Christ has risen, because they hold it to be antecedently impossible that He should rise. St. Peter, on the other hand, almost speaks as if he could dispense with any evidence, so certain is he that Jesus Christ must rise. In point of fact, as we know, St. Peter had his own experience to fall back upon;[a] he had seen his Risen Master on the day of His Resurrection, and often since.

[a] St. Luke xxiv. 34.

But so far was this evidence of his senses from causing him any perplexity, that it only fell in with the anticipations which he had now formed on other and independent grounds. "It was not possible," he says, "that Christ should be holden, or imprisoned, by death." It will do us good, my brethren, as fellow-believers with St. Peter, to spend some little time upon his grounds for saying this; to consider, so far as we may, the reasons of this Divine impossibility.

And here, first of all, we find the reason which lay, so to speak, closest to the conclusion, and which was intended to convince the Apostle's hearers, in the sermon itself. "It was not possible that Christ should be holden of death; *for* David speaketh concerning Him." It was then Jewish prophecy which forbade Christ to remain in His grave, and made His Resurrection nothing less than a necessity. As to the principle of this argument there would have been no controversy between St. Peter and the Jews. The Jews believed in the reality and force of prophecy—of that variety of prophecy which foretells strictly future events—just as distinctly as did Christians. The prophets, in the belief of the Jews, were the confidants of God. He whispered into their souls, by His Spirit, His secret resolutions for the coming time. "Surely," exclaims the prophet Amos, "surely the Lord will do nothing, but He revealeth His secret unto His servants the prophets."[a] And when once God had thus spoken, His word, it was felt by Jews and Christians, stood sure.[b] His gifts and calling were without repentance.[c] The prophetic word became, in virtue of God's Moral Attributes, a restraint upon that liberty of which it was the product, until it was fulfilled. It con-

[a] Amos iii. 7.   [b] Numb. xxiii. 19.   [c] Rom. xi. 29.

stituted within the limits of its application a law of necessity, to which men and events, and, if need were, nature had to bend. And for all who believed in its Author, the supposition that it would come to nothing after all, was, to use St. Peter's phrase, "not possible." It could not return empty; it must accomplish the work for which God had sent it forth; since it bound Him to an engagement with those who uttered and with those who heard His message.

Obviously enough, the true drift of a prophecy may easily be mistaken. God is not responsible for the eccentric guesses as to His meaning in which well-meaning men of vagrant imaginations may possibly indulge. We have lived in this generation to hear some very confident guesses, based on the supposed meaning of prophecy, respecting the end of the world, or some impending general catastrophe. But the dates assigned for such occurrences have passed. And religion would be seriously discredited, if the Sacred Word itself were at fault, instead of the fervid imagination of some incautious expositor. But where a prediction is clear, it does bind Him Who is its real Author to some fulfilment, which, in the event, will be recognised as such. And such a prediction of the Resurrection of Messiah St. Peter finds in Psalm xvi., where David,—as more completely in Psalm xxii.,—loses the sense of his own personal circumstances in the impetus and ecstasy of the prophetic spirit, and describes a Personality of Which indeed he was a type, but Which altogether transcends him.

> "Therefore My heart is glad,
> And My glory rejoiceth:
> My flesh also shall rest in hope.
> For Thou wilt not leave My Soul in hell;
> Neither wilt Thou suffer Thine Holy One to see corruption.

Thou wilt show Me the path of life:
In Thy Presence is fulness of joy;
At Thy Right Hand there are pleasures for evermore."[a]

David, so argues St. Peter, utters these words; but they are not strictly true of David. "David," he says, "is both dead and buried, and his sepulchre is among us unto this day." Or, as St. Paul states, when appealing to this very Psalm in his sermon at Antioch in Pisidia, "David, after he had served his own generation by the will of God, fell on sleep, and was laid unto his fathers, and saw corruption. But He, Whom God raised up, saw no corruption."[b] The meaning of the Psalm was so clear to some Jewish doctors, that, unable as they were to reconcile it with David's history, they invented the fable, that his body was miraculously preserved from corruption. David, however, was really speaking in the Person of Messiah. And his language created the necessity that Messiah should rise from the dead; or, as St. Peter puts it, his language made it impossible that Messiah should be holden by death. God had spoken, in other passages, no doubt. But He spoke with great clearness in this. And His Word could not return unto Him empty.

Observe, here, that St. Peter had not always felt and thought thus. He had known this Psalm all his life. But long after he had followed Jesus Christ about Galilee and Judæa he had been ignorant of its true meaning. Only little by little do any of us learn God's truth and will. And so lately as the morning of the Resurrection, St. John says of both St. Peter and himself that "as yet they knew not the scripture, that He must rise again from the dead."[c] Since then the Holy Spirit had come down, and had poured a flood of light into the minds

[a] Ps. xvi. 9-11.   [b] Acts xiii. 36, 37.   [c] St. John xx. 9.

of the Apostles and over the sacred pages of the Old Testament. And thus a necessity for the Resurrection, which even Jews ought to recognise, was now abundantly plain to them. May that same Eternal Spirit teach us, as then He taught our spiritual forefathers, the full meaning of His Word!

A second reason which would have shaped St. Peter's language lay in the character of his Master Jesus Christ. It was our Lord's character not less assuredly than His miracles which drew human hearts to Him, and led or forced them to give up all that this world could offer for the happiness of following and serving Him. Now, of our Lord's character a leading feature was its simple truthfulness. It was morally impossible for Him to hold out prospects which would never be realised or to use words which He did not mean. Nay, He insisted upon simple sincerity of language in those who came into His company. He would not allow the young man to call Him "Good Master,"[a] when the expression was a mere phrase in his mouth. He would not accept professions to follow Him whithersoever He went, or aspirations to sit on His right hand and on His left in His kingdom till men had weighed their words, and were sure that they meant all that such words involved. Unless then He was like those Pharisees whom He censured for laying burdens upon others which they would not touch themselves, it might be taken for granted that if He promised He would perform; that His promise made performance morally necessary, and non-performance morally impossible. This was the feeling of His disciples about Him. He was too wise to predict the impossible. He was too sincere to promise what He did not mean.

[a] St. Mark x. 17.

The Resurrection inevitable.

Now Jesus Christ had again and again said that He would be put to a violent death, and that after dying He would rise again. Sometimes, as to the Jews in the Temple, when He cleansed it in the early days of His ministry, He expressed His meaning in the language of metaphor. "Destroy," He said to them, "this Temple, and in three days I will raise it up."[a] The Jews rallied Him on the absurdity of undertaking to reconstruct in three days an edifice which it had taken forty-six years to build. The drift of the words may have been made plain to the disciples by a gesture which accompanied them; and in later years they understood the sense in which He termed His Body a Temple, namely, because in Him dwelt all the fulness of the Godhead bodily.[b] Sometimes He fell back upon ancient Hebrew history, and compared that which would befall Himself to the miraculous adventure of the prophet who shrank from the mission assigned to him by God. When the Pharisees, irritated at His stern rebuke of their blasphemous levity in ascribing His miracle on the blind and dumb man to the activity of Beelzebub, asked Him for a "sign," that is, for some credential of His mission, He contented Himself with saying that as Jonah had been three days and three nights in the whale's belly, so would the Son of Man be in the heart of the earth.[c] In other words, His right to speak and act as He did would be proved by His rising from the dead. With His disciples He used neither metaphor nor historic parallel. He said simply, on three occasions at the least,[d] as the hour of His sufferings approached, that He should be crucified, and should rise again from death. Peter himself had, on the first of these occasions, rebuked Him, as we know, and had been rebuked in turn.[e] Thus He

---
[a] St. John ii. 19.   [b] Col. ii. 9.   [c] St. Matt. xii. 40.
[d] St. Matt. xvi. 21; St. Mark ix. 31; x. 32-34.   [e] St. Matt. xvi. 22, 23.

was pledged, if we may reverently say so, to this particular act. He was pledged to the Jewish people, pledged to its ruling classes, pledged especially to His Own chosen band of faithful followers. He could not have remained in His grave—I will not say without dishonour, but—without causing in others a revulsion of feeling such as is provoked by the exposure of baseless pretensions.

It may indeed be urged that the Resurrection foretold by Christ was not a literal resurrection of His dead Body, but only a recovery of His ascendency, His credit, His authority; obscured as these had been for a while in the apprehension of His disciples and of the world, by the tragedy of the Crucifixion. The word Resurrection, according to this supposition, is in His mouth a purely metaphorical expression. It is used to describe not anything that affected Jesus Christ Himself, but only a revolution of opinion and feeling about Him in the minds of others. Socrates had had to drink the fatal hemlock; and the body of Socrates had long since mingled with the dust. But Socrates, it might be said, had risen, in the intellectual triumphs of his pupils, and in the enthusiastic admiration of succeeding ages; the method and words of Socrates had been preserved for all time in a literature that will never die. If Christ was to be put to death by crucifixion, He would triumph, even after a death so shameful and degrading, as Socrates and others had triumphed before Him. To imagine for Him an actual exit from His tomb, is said to be a crude literalism, natural to uncultivated ages, but impossible, when the finer suggestiveness of human language has been felt to transcend the letter.

An obvious reply to this explanation is, that it arbitrarily makes our Lord use literal and metaphorical language in two successive clauses of a single sentence.

He is literal, it seems, when He predicts His Crucifixion; there is no doubt about that. The world has always agreed with the Church as to the fact of His being crucified. Tacitus[a] mentions His death as well as the Evangelists. But if our Lord is to be understood literally, when He foretells His Cross, why is He to be thought metaphorical when He foretells His Resurrection? Why should not His Resurrection, if it be only metaphorical, be preceded by a metaphorical crucifixion; a crucifixion of thought, or will, or reputation,—not the literal nailing of a human body to a wooden cross? Why does this fastidious temper, which shrinks from the idea of a literal rising from a literal grave, not shrink equally from a literal nailing to a literal cross? It is impossible seriously to maintain on any grounds consistent with an honest interpretation of His words, that our Lord Himself could have meant that He would be literally crucified, but would only rise in a metaphorical sense. Surely He meant that the one event would be just as much or just as little a matter of fact as the other. And any other construction of His words would never have originated except with those who wish to combine a lingering respect for His language, with a total disbelief in the supreme miracle which has made Him what He is to Christendom. No; it is clear that, if Jesus Christ had not risen from the grave He would not have kept His engagements with His disciples or with the world. This was the feeling of those who knew and loved Him best. This was the feeling of St. Peter, ripened no doubt but lately into a sharply-defined conviction, but based on years of intimate companionship;—when Christ, so scrupulously truthful and so invariably wise, had once said that He would rise from death, any other event was simply impossible. All was really staked on His

[a] *Annal.* xv. 44.

rising again. And when He did rise, "He was declared to be the Son of God with power, in respect of His Holy and Higher Nature, by the Resurrection from the dead."[a] Those who cling to His human character, yet deny His Resurrection, would do well to consider, that they must choose between their moral enthusiasm and their unbelief; since it is the character of Christ, even more than the language of prophecy, which made the idea that He would not rise after death impossible for His first disciples.

Not that we have yet exhausted St. Peter's reasons for this remarkable expression. You will remember, my friends, that in the sermon which St. Peter preached to a crowd, after the healing of the lame man at the Beautiful gate of the temple, he went over much of the ground which is traversed in this first sermon on the Day of Pentecost. He told his hearers among other things that they had "killed the Prince of Life, Whom God raised from the dead."[b] Remark that striking title, "The Prince of Life." Not merely does it show how high above all earthly royalties was the Crucified Saviour in the heart and faith of His Apostle. It connects the thought of St. Peter in this early stage of his ministry with the language of his Divine Master on the one side, and that of His Apostles St. Paul and St. John upon the other. Our Lord had said, "I am the Way, the Truth, and the Life;"[c] He had explained the sense of this last word "Life" by saying that "as the Father hath Life in Himself, so hath He given to the Son to have Life in Himself."[d] He had complained to the men of His time, "Ye will not come unto Me that ye might have life."[e] And St. John said of Him that "in Him was Life:"[f] and St. Paul, in

[a] Rom. i. 4.   [b] Acts iii. 15.   [c] St. John xiv. 6.
[d] St. John v. 26.   [e] St. John v. 40.   [f] St. John i. 4.

to-day's Epistle, calls Him "Christ, Who is our Life."[a] When, then, St. Peter names Him the "Prince of Life," he is referring to this same truth about his Master. And it is in fact the keynote of the Gospel.

What is life? That is a question which no man even now can answer. We do not know what life is in itself. We only register its symptoms. We see growth; we see movement; and we say, Here is life. It exists in one degree in the tree; in a higher in the animal; in a higher still in man. In beings above man, we cannot doubt, it is to be found in some yet grander form. But in all these cases it is a gift from another: and having been given, it might be modified or withdrawn. Who is He in Whom life resides originally; He Who owes it to no other; He from Whom no other can withdraw it? Only the Self-Existent lives of right. He lives because He cannot but live; He lives an original as distinct from a derived life. This is true of the Eternal Three, Who yet are One. But Revelation assures us that it is only true of the Son and the Holy Spirit, because by an unbegun, unending communication of Deity, They receive such Life from the Eternal Father. Hence our Lord says, "As the Father hath Life in Himself, so hath He given to the Son to have Life in Himself."[b] Not merely Life, but "Life in Himself." Thus, with the Eternal Giver, the Eternal Receiver is Fountain and Source of Life. With reference to all created beings, He is the Life,—their Creator, their Upholder, their End. "For," says St. Paul, "by Him were all things created, that are in heaven, and that are in earth, visible and invisible; whether they be thrones, or dominions, or principalities, or powers: all things were created by Him, and for Him: and He is before all things, and by Him all things consist."[c]

[a] Col. iii. 4.   [b] St. John v. 26.   [c] Col. i. 16, 17.

This then is the full sense of St. Peter's expression, "The Prince of Life." And in the truth which it teaches as to our Lord's jurisdiction over life, based on the truth of His Eternal Nature, we may trace a third reason for St. Peter's expression in the text. How could the very Lord and Source of Life be subdued by death? If, for reasons of wisdom and mercy, He subjected the Nature which He had made His Own to the king of terrors, this was surely not in the course of nature; it was a violence to nature that this should be. And therefore when the object had been achieved, He would rise, St. Peter implies, by an inevitable rebound, by the force of things, by the inherent energy of His irrepressible Life. From St. Peter's point of view, the real wonder would be if such a Being were not to rise. The pains of death were loosed, —not by an extraordinary effort, as in your case or mine —but because it was impossible that He, the Prince of Life, should be holden of it.

Observe, then, my friends, how St. Peter deals with this great subject. He now looks at it from above, so to say, rather than from below. He here asks himself what his faith about the Son of God points to, rather than what history proves to have taken place. He is for the moment more concerned for his Master's honour than with the significance and value of His acts for us. To St. Peter it is less strange that there should be an innovation upon nature such as the resurrection of a dead body than it would be if such a Being as Jesus Christ, having been put to death, did not rise. St. Peter is very far from being indifferent to the proof that Christ did rise; indeed he often and earnestly insists on it. But just as St. John always calls Christ's miracles His "works,"[a] meaning that they were only what such an One as He

[a] St. John vii. 3, 21; x. 25, 32; xiv. 12; xv. 24.

might be expected to do; so St. Peter treats His Resurrection from the dead as perfectly natural to Him; nay, as an event which any man or angel with sufficient knowledge might have calculated beforehand, just as astronomers predict unerringly the movements of the heavenly bodies. God hath raised Jesus from the dead, he says, because it was impossible that death should continue to hold Him.[a]

III.

Yes. The buried Christ could not really remain in His grave. He was raised from it in virtue of a Divine necessity; and this necessity, while in its original form strictly proper to His case, points to kindred necessities which affect His servants and His Church. Let us in conclusion briefly consider them.

Note, first, the impossibility, for us Christians too, of being buried for ever in the tomb in which we shall each be laid at death. We too, after the death and burial which awaits each one of us, shall rise; nay, we must rise. In this, as in other matters, "as He," our Lord, "is, so are we in this world."[b] To us as to Him, although in a different way, God has pledged Himself. There is a difference indeed, such as might be expected between our case and His. In Him an internal vital force made Resurrection from death necessary; in us there is no such intrinsic force, only a power guaranteed to us from without. He could say of the temple of His Body, "I will raise it up in three days:" we can only say that God will raise us up, we know not when. But this we do know, that "if the Spirit of Him that raised up Jesus from the dead dwell in you, He that raised up Christ from the dead

[a] Acts ii. 24.   [b] 1 St. John iv. 17.

shall also quicken your mortal bodies by His Spirit that dwelleth in you."ᵃ This we do know, that "we must all be made manifest before the judgment-seat of Christ, that every one may receive the things done in the body, according to that which he hath done, whether it be good or bad."ᵇ The law of justice and the law of love combine to create a necessity which requires "a resurrection of the dead, both of the just and of the unjust."ᶜ

It is not always easy even for believing Christians to do justice to this solemn and certain truth. The gradual decay of vital force during illness, the dissolution and corruption of the body after death, the chemistry not less than the pathos of the grave, combine to make us forget Whose word it is that warrants for each one of us a Resurrection. And yet He "will change our vile body, that it may be fashioned like unto His glorious Body, according to the mighty working whereby He is able even to subdue all things unto Himself."ᵈ Death is not an eternal sleep; the Tomb is not the final resting-place of the bodies of those whom we have loved. The empty Sepulchre at Jerusalem on Easter morning is the warrant of a new life, strictly continuous with this, and, if we are faithful, much more glorious.

See here, also, the principle of moral resurrections in the Church of Christ. As with the bodies of the faithful so it is with the Church of Christ. The Church of Christ is, according to St. Paul's teaching, Christ Himself in history. St. Paul says as much when he tells us that "as the body is one, and has many members, and all the members of that body, being many, are one body, so also is Christ."ᵉ The Church is Christ's Body, the fulness of Him

---

ᵃ Rom. viii. 11.   ᵇ 2 Cor. v. 10.   ᶜ Acts xxiv. 15.
ᵈ Phil. iii. 21.   ᵉ 1 Cor. xii. 12.

That filleth all in all.[a] But the force of this language is limited by the fact, equally warranted by Scripture—that the Church has in it a human element, which, unlike the Humanity of Christ, is weak and sinful. The Church of Corinth itself, to which St. Paul wrote the sentence which I just now quoted, was filled with strife,[b] irreverence,[c] even worse sins than these.[d] Again and again in the course of her history large portions of the Christian Church have seemed to be dead and buried,—buried away in some one of the lumber-rooms of the past. And the world has gone its way, rejoicing as if all was over; as if henceforth unbelief and ungodliness would never be disturbed in their reign on earth by any protest from Heaven. But suddenly the tomb has opened; there has been a moral movement, a profound agitation in men's consciences, a feeling that all is far from right. And then has arisen a new spirit of devotion, social stir, literary activity, conspicuous self-sacrifice; and, lo! the world awakes to an uneasy suspicion that "John the Baptist has risen from the dead, and that mighty works do show forth themselves in him."[e] The truth is that Christ has again burst His tomb and is abroad among men. So it was after the moral degradation of the Papacy in the tenth century; so it was after the recrudescence of Paganism by the Renaissance in the fifteenth; so it was in this country after the great triumph of Puritan misbelief and profanity in the seventeenth century, and of indifference to vital religion in the eighteenth. The oppression, the degradation, the enfeeblement, of the Church of Christ is possible enough; too generally, the world only binds and makes sport of Samson, because Samson has yielded to the blandishments

[a] Eph. i. 22, 23.   [b] 1 Cor. iii. 3.   [c] 1 Cor. xi. 18-22.
[d] 1 Cor. v. 1.   [e] St. Matt. xiv. 2.

of Delilah. But there is a latent force in the Church of Christ, which asserts and must assert itself, from generation to generation. If the Crucifixion is re-enacted, in the Holy Body; if, as St. Paul puts it, we fill up, from century to century, that which is behind of the afflictions of Christ;[a] the Resurrection is re-enacted too. It is not possible that the Body of Christ, instinct with His force and vital Spirit, should be holden of death; each apparent collapse and failure is followed by an outburst of energy and moral glory, which reveals the presence of the Living Christ; His Presence Who, if crucified through weakness, yet liveth by the Power of God.[b]

Thirdly, note here what is or ought to be the governing principle of our own personal life. If we have been laid in the tomb of sin, it ought to be impossible that we should be holden of sin. I say "ought to be;" because, as a matter of fact, it is not impossible. God only is responsible for the resurrection of the Christian's body, and for the perpetuity, through its successive resurrections, of the Christian Church; and therefore it is impossible that either the Church or our bodies should permanently succumb to the empire of death. But God, Who raises our bodies whether we will or not, does not raise our souls from sin, unless we correspond with His grace; and it is quite in our power to refuse this correspondence. That we should rise then from sin is a moral, not a physical necessity; but surely we ought to make it as real a necessity as if it were physical. For any who feels in his soul the greatness and love of Jesus Christ it ought to be morally impossible to remain in the tomb: "Like as Christ was raised from the dead by the glory of the Father, even so we also should walk in

[a] Col. i. 24. [b] 2 Cor. xiii. 4.

newness of life."[a] If Lent is the season for mourning the past, Easter is the season for those bracing definite resolutions and vigorous efforts which control the future. If we were unaided and alone, such efforts and resolutions would be failures indeed; like the vain flutterings of a bird against the wires of the cage which imprisons it. But He Who has "broken the gates of brass, and smitten the bars of iron in sunder,"[b] will not fail us, if we ask and seek His strength; and the permanence and splendour of His Life in glory may, and should be, the warrant of our own.

One word more. A real Resurrection with Christ will make and leave some definite traces upon life. Let us resolve this day to do or leave undone some one thing which will mark a new beginning: conscience will instruct us, if we allow it to do so. If any of you are looking out for a way of showing gratitude to our Risen Saviour, let me suggest that you should send the best contribution you can afford to the Mission at Zanzibar on the east coast of Africa. There a small band of noble men, under the leadership of a bishop of Apostolical character,[c] is making efforts worthy of the best days of the Church to propagate the Faith among races, to whom no depths of degradation and misery that are possible for human beings are unknown, but who are as capable as ourselves of rising with Christ to a new life of moral and mental glory. According to accounts which have just reached this country, at the very moment when new and unanticipated opportunities are presenting themselves, and such an inroad upon heathendom, and the slavery and vices which mark its empire, is possible, as has never been possible before, their scanty means altogether fail

---

[a] Rom. vi. 4.   [b] Ps. cvii. 16.
[c] The late Bishop Steere, who has since gone to his reward.

these noble missionaries. They literally have not enough to eat; much less can they attempt the new enterprises of Christian charity which their circumstances imperatively demand. Shall we leave them to despondency, to retreat, to failure; with the heathen before them stretching out their hands unto God, and with the impure imposture of the false prophet hard by, ready to take a cruel advantage of our supineness? Surely it cannot but be that some who hear me will make an effort worthy of our Easter gratitude in behalf of an object, than which none can well be imagined more truly Christian and philanthropic, more worthy of men who humbly hope that they have part in the First Resurrection, and in all that it implies.

SERMON VII.

THE REALITY OF THE RESURRECTION.

St. Luke xxiv. 39.

Behold My Hands and My Feet, that it is I Myself: handle Me, and see; for a spirit hath not flesh and bones, as ye see Me have.

THIS saying of our Risen Lord to the ten Apostles and their associates is not to be confused with a somewhat similar but distinct saying to St. Thomas, "Reach hither thy finger, and behold My Hands; and reach hither thy hand, and thrust it into My Side: and be not faithless, but believing."[a] The occasions were different. One was on the evening of the day of the Resurrection; the other a week later. The states of mind to which our Lord addressed Himself were different. The ten were in a state of terror and perplexity: Thomas a hard-headed doubter. The words are different. The ten are only invited to handle the limbs of Christ: Thomas is to thrust his hand into the open side. To the timid Apostles our Lord offers consolation: to the sceptical Thomas He presents the opportunity of a verifying experiment. With Thomas He expostulates: with the ten He soothes. To Thomas He says: "Be not faithless, but believing;" to the ten, "Why are ye troubled, and why do thoughts arise in your hearts?"[b]

[a] St. John xx. 27.   [b] St. Luke xxiv. 38.

It is easy to understand the anxious thoughts, the terror and affright, of the Apostles. They had met, together with a few adherents, possibly at the house of Zebedee, where they might feel safe from the violence of the Jewish mob. They had met together, with full hearts, that they might talk over one with another the events of that momentous day. They had heard the report of the Holy Women. They were saying one to another, as if to re-assure each other by the act of repetition, "The Lord is risen indeed, and hath appeared unto Simon."[a] They had just learned what had happened on the Emmaus road, and how, when the walk was over, the Divine Stranger had been recognised, and how He had taken His leave. They were filled with conflicting emotions, no one of which had as yet the mastery,—with hope, delight, apprehension, fear. They were still listening to or discussing the report of the disciples from Emmaus; and the doors were fast shut so that no stranger or spy might betray their precious secret, when, lo! "as they thus spake, He Himself stood in the midst of them, and said, Peace be unto you."[b] The doors had not opened; there had been no movement as from the entrance to the midst of the apartment. At one moment there was vacancy, at another He was there, and in the act of blessing them. Nor was this the impression, the illusion, as it might have been thought, of a single mind. They all saw Him; they all heard Him; and their first and common feeling was one of terror.

What was the cause of their terror? It was their belief that they were close to a disembodied spirit, which, for the moment, had simulated bodily form, and had uttered a human voice. However we may explain it, there is no doubt that the real or fancied appearance of a human spirit, without the body, has, in all ages, been more than

[a] St. Luke xxiv. 34.   [b] St. Luke xxiv. 36.

unwelcome to man; it has been terrible. It may be that to a composite being such as ours, in which body and soul are so subtly and intimately intertwined, the divorce between the two, when thus vividly brought before us, seems to suggest unnatural violence as nothing else can. It may be that our ignorance of the capacities of a disembodied spirit, of its power to affect ourselves in a hundred ways now that it lives under totally new conditions, may explain the universal dread which it inspires. It may be—nay rather, it probably is—the case, that the quickened sense of the nearness and reality of the invisible world has a terror for us sinners, because we know that we are sinners. A perfectly sinless man would gaze at a ghost with reverent but untroubled curiosity. Certain it is that, for ordinary men, as in the days of Eliphaz the Temanite, so in all ages of the world's history, to see, or think we see, a disembodied spirit inspires dread:—

> "Fear came upon me, and trembling,
> Which made all my bones to shake.
> Then a spirit passed before my face;
> The hair of my flesh stood up:
> It stood still, but I could not discern the form thereof:
> An image was before mine eyes." [a]

"Why are ye troubled, and why do thoughts arise in your hearts?" Our Lord had not to wait for an answer to His question. His next words show that He knew how the Ten would have answered it. "Handle Me, and see; for a spirit hath not flesh and bones, as ye see Me have." They were not, as they fancied, in the presence of a spirit divorced from its earthly tenement by the rude hand of death. He Who stood before them was death's Conqueror, and bade them test the reality of His recovered life.

My brethren, death would seem this year to have

[a] Job iv. 14-16.

been more busy than is his wont in striking down those whose disappearance from our midst makes us all think more seriously of the lessons of Easter. On Easter Day we had to deplore the loss of a man [a] who had presided over the great profession of the law with signal ability and distinction; and to-day his widowed successor mourns one whose graces and virtues justly endeared her to a wide circle of friends and dependants, and who, it is believed, laid the foundation of the illness which has brought her to her grave, by her benevolent labours among the sick and poor at the East end of London.[b]

But to-day, also, it would be impossible to forget another public loss which yet more closely touches us, who pass our lives under the shadow of this great Church.[c] More than a hundred years have passed since a Lord Mayor of London last died during his year of office. The incessant demands upon the time and strength of the Chief Magistrate of this great city, which bring him before the country and the world more often and more prominently than any Englishman who is not directly concerned in the business of Government, are so little in harmony with the thought of death, that they might almost seem to bar his approach. As the bell of St. Paul's tolled forth its mournful message yesterday morning, we Londoners reflected, that in the late Lord Mayor we had lost a civic ruler, who had already given ample proof that he was equal to the exacting duties and to the splendid opportunities of his great position. His ready sympathy with the best enthusiasms that stir the heart of the country, and with every effort of public or private bene-

---

[a] Earl Cairns, late Lord Chancellor, died April 2, 1885.
[b] The Countess of Selborne, died April 10, 1885.
[c] George Swan Nottage, Esq., Lord Mayor of London, died at the Mansion House, on Saturday, April 11, 1885.

VII] *The Reality of the Resurrection.*

volence, and his conscientious devotedness to the more immediate claims of his office, and to the interests of his fellow-citizens, had already won for him general good-will and respect, and had created a confident anticipation that his year of rule would hereafter rank with the most useful and distinguished of those which had preceded it. But, once again, we have learnt the lesson, that death, like God, is no respecter of persons; and that no position, however distinguished, no devotion to duty, however assiduous, no tribute of respect and popularity, however general, well deserved, and sincere, can insure any man against his assaults. Certainly this year the lessons of Easter, always solemn, have been illustrated for us in London by events of unwonted solemnity.

I.

Let us return to the Upper Chamber, and note, first of all, the nature of our Lord's Risen Body. It was the Body Which had been born of the Virgin Mary, and had been nailed to the cross; the Body from Which life had been expelled by the painful death of crucifixion, ere It had been buried in the grave of Joseph of Arimathæa. This identity is insisted on by our Lord. He pointed to the Wounds which had been made on the preceding Friday: "Behold My Hands and My Feet, that it is I Myself." And then, to meet the suspicion that a spiritual essence of some kind was personating a bodily form, He adds: "Handle Me, and see; for a spirit hath not flesh and bones, as ye see Me have." Mark that "flesh and bones." It sets aside the notion that the Body of the Risen Saviour was somehow a body, but not real flesh; bodily form, without nerves and veins, without bodily substance; an etherealised likeness of the Body Which had been crucified, not the crucified

Body Itself. "A spirit hath not flesh and bones, as ye see Me have." And this literal identity of the risen with the crucified Body of Jesus was made good by another test. When our Lord had shown to His disciples His Hands and His Feet, and they yet believed not for joy, and wondered, He said unto them, "Have ye here any meat?" He would show that the digestive and nutritive functions of His Risen Body were intact. At the great festivals, fish was brought to Jerusalem in quantities from the Sea of Galilee and the Mediterranean coast; and, if it were to be had anywhere, it would be forthcoming at the house of Zebedee. So "they gave Him a piece of a broiled fish, and of an honeycomb; and He took it, and did eat before them."[a]

Our Lord's Risen Body, then, was literally the very Body Which had been crucified; and yet It had properties attaching to It which distinguished It. We cannot indeed say of His Body, as of our own, that it was sown in corruption; since corruption is the brand and note of sin, and God would not suffer His Holy One to see corruption. It was indeed sown in dishonour and raised in glory. It was sown in weakness and raised in power. But especially, It was sown a natural body, that is, a body governed by ordinary natural laws; and raised a spiritual body, that is, a body which, while retaining physical substance and unimpaired identity, was yet endowed and interpenetrated with some of the properties of spirit.[b] Of this our Lord had given proof in His sudden disappearance from the two disciples at Emmaus, and in His presenting Himself as suddenly to the astonished disciples in Jerusalem, while the doors were shut, and without any movement to the spot at which He appeared. And if it be asked, how could a solid and palpable Body, Which men could handle, Which could eat and converse, thus vanish and

[a] St. Luke xxiv. 42, 43.   [b] 1 Cor. xv. 42-44.

reappear, like a ghost, it is better at once to say that we do not know. Only, our ignorance of the explanation of such a matter as this by no means proves that no explanation could be given, still less that the supposition of a physical body traversed by spiritual properties is an impossible supposition. Impossible indeed! What do we know of the possibilities—the abstract possibilities of being,—to decide, on the strength of our narrow experience, that this or that mode of existence is impossible? Impossible! Have we not, I will not say sufficient humility, but sufficient imagination, to conceive that the Infinite Creator is not limited in resources; that we ourselves need not have had these bodies, of this particular shape, or these minds, with this particular assortment of faculties; and that if He pleases to enrich a Body such as ours with one or more properties belonging to another order or sphere of being, He is not debarred from doing so by the observations which we have made, in our notebooks or our memories, respecting His ordinary rules of working? Undoubtedly our Lord's Risen Body had properties which belong to spirit; but they did not suspend or impair Its reality as a body; as the Body Which had been born of Mary, and had been nailed to the cross.

And this leads me to notice a remark of a very interesting and accomplished writer, which it were better perhaps to leave unnoticed, unless attention had already been directed to it very prominently. He complains that Christ's Resurrection is understood by Christians in what he calls a "carnal" sense; he asks how a "carnal" resurrection could benefit us; he holds that to be a good Christian it is enough to believe in what he calls Christ's spiritual Resurrection; and he regrets that the Jews buried and did not burn their dead, for in the latter case, he thinks, the Christian idea of the Resurrection would have remained far more spiritual.[a]

Here we really have to do with a use of terms which is, to say the least, ambiguous. What do we generally mean by "carnal"?

"Carnal" is a word which has acquired a bad sense from its association in St. Paul's writings with the idea of sin. The flesh, St. Paul teaches, is the seat of sin, and carnal is that which belongs to the flesh. Our author employs a word which has these damaging associations connected with it; but what does he really mean by it? Sin has no place in our Lord; and our author means by a "carnal" resurrection simply a literal, matter-of-fact, real resurrection. And what does he mean by "spiritual"? Not, I fear, even that which belongs to a spirit independent of that of the person who is thinking about the Resurrection. He means by spiritual something that presents itself attractively to the thinking mind, but has no certain place in the sphere of external facts. And if this is his meaning, then we must say unshrinkingly that a Resurrection, to be real, must be carnal, in the sense of being "a resurrection of the flesh;" if it is not, in this sense, carnal, it is no resurrection at all. A resurrection of a body, if it be real, is the restoration to life of the flesh which composes

[a] Max Müller, *Biographical Essays* (London, 1884), pp. 139, 140. "And as to Christ's real resurrection, is it credible that when we are told again and again that Christ came to bring life and immortality to light, the simple words that Christ rose from the dead should be taken in a carnal, not in a spiritual sense? How would a carnal resurrection and ascension benefit us? . . . Of this I am perfectly certain, that if you had said to Stanley, 'Am I a Christian if I believe only in the spiritual Resurrection of Christ?' he would have said, 'Yes, and all the more if you do not believe that His body was taken up to the clouds.' I often regret that the Jews buried, and did not burn their dead, for in that case the Christian idea of the Resurrection would have remained far more spiritual."

that body. It is not the presentation of something else, whether it be a spiritual essence, or a vital truth, or a conviction, or a hope in the minds of others. The substitution of anything else for the material of the body destroys the fact of a real resurrection; the word becomes misleading and dishonest. To call a resurrection spiritual, which is in fact no true resurrection at all, but only a particular effect upon the minds of certain living people, is to abuse the term "spiritual:" but our Lord for Himself repudiates the idea that His Resurrection was spiritual in any sense which excluded the quickening of His very flesh. "Handle Me, and see," cries the Risen Jesus, "for a spirit hath not flesh and bones, as ye see Me have." As for cremation, Christian reverence shrinks from discussing the cremation of our Lord's Sacred Body; but cremation, had it taken place, could have made no difference, except in the sphere of imagination. The resurrection of a body from its ashes is not a greater miracle than the resurrection of an unburnt body. Each must be purely miraculous, and there is no more to be said. Faith would have been as clear and strong if the former usage had prevailed in those ages and countries instead of the latter.

The truth, as we have seen, is that our Lord's Resurrection was, in the words of this writer, both carnal and spiritual. Carnal, because His Body, and nothing else that was substituted for it, actually rose; spiritual, in so far as His Body was endowed with new properties, which traversed and suspended the ordinary laws of matter.

II.

Now, corresponding to the twofold character of our Lord's Risen Body, visible and palpable on the one hand,

and spiritual on the other, is the character of the Religion which represents Him among men.

Religion is like a sacrament: it has its outward and visible signs and its inward fact, or thing signified. Of these, the latter is, beyond dispute, the more important. Religion, the bond between the soul and God, lives in the habits, or acts, whereby the soul adheres to, and communes with, the Infinite Source of life. It is made up of faith, hope, and love, pouring themselves forth at the feet of the Invisible King; it is by turns aspiration, worship, resolve; it expends itself in a thousand unheard, unuttered acts, whereby the human spirit holds converse with its Creator. Sometimes it has its eye on the Divine Justice, and it is forthwith godly fear; sometimes on the beauty and perfection of God, and it melts into love; sometimes on the soul's manifold sins and ingratitude, and then it becomes shame and confusion; sometimes on the promises of God's mercy in Jesus Christ, and then it is repentance, contrition, self-condemnation, resolutions to amend. Religion, as it beholds the transcendent Majesty of God, prompts the soul to a thousand acts of adoration, praise, and thanksgiving; it summons the angels and the saints, and the whole world of sentient and even inanimate creatures to sympathy and co-operation in the work of praise; it bids the soul offer all that it has and is to His service and His glory; it congratulates Him that He is what He is, and rejoices that any other creatures exist to set forth His praise; it desires that all may be brought to know and love Him; it is full of zeal for the advancement of His kingdom, and the doing of His will. Above all, Religion is a humble and resigned temper, which sees in the ills of life the just reward of personal sin, and would take up the Cross, less from a sense of necessity, than from a sense of justice; its inmost spirit is that of the

VII]   *The Reality of the Resurrection.*   113

Psalmist: "a broken and contrite heart, O God, Thou wilt not despise."[a]

Religion is thus in its essence altogether removed from the province of sense; we cannot feel, or see, or hear these acts of the soul, which assert its presence. It belongs to the purely immaterial world: it is hid with the Father, Who seeth in secret, and Who is worshipped, if at all, in spirit and truth.

On the other hand, Religion has another aspect. It steps forth from the sphere of the supersensuous, which is its congenial home; it takes bodily form and mien, and challenges the senses of hearing, and sight, and touch. It appeals through the human voice to the ear of sense. It meets and fascinates the eye; it even presents itself, as in the outward elements of a sacrament, to the touch. It is represented by a visible society,—the Church. This society has its ministers, its assemblies for worship, its characteristic rites, its public buildings—all of which fall within the province of sense. The visible Church is, as our Lord said, a city set on a hill, which cannot be hid.[b]

Again, Religion is represented by a book,—the Bible. The Bible, too, belongs to the world of sense, just as much as the Church. We see it, handle it, read it. It brings Religion visibly into the area of history, of poetry, of philosophy, as embodied in a large ancient literature.

In the same way, Religion takes an outward shape in the good works and characters of individual Christians. They arrest observation; they invite comment, examination, discussion; they belong just as much to the public life of mankind as do the lives of worldly or wicked men. By them, too, Jesus Himself stands in the midst of human society.

In short, Religion in the world has this double character,

[a] Ps. li. 17.   [b] St. Matt. v. 14.

VOL. I.   H

outward and inward. Its organisation among men in a visible Church, its embodiment in a sacred literature, its exhibition in the productive lives of Christians, are the outward and visible signs of a world beyond, in which the convictions and motives to which it appeals have their sway and empire. It is easy enough to make too much of the outward and visible side of Religion. We may think so much of the visible portion of the Church as to forget that larger invisible portion of it which is beyond the veil. We may be so enamoured of the literary beauty of the Bible as to forget its real claims as the Handbook of Revelation, and the Handbook of Religion. We may be so delighted with the purely material side of Christian benevolence, with the long train of earthly blessings which a good man, who has the opportunity of doing so, leaves behind him, as he moves forward through life towards the goal of his career, as to forget that which is greater than anything material; that which is true in conviction, and lofty in character, and disinterested in motive; in short, all that really connects the servant of God with the invisible world.

But the palpable, material side of Religion is like the visible form of the Risen Jesus in the house of Zebedee; it is a warrant of the realities of the invisible. When the Ten gazed upon the open Wounds in the Hands and Feet of the Redeemer; when, in response to His unspeakable condescension, they handled Him, and knew from contact that He had indeed a Body of flesh and bones; they knew that, if a few hours, perhaps a few minutes later, He should have vanished from their sight, He would still be with them, although invisibly. When our eyes rest on the visible accessories of Religion, on its representation in a great society of human beings, on its splendid literature, on its representative efforts, on its temples and its worship, on its solemn rites and ordinances, on its whole machinery of action in a Christian country, let us reflect that these would not be here, unless there were a solemn truth behind. If they belong to the world of sense, they witness to the supersensuous; they assure us that Religion is no phantom, but has the flesh and bones of substance and reality.

III.

Our Lord's precept, "handle Me, and see," is addressed to two different classes of men.

a. It is an encouragement for the timid. The Eleven were thoroughly frightened at the sudden appearance of the Risen Jesus: they were bidden draw near, handle Him and see if there was aught to terrify them. He did not always speak thus. When, in the early morning of that very day, the impulsive Magdalene, in her passionate and eager love, would have laid hold on Him, He checked her: "Touch Me not; I am not yet ascended unto My Father."[a] This intimate contact is a privilege for the hesitating and the unpresuming.

There are in every generation some men who are afraid to come near enough to Religion to do it justice. It inspires them with a certain curiosity, but with less curiosity than apprehension. There is something mysterious about its language, its services, its ministers, which attracts and yet repels them,—repels them sufficiently to prevent their investigating its claims. We all of us must have met in life men who look into a Bible now and then, enter a church now and then, engage in a religious conversation now and then; but who on the whole are suspicious, distant,

[a] St. John xx. 17.

unwilling to commit themselves. They listen to a sermon; and its phraseology, necessarily differing, as much of it does, from that in which we conduct the affairs of civil life, seems weird and strange to them. They are present in a church while the Holy Sacrament is being celebrated; and the successive stages of the service, and the posture of the worshippers, and the mysterious acts of Consecration and Communion, seem to belong to an order of ideas which inspires apprehension, or at least awe, rather than love and confidence. To such our Lord says, '"Handle Me, and see." The Sacrament of My Death, and the words of My Gospel, can only thus alarm you, while you keep at a distance from them. To come closer is to know that here is the flesh and bones, the warrants of the reality of a Religion which can satisfy the deepest needs of the soul of man.'

β. "Handle Me, and see." It is a direction for the perplexed. The Eleven could not reconcile the presence of Jesus there in the midst of them with the fact that the doors were closed. How did He come there? Or was He there at all? were they looking on something that only resembled Him, although it resembled Him exactly? They did not know; they could only wonder.

There are many men who, if they were asked what is the leading characteristic of Religion, would answer, 'The perplexities which surround it.' To them it appears to be, beyond any other subject, uncertain. They do not reject, but neither do they admit, its claims. They pass weeks, months, years, in an attitude of indecision; and too often they end their lives by dying undecided. Religion is of course only of value to those who heartily accept its claims; and the question arises, Why do men of this kind thus forfeit its assistance and its blessings? It may be replied that Christendom is so divided that they do not know what to believe. Very well, let them begin by believing all the truths on which Christendom, with all its divisions, is agreed: to believe these truths, and act on the belief, will soon carry them further. May it not be that their perplexity is due, at least in part, to a want of serious purpose in examining the claims and substance of Religion at all? Who has not felt on an August day, when a wide landscape lies stretched out under the rays of a summer sun, how at first everything seems to be indistinct and blurred; and then, as the spectator steadily and intently gazes, outline and form gradually emerge from the haze; here appears a hill, there a wood, yonder a river, then a church tower, and a mansion, and the houses of the cottagers nestling among the trees? Five minutes ago all seemed misty and indefinite; only let the eye resolutely scan it, and the harmonies as well as the features of the prospect become clear, and all doubts as to its range, and beauty, and characteristics are at an end. In many cases—I do not say in all,—Religion is only perplexing because it is never examined closely; because men look at it only as a sort of by-play, in the spare moments of a busy life, and assume too hastily that it is unsubstantial, when its reality does not flash forth irresistibly upon their inert intelligence. They must handle it if they would see that it has the flesh and bones, which distinguish a creed that has come from heaven from a creation of the fancy or of the fears of men.

And this may lead us to consider one practice in particular by which our Lord's command may be obeyed in its spirit and drift,—I mean, Meditation. The Bible says a great deal about meditation, that is, the fixing the mind steadily on some one religious truth or fact, with a view to extracting from it all the meaning and guidance that we possibly can. Many Christians who say their prayers regularly never meditate. The very word seems to them rather to belong to religious phraseology, than to describe anything actual and practical in a Christian's life. Yet they little know how much they lose, especially with reference to the life of our Lord and Saviour, by neglecting this most healthful and fruitful exercise. You say you do not know how to set about it. Very well, try something of this kind. After saying your morning prayers, open a New Testament, and ask God to enable you to realise His Presence, and to send His Holy Spirit to enlighten and guide you. Then read two or three verses, or a short paragraph, a miracle, a parable, a part of a discourse, as the case may be. Do not think of its grammatical, or historical, or literary aspects: but say, 'What do these words say to me? What truth do they teach? What fault do they correct? What effort do they prescribe or encourage? What resolutions do they make necessary?' If earnest, you will soon see your way. Scripture is so full of meanings that the real difficulty is which to select out of its abundance. Then, having decided on the main lessons of the passage, pray earnestly that you may practically remember them, and turn them in whatever way to the best account. The whole exercise need not take up more than ten minutes; but at the end of a year, it will, if regularly practised, have made a great difference in matters which most intimately concern the soul. It is one way of so handling the Gospel History as to become convinced of its truth from perceiving its intimate sympathy with, and adaptation to, our own case. Instead of a vague, half-remembered, less than half-comprehended, story, the life of Jesus, steadily meditated on, passes into the life of the Christian, by an insensible but real transfusion. It is turned *in succum et sanguinem;* into the very substance of all that is truest and deepest in thought and heart. It illuminates, it warms, it invigorates; and by doing this it gives that inward proof of its own reality, which has been most highly prized by the most devoted servants of God. As of old, so now it is true that the man is blessed whose delight is in the revealed law of the Lord, and who meditates in it day and night; since he shall be like a tree, planted by the water-side, who will bring forth his fruit in due season; his leaf also shall not wither, and look, whatsoever he doeth, it shall prosper.[a]

[a] Ps. i. 2, 3.

SERMON VIII.

OUR LORD'S RESUMPTION OF LIFE.

St. John x. 18.

I have power to take it again.

OUR Lord is speaking of His Life, and of His power, or, more strictly, His authority over it. This authority to dispose of it includes the laying it down in death, and the taking it again by Resurrection. "No man," He says, "taketh My Life from Me; but I lay it down of Myself. I have power to lay it down, and I have power to take it again." Both in death and in Resurrection His Will is free, and all-powerful. He died when and as He willed to die; "I lay My Life down of (or from) Myself." He rose when and as He willed to rise: His Life had not escaped beyond His control, because He had laid it down in death: "I have power to lay it down, and I have power to take it again."

I.

In no other passage of the Gospels is the Majesty of our Lord's Divine Person more plainly revealed in His words than here. "No man taketh My Life from Me: but I lay it down of Myself."

Could you or I make these words our own? There is indeed much in life that we can control: but can we control our way of leaving it? Death comes to us in an hour that we think not, in some place that we have never thought of, through some cause or agency which we have never anticipated. It finds us, not in command of the situation; but passive, helpless, alas! too possibly, unprepared. So far from laying our life down, we yield it up. It is wrung from us by the dreadful ravages of disease, or by the hand of violence, or by an accident, as we call it, by a railway collision or by a street vehicle, which shatters the feeble physical frame, and dismisses the spirit to the judgment-hall of its Creator. No men of this century have wielded such power in Europe, at certain moments of their lives, as the first and the third Napoleon; they little meant to die, the one at St. Helena, the other at Chislehurst. The late Bishop Wilberforce once said that he never entered a railway carriage without reflecting that he might never leave it alive. He was a fearless horseman. And he met his death, as all the world knows, by a fall from his horse, when riding it at a walking pace, and engaged in conversation with a friend.

Perhaps it occurs to some who hear me, that a man may, if he chooses to do so, lay down his life at pleasure. The old Stoics taught that when life had become, for whatever reason, unbearable, a wise man would leave it by an act of self-destruction. As a matter of physical possibility this, of course, is true. We can, if we will, break away from the moral control of our Creator, and rush all unprepared, or rather with an act of deadly sin upon our souls, into His awful Presence. Every day, indeed, the newspapers remind us that suicide is, physically speaking, only too possible: but what can be said of its morality? Morally, it is at once cowardice and murder; not the less cowardice because, possibly, as with Cato or Seneca, it is draped in a subtle personal pride; not the less murder, because the murderer is also the victim.

Certainly a good man may find himself in circumstances in which it is a moral duty knowingly to face or accept death at the hands of others. The heathen knew that a man can sometimes only live at the cost of the true reasons which justify life. So it has been with great patriots in all ages of the world. So it has been with thousands of martyrs whose names are dear to the Christian Church. These men had moral power to lay down their lives. But they could not control the circumstances which made death a duty. If our Lord lays down His life, His act differs from that of the suicide in its moral elevation; it differs from that of the martyr in His command of the situation. As the Good Shepherd, He gives His life for the sheep;[a] it is in this character that He is speaking. As the Lord of life, He speaks of His Own Human Life as His creature. It falls as entirely under the control of His Sovereign and Creative Will as does the life of every human being under the Will of God. When God recalls or cancels a life to which He has given existence, we know that He is doing what He wills with His Own. "Hath not the potter power over the clay?"[b] And when our Lord appoints the Human Body which He had made His Own to suffering and to death, He too is dealing with His Own Creature; though It was for ever united to Himself.

"I have power to take it again." Here our Lord's Majesty is much more apparent than in the former part of the sentence. For here He speaks as having a control over His Life, which no mere man can possibly, in any

[a] St. John x. 11.   [b] Rom. ix. 21.

circumstances, pretend to have. We know that when soul and body are sundered by death, the body is resolved into its original elements. And there is in the soul no such force as can reconstitute the body, or make it again the dwelling-place and instrument of the soul. Scripture tells us that in certain cases life has been recalled to bodies from which it had fled; as to the widow's son whom Elisha raised,[a] and the dead man who touched the bones of Elisha,[b] and the daughter of Jairus,[c] and the son of the widow of Nain,[d] and, above all, Lazarus.[e] But in all these cases the restoration to life was effected, not from within, but from without. God put forth His creative or re-creative power, through some human agency, or, as in the case of our Lord's miracles, directly: and that which poor stricken humanity, lying in the strong and humiliating grasp of death, could never do for itself, was done for it by the Power to Whom Nature owes its being, and Whom it must obey.

Here, I say, barbarism and civilisation, the ancient and the modern world, are on a level. Our Science has no doubt done wonders: it has brought first one and then another of the powers of Nature under man's control. But no man of science cherishes even a distant hope that it is reserved for him to startle the world by undoing the work of death, or even by keeping death indefinitely at bay. When you and I lie down to die, our bodies and spirits will be parted asunder; but, most assuredly, not at our discretion. And then will succeed a period during which the spirit, conscious of its separate life, remembering its past life, capable as before of all that is implied in intelligence and resolve, may survey, we know not how closely, as from another sphere of being, the gradual decay of its

---

[a] 2 Kings iv. 32-35.   [b] 2 Kings xiii. 20, 21.   [c] St. Luke viii. 49-55.
[d] St. Luke vii. 11-15.   [e] St. John xi. 38-44.

old and intimate companion, the body. But, for all purposes of reconstructing the body's life, the living spirit will be as powerless as the decaying body itself. Death can only be conquered by One Who, if He belongs to the Human Family, also transcends it, and Who has, it may be said, an independent and higher position outside it, which gives Him the necessary leverage for His work. And this it is which lies in our Lord's words, and which was realised at His Resurrection. When He claims to take His life again, He stands in a relation towards His Life, which is inconceivable in any mere man; which is only intelligible if we believe Him to be personally the Everlasting Son of God. For Him, it is plain His Human life is not a necessary condition of activity, but something to be acted on, disposed of, controlled. He speaks of it as we might speak of a dress, or of a social position which may be laid aside and then resumed at will. That which invests our Lord's Resurrection with its distinctive glory is the fact that He raised Himself from the dead by His Own will and act.

II.

There is indeed another aspect of the Resurrection which is more often brought before us in Holy Scripture. Our Lord is said to have been raised up by God the Father. This was St. Peter's language in his sermon on the Day of Pentecost,[a] and when addressing the people, after the miracle at the Beautiful gate of the temple.[b] This was the expression he employed, when defending himself before the Sanhedrin, both on the first[c] and second[d] occasion of his appearing before it. This is the phrase which is used in St. Peter's address to Cornelius,[e] and not

[a] Acts ii. 24.   [b] Acts iii. 15.   [c] Acts iv. 10.
[d] Acts v. 30.   [e] Acts x. 40.

less than four times in St. Paul's sermon in the synagogue at Antioch in Pisidia.[a] It is indeed St. Paul's common way of referring to the Resurrection: he is wont to speak of the Resurrection as the work of God the Father. So it is in the first epistle that he ever wrote; that to the Thessalonians.[b] So it is in the last, his second letter to Timothy.[c] So it is in each of the four letters which mark the most active period of his life; those to the Romans,[d] the Galatians,[e] the two to the Corinthians.[f] So it is in two out of the four epistles written in his first imprisonment;[g] although he also sometimes refers to the Resurrection, without reference to the agency by which it was effected.[h]

On the other hand, on two occasions when our Lord is reported by the second[i] and third[k] Evangelists to have predicted His Resurrection, he speaks of it as of an act distinctly His Own. And in like manner, He had, during an earlier visit to Jerusalem, used the momentous words, "Destroy this temple, and in three days I will raise it up."[l] The Jews understood Him to be speaking of the building on which they were looking. But the Evangelist explains that He meant the temple of His Body; and this expression implies that the act of rising was His Own no less than His saying, "I have power to take My life again."

There is here, at first sight, a contradiction; but only at first sight. The Resurrection does not cease to be our Lord's act, because it is also the act of the Father. When God acts through mere men, He makes them His instru-

---

[a] Acts xiii. 30, 33, 34, 37. [b] 1 Thess. i. 10. [c] 2 Tim. ii. 8.
[d] Rom. iv. 24, 25; vi. 4; viii. 11. [e] Gal. i. 1.
[f] 1 Cor. xv. 15; 2 Cor. iv. 14. [g] Eph. i. 20; Col. ii. 12.
[h] Rom. vi. 9; vii. 4; 1 Cor. xv. 20, etc. [i] St. Mark x. 34.
[k] St. Luke xviii. 33. [l] St. John ii. 19.

ments; their acts are His. He saves Israel by Moses. He conquers Canaan by Joshua. There is no contrast between His mighty Arm and the agent whom He employs; the result is variously ascribed to the agent or to the Employer. This is not indeed strictly analogous to, but it enables us to understand, the case before us. Our Lord raised Himself from the dead, because, "as the Father hath life in Himself, so He hath given to the Son to have life in Himself:"[a] the Power which immediately effected the Resurrection is as old as the Eternal Generation of the Son. But it is also the Father's Power, since from Him it is thus eternally derived. And so far from there being any opposition between the two, the one necessarily implies the other, in virtue of the Unity, not merely of Will, but of Essence, between the Everlasting Father and the Everlasting Son. If we believe our Lord when He says, "I and My Father are One,"[b] we see no difficulty in being told that Christ was raised from the dead by the Father, while yet He Himself refers to His Resurrection as to an act strictly His Own.

It is important to remember this on Easter Day, as showing the true character of our Lord's Resurrection. His Resurrection was His Own act. He rose from the dead, as He spoke, or ate, or walked, or sat down; because He willed to do so. There must have been a moment, which imagination under the conduct of Christian faith endeavours, but in vain, adequately to realise, when the Human Soul of our Lord, surrounded by myriads of angels, on His return from the home of the ancient dead, came to the grave of Joseph of Arimathæa to claim the Body That had hung upon the Cross. Sure we may be that the highest intelligences of heaven bent low in adoration, when the Soul of Jesus

[a] St. John v. 26.   [b] St. John x. 30.

> Paused at the Body's wounded side,
> Bright flashed the cave, and upward rose
> The living Jesus glorified.

Such a moment there was, in the history of this our world, when our Lord asserted His power over death; and Easter is indeed poorly kept, if we fail to bear in mind what must have been the most original and overwhelming incident of the mystery which it commemorates.

III.

Of the considerations which our Lord's Self-resurrection suggests, let us content ourselves with three.

We are reminded, first of all, of what Christianity really and truly means. It does not mean mere loyalty to the precepts of a dead teacher, or admiration of a striking and unworldly character that lived upon this earth eighteen centuries ago. True Christianity is something more than literary taste; it is more than a department of moral archæology.

It is, before all things, devotion to a living Christ; to a Christ Who lives now as energetically as on the morning of the Resurrection; to a Christ Who proved His indestructible vitality by raising Himself from the dead. If Christianity were a false religion, literary men might still endeavour to reconstruct the history of its earliest age, by their profound researches, their vivid descriptions, their cultivated historical imagination, their artistic wordpainting. This is what is done with the great teachers of Pagan antiquity; with Socrates, Plato, Marcus Aurelius, Epictetus, not less than with Him Who is the subject of the Gospels. But there is this difference. What the great heathens were is all that we can hope to know in this life. What they are, and where, we cannot know. Somewhere indeed their spirits are in God's Universe, waiting for the last award; but assuredly not more capable of helping others, not themselves less helpless and incapable, than the millions who have admired their acts or their sayings since they departed hence. But how utterly different is the case with Christ our Lord! He Who could, at will, resume the life, which He had willed to lay down, is not thus powerless among the spirits of the dead: and as faith listens, she hears His Voice sounding from the depths of the Eternal World, "I am He that liveth, and was dead; and behold, I am alive for evermore; and have the keys of hell and of death."[a] In the fulness of that living and indestructible power which He asserted by His Resurrection, He still rules and holds communion with His Church, and with every living member of it. And our relation to Him, so far from being that of mere students towards an ancient literature, is really that of members of a great family, living in intimate association with an unseen but watchful and most tender Parent, Whose power to aid is never doubtful to those who remember that on Easter morning He raised His Own Body from the grave.

Do not mistake me. Literature has done, and may yet do, great service to Christianity, by investigating and exhibiting its early history. But a literary Christianity is one thing, and a living Christianity is another. A living Christianity means a living Christ. And unless, in our acts, and words, and thoughts, we have renounced the fatal mistake of treating Him as merely the subject of an ancient literature, while forgetting that He is at this moment just as much alive, and just as present, and very much more aware of all that is going on around and

[a] Rev. i. 18.

within us than the person who sits next to each one of us on the floor of this Cathedral, we have not learnt the very first lesson of Easter Day.

Next, we see here the foundation of our confidence in the future of Christianity. Based as it is on a Risen Christ, on a Christ Who raised Himself from death, it cannot pass away. Great teachers there have been, upon whom mankind has lavished the enthusiasm of a passionate admiration; but they have died and been forgotten. The age in which they lived, perhaps, proclaimed that the dust of their writings was gold: a succeeding age scarcely opens their folios. Why are we Christians certain that this fate does not await the Great Teacher Whom we worship? Because men's loyalty to Him rests from age to age, not mainly on His words, not even on His example, but on His Person. "Christ," it has been finely and profoundly said, "is Christianity:" not Christ's words, not Christ's example, but Christ. And why is it that in thus clinging to His Person, Christian faith is so sure of the future? Why is it that faith is undismayed in days of declension, darkness, weakness, division, apparently hopeless failure and collapse? Because she has before her not a Christ who was conquered by death, not a Christ whose spirit was dismissed to find a place somewhere near Plato or Confucius, while his corpse rotted in a rocky grave beneath the Syrian sky, but a Christ Who, when to the eye of sense He seemed to have succumbed to the agencies which drag or thrust us to the tomb, suddenly, as a Psalmist says of God in Providence, "awaked as one out of sleep, and as a giant refreshed with wine, and smote His enemies,"* sin, death, hell, "on the hinder parts, and put them to a perpetual shame."

* Ps. lxxviii. 65.

Of that decisive victory the effects are not transient; since He Who then rose from the sleep of death dies no more.

Had it been otherwise Christianity might well have perished, more than once. It might have died outright of the public and astonishing wickedness of the Roman Court in the tenth century. It might have been crushed out of being by the hordes of Islam in the first flush of their conquests, or by the great Turkish Sultans of the fifteenth and sixteenth centuries. It might have sunk beneath the accumulated weight of corruption which invited the Reformation: it might have disappeared amidst the Babel of self-contradicting voices which the Reformation itself produced. At one time it has been threatened with death, by the relation of the Church to corrupt or absolute governments; at another by the rash levity or by the dishonest enterprises of speculative and unbelieving theologians. Men said that the Church was killed, under Decius and Diocletian: they said so again, with greater confidence, after the literary blasphemies and moral outrages of the first French Revolution. But, practically, each reverse, each collapse, each period of sickness and decline, is followed by revival, reinvigoration, victory. Why is this, but because Christ is incarnate in Christendom; and Christendom reproduces in its history His momentous words? Again and again in history He might seem to lay down His life, and lo! presently He takes it again; the heaviness of His people may endure for a night, but joy cometh in the morning. For He is there Who died on Good Friday, and lay in the grave on Easter Eve and rose, when He willed to rise on Easter morning, as Master of the life which for His Own high purposes He thus could lay aside and thus resume.

Once more, Easter is one of the days on which the

dead must have a great place in the thoughts and prayers of Christians. Of every anniversary, to a certain extent, this holds good. Each birthday recalls those who shared it with us last year, or in years that preceded it, and who are no longer on earth. Each family gathering reminds us by its gaps that of those who are nearest to us by blood, some are no longer present in the flesh, but have passed into that sphere of being which awaits us all. And public holidays and Church holidays have the same mournful reflections inevitably attached to them; we cannot help thinking of any who was here one or five or ten years since, and who is here no longer. Easter Day, the queen of festivals, brings with it this sad and piercing thought, but it also brings with it a consolation which no serious Christian will miss. They have passed away—those whom we have known and loved, it may be, better than any who yet remain,—they have passed into the world of disembodied spirits; they are waiting, unchanged in all that belongs to essential character, with that simplicity, that disinterestedness, that affectionateness, that generosity, that lofty and intrepid purpose, that lowly and penetrating sympathy which won our hearts while they were still on earth. They are waiting, in a scene which we cannot even imagine, but which we shall one day gaze upon; until another change shall restore them to the completeness of their past selves. And of the reality of this change, Easter is the guarantee. He Who could, at will, resume the life which He had laid down upon the Cross, can surely quicken at pleasure the bodies which have mingled with the dust; He can reunite them to the spirits, with which they were joined from the earliest moments of life. He Who could achieve the greater can achieve the less. We cease to marvel at His raising Lazarus, when we remember that He raised Himself.

It is this conviction which makes life to a believing Christian so entirely different a thing from that which it is to a man who has never shared or who has lost a Christian's faith. The world has been reading the papers in which that distinguished man of letters, the late Mr. Carlyle, has left on record his thoughts and feelings about several of his contemporaries, and especially those members of his family who had a first place in his affections. Those papers are marked by all the writer's undisputed originality: and they have naturally aroused a degree of interest that is seldom commanded by any publication of the kind. It is instructive to listen to the comments that they provoke, and to the points in them which are selected as specially worthy of attention. One man dwells on the writer's power of vividly hitting off character, by a few decisive touches, such as might befit a print of Dürer's. Another insists, and with great justice, upon the revelations which they contain of a very tender heart; of a filial piety which is none too common in our day, and which is always beautiful. Another complains of the harsh, bitter, unwarranted judgments which disfigure them, and which are said, perhaps with reason, to be at variance with the language used by the writer at other times and in other circumstances. A fourth calls attention to the simplicity, which is here, as always, a note of strength; or to the stern independence, or to the pathetic self-reproach, which are again and again noticeable in these pages. But for us Christians, there is, it seems to me, a lesson in them which is more painfully and unfortunately interesting than any other. It is the bearing of this remarkable and gifted man in the presence of death. Carlyle does not here tell us why he had renounced the Christian beliefs in which he had been brought up: and we may well hope that his responsibility in this grave matter is less than it would have been, if as a boy he had learnt the faith of St. Paul and St. John undisfigured by the mistaken traditions of his northern home. However this may be, we see him in these pages face to face with those great sorrows which sooner or later await us all. And he shows us how little even genius avails, at these crises of our lives, to afford the peace and strength which faith only can command. None surely can mark the deeply troubled phrases,—echoes of a suppressed wail of agony that again and again finds vent in words,—when the writer thinks of a scene in the chamber of death as really the last scene of all, without bitterly regretting that a mind, in many ways so noble and so true, should have forfeited the great consolations which are the right of every believer in a Risen, or rather a Self-raised, Christ.

Faith forbids us Christians thus to sorrow, as those who have no hope, for them that sleep in Him. "For if we believe that Jesus died, and rose again, even them also which sleep in Jesus will God bring with Him."*

"I have power to take My Life again." May God teach each one of us something of the meaning of these words of our Lord Jesus Christ on this His Resurrection Festival, to the greater glory of Him our Redeemer, and to our own endless peace!

* 1 Thess. iv. 14.

SERMON IX.

THE POWER OF RECOVERY.

PSALM CXVIII. 17.

I shall not die, but live, and declare the works of the Lord.

THIS buoyant and hopeful language is obviously in place on Easter Day. The Psalm which contains it has just been sung; we have been placing ourselves among the Jews just restored to their homes after the Babylonish Captivity. It was sung for the first time either at laying the foundation-stone of the new temple, or at its dedication: and it breathes, in every line, the spirit of thankfulness, of triumph, of hope. It is the Hymn of the Deliverance from the Captivity, just as Miriam's song is the Hymn of Deliverance from Egypt:[a] it is such a *Te Deum* as was possible when as yet the Gospel had not been revealed.

The situation is implied rather than described. Heathendom has done its worst; but Israel has triumphed. The heathen had compassed Israel about "like bees,"[b] in countless, thronging numbers; they had "thrust sore"[c] at Israel: but "the voice of joy and salvation was now heard in the dwellings of the righteous:"[d] the "right hand of the

---

[a] Exod. xv. 20, 21.
[b] Ps. cxviii. 12.
[c] Ib. 13.
[d] Ib. 15.

Lord had brought mighty things to pass."[a] The bondage
of seventy years is over: God has "broken the gates of
brass, and smitten the bars of iron in sunder:"[b] the perils
of the desert have been safely traversed; and Israel is again
in the home which, it had seemed, had been left for ever.
And the people are keeping high festival: the day itself
is consecrated. The temple gates are bidden open before
the advancing procession; the "gates of righteousness," as
they are called, must open, for they lead the way to the
altar of the All-Holy. And then as the throng passes
within, the Psalmist notes a circumstance which forms a
leading feature in his poem. In building the new temple,
some block of stone had been, at first, laid aside as useless,
and then, on fuller consideration, it had been lifted up to
fill one of the most important positions in the structure.[c]
In the Psalmist's eyes, this was a parable, setting forth
the recent history of the Jewish people. That people had
seemed, as it went into its exile, to be laid aside as no
longer of any account in the work of building up the
moral and religious future of the world: it had had its
day; and it was forgotten. But lo! in the Hands of the
Great Builder of the temple of human history, there is a
sudden shifting and readjustment of the materials of
Empire; Babylon itself dissolves in ruins; Persia becomes
mistress of the East: and the nation which was but now
cast aside as worthless by Nebuchadnezzar, is honourably
replaced in its ancient and consecrated home by Cyrus.
And thus the stone which the human builders of the
world's politics rejected, the same is made the head of
the corner: only no merely human foresight could have
foreseen, no merely human power could have compassed
such a result: "This is the Lord's doing, and it was marvellous in the eyes" of His servants.[d] Nor is this all.

[a] Ps. cxviii. 16.   [b] Ps. cvii. 16.   [c] Ps. cxviii. 22.   [d] *Ib.* 23.

Still around the restored people were hovering many and implacable enemies; the old vindictive animosities which, in "the day of Jerusalem,"[a] had hailed with delight the Babylonian triumph, were irritated into new life by the spectacle of the Restoration; Edom, Ammon, Moab, the Arabian tribes, threatened mischief, if only and whenever they might have opportunity. But the Psalmist, impersonating the restored nation, is hopeful—nay, confident. The recent deliverance was itself the warrant of triumphs to come. Let Israel only be true to its high destiny, and He Who had done so much for His people will not leave them a prey to the enemies around: "I shall not die, but live, and declare the works of the Lord."

And indeed this confidence stood the Jewish people in good stead. It carried them through the vicissitudes of the Persian rule, through the cruel oppressions of Antiochus Epiphanes, through the troubled days of the Herodian dynasty. It was only forfeited when they virtually rejected its true ground and basis; when they broke, as St. Paul showed them,[b] with all the antecedents of their history, by rejecting that Son of David, Who was also David's Lord, and in leading up to Whom Israel had fulfilled its appointed destiny.

Thus we have in the words, and indeed throughout the Psalm, a buoyant sense of recovered power, which looks hopefully forward into the uncertain future. And of this the secret is a quickened conviction of the presence of God among His people. Just as some two centuries earlier, when Sennacherib was threatening Jerusalem, a Psalmist had sung that "God is in the midst of her, therefore shall she not be removed: God shall help her, and that right early;"[c] so now the warrant of confidence is the same.

[a] Ps. cxxxvii. 7.   [b] Acts xiii. 16-41.   [c] Ps. xlvi. 5.

"The Lord is on my side: I will not fear what flesh can do unto me."[a] The Psalm passes from stanza to stanza in an ever-swelling volume of thankful hope: "The Lord is my strength and my song, and is become my salvation."[b] "The Lord hath chastened and corrected me: but He hath not given me over unto death."[c] "This is the day which the Lord hath made: we will rejoice and be glad in it."[d] "I shall not die, but live, and declare the works of the Lord."

I.

Had this however been all that there is to be said about the words before us, it would have been better to have gone elsewhere for an Easter text. What did these words mean in the mouth of our Lord Jesus Christ? It may be said at once, and confidently, that He made the words His Own. During His earthly life, the Book of Psalms was His Prayer-book. And those Psalms, we may be sure, which were believed to refer to the promised Messiah, were often in His heart and on His lips. To Him the immediate historical reference was less than the deeper although secondary sense of the words: He knew the meaning of His Own Spirit better than did the Psalmist whom His Spirit had inspired. So He ignores the reference to the rejected and restored people: He is, Himself, the corner-stone. Had not Isaiah said that Israel's Saviour was to be "despised and rejected of men,"[e] before the hour of triumph came when He should "divide the spoil with the strong"?[f] and was not this fulfilled accurately in the earthly life of Jesus? And therefore when, four days before His Passion, He had uttered in the temple that

[a] Ps. cxviii. 6.   [b] Ib. 14.   [c] Ib. 18.
[d] Ib. 24.   [e] Isa. liii. 3.   [f] Isa. liii. 12.

solemn parable of the husbandmen, who after beating and killing and stoning their Master's servants, end by slaying the son, and casting him out of the vineyard,[a] He desired to bring the reality sharply home to the consciences of His hearers, and at the same time to announce the certain but unsuspected issue of all that they were then meditating. Therefore He suddenly asked them, "Did ye never read in the scriptures, The Stone Which the builders rejected, the same is become the Head of the corner?"[b]

Thus we see what was the meaning of this Psalm as used by our Lord. The Cross and grave have taken the place of the Babylonian bondage; the Restoration to Palestine is forgotten in the Resurrection. This single verse throws light on all the rest; and we cannot doubt what our Lord meant by saying, "I shall not die, but live, and declare the works of the Lord." Before His Crucifixion the words were a prophecy of the Resurrection. Unlike ourselves, our Lord throughout His earthly life knew what was before Him. From us the future is hidden in mercy: we could not bear the sight, it may be, if the veil were lifted. But our Lord surveyed everything. He contemplated each detail of the Passion for years before it was undergone; and of course He accentuated and extended His sufferings by the contemplation. The motto of this period of His life was, "I have a baptism to be baptized with, and how am I straitened till it be accomplished!"[c] And yet the foreknowledge which surveyed His coming agony surveyed also the peace and triumph beyond. "Behold, we go up to Jerusalem, and all things that are written by the prophets concerning the Son of Man shall be accomplished. For He shall be delivered unto the Gentiles, and shall be mocked, and spitefully entreated,

[a] St. Matt. xxi. 39.   [b] St. Matt. xxi. 42.   [c] St. Luke xii. 50.

and spitted on: and they shall scourge Him, and put Him to death: and the third day He shall rise again."[a] He was to die, yet He was to rise; it was the prospect of death modified by the prospect of triumph over death; it was Calvary, but already irradiated by the Resurrection morning. "I shall not die, but live, and declare the works of the Lord." But after the Resurrection the words must have a fuller meaning; they became to Him more literally true. "Christ being raised from the dead dieth no more."[b]

This is indeed the crowning glory of the Easter Victory: it is final. The sorrow of Gethsemane, the humiliations of the judgment-hall, the lingering torture on Calvary, are passed for ever; they never can be renewed. "For in that He died, He died unto sin once; but in that He liveth, He liveth unto God."[c] We have heard of victories which are no sooner achieved than other victories become necessary in order to secure their advantages. But when Jesus rose from His grave on Easter Day, the sting of death was extracted, and the power of the grave conquered, once for all. "I am He that liveth, and was dead; and, behold, I am alive for evermore."[d] Henceforth He will declare the works of the Lord. For forty days He will hold converse with His Apostles as to the things concerning the kingdom of God. And then He will send the Holy Spirit, the Comforter, "to take of" what He had already taught in parable or epigram, and "show it to" His Church, in its full significance of creed and doctrine.[e] And His envoys, speaking in His Name, and as His mouthpieces, shall "go into all the world, and preach the Gospel to every creature,"[f] even to the end of time.

Yes! He is living now. We do not see Him: He has

---

[a] St. Luke xviii. 31-33.   [b] Rom. vi. 9.   [c] Rom. vi. 10.
[d] Rev. i. 18.   [e] St. John xvi. 15.   [f] St. Mark xvi. 15.

withdrawn Himself beyond the veil; but tokens are not wanting which go to show that He is within hearing, that He watches and shapes the course of the world, and the destinies of His Church, and the lives of His servants. He has a better reason for His confidence than had Israel after the Restoration. The Presence of God in Israel was liable to forfeiture by disloyalty; it was, as we know, forfeited in the sequel of events. In our Lord and Saviour this Presence is linked to His Manhood, by a union, personal and indissoluble. He speaks as Man, for ever united with Deity; and His sense of possessing an imperishable life becomes, when deposited in the heart of His Church, a power of recovery and survival which yields a new meaning to the words that may well engage our attention.

II.

"I shall not die, but live, and declare the works of the Lord."

We listen here to an utterance of the heart of the Christian Church, again and again heard during the centuries of her eventful history. In many ways the Passion and Resurrection of Christ have been reflected in the later fortunes of Christianity; and especially the Church's power of recovery from weakness and disaster is a note and proof of her union with Christ. This her vital and recuperative energy is His Who "was crucified through weakness, yet liveth by the power of God."[a]

In three ways, the Church of Christ has been, from time to time, brought down, to all appearance, to the chambers of the dead, and from this deep depression she has risen again to newness of life.

[a] 2 Cor. xiii. 4.

First, there has been the distress and suffering produced by outward persecution. For nearly three hundred years the Imperial Government of Rome was engaged in an almost uninterrupted attempt to stamp out the Church by physical force. No forms of torture were unemployed in order to expel religious conviction from the souls of Christians. Old men and maidens, young men and children, gave their witness, on scaffolds, in amphitheatres, in deserts, on mountain-sides, to the Name of Jesus. One Emperor failed in the enterprise; but another took up the task. After Nero came Domitian, after Decius, Diocletian. At last the arms of the old Empire became enfeebled by age; and the wild cries of the barbarians were heard more and more distinctly along a thousand miles of frontier; and Paganism in its decay could persecute no more. Yet at times it had seemed that the Faith might be killed out from among men. It was natural to take this view of things, if men had no adequate idea of the forces and principles in conflict;—organised physical might on one side, and a Creed, resting only on unseen realities, on the other.

But all through these dark and dreary years, the secret leaven of the Resurrection power of Jesus was working in the heart of Christendom. Never was the darkness so thick that no ray of light reached the soul of the suffering Church. Never was her cause so desperate but that she could, not boastfully or in scorn, but in the clear, albeit broken accents of faith and hope, utter her unfailing conviction; 'The Empire will pass, but Jesus Christ remains; "I shall not die, but live, and declare the works of the Lord."'

Next, the Church has been exposed more than once to a more formidable danger,—the decay of vital convictions within her fold.

This happened in the early part of the thirteenth century, when the Arabian philosophers of Moorish Spain were so widely read in the Universities of Europe, and caused for some years a secret but profound unsettlement of faith in the leading truths of Christianity. So again, at the revival of letters in the fifteenth and sixteenth centuries, especially in Italy. So also, and conspicuously in the eighteenth century, we may almost say, throughout Europe. The great anti-Christian campaign was opened in England by Bolingbroke, Tindal, and the English Deists. It was carried on in France by their pupil—for such virtually he was—Voltaire, and the Encyclopædist writers. It found a powerful patron in Frederick the Great of Prussia. It closed, in Germany, with Lessing, who mistook criticism for faith, and to whom the search for truth seemed better than its possession; and with Nicolai, and other writers of the "enlightenment" period; while on the western bank of the Rhine, the worship of the goddess of Reason was keeping time with the horrors of the Revolutionary Tribunal and of the Reign of Terror. "I am tired," Voltaire once said, "of hearing that it took only twelve men to set up Christianity in the world; I will show that it needs but one man to destroy it." There were Christians to whom it seemed that Christianity had had its day; that God must have withdrawn His protective survey from the world of human thought; and that all the waves and storms of insurrectionary blasphemy were at last burying out of sight and for ever the Gospel of Christ. But that age was also the age of not a few saintly Christians, both in England and elsewhere. And they were sure that the Faith and Church of Christ had not forfeited the power of recovery which is lodged in them by Christ's Resurrection. Years passed, and men who were not religious came to see that, whatever were

Voltaire's powers in other directions, his shallow scornful treatment of the Bible resembled the art of the schoolboy who earns the cheap laughter of his fellows by painting a moustache on a fine antique, and running away. Years passed, and theories which were merely negative, and had no substantial truth or help to give whereby minds might be illuminated and wills invigorated, and souls refreshed, were seen in their real poverty and nakedness. And thus men turned their eyes back to the creed of their forefathers and to the spiritual mother that had blessed them in their infancy. But all through that dreary century, in the heart of the Church was repeated the profound unsurrendered conviction: 'These writers may say what they will: and yet "I shall not die, but live, and declare the works of the Lord."'

Once more, and worst of all, the Church has been exposed to moral corruption. So it was, we know, within certain limits, under the eyes of the Apostle himself at Corinth. So it was in the tenth century, when the highest places in the hierarchy were controlled by the unhappy Theodora and Marozia.[a] We need not multiply illustrations; but here surely is an evil more perilous far than any persecutor's sword, or even than any form of intellectual rebellion. And yet in times like these, however grave has been the scandal, or deep-seated the disease, the heart of the Church has remained sound. The thousands or millions of simple folk, who have been true, on the whole, to the light which God has given them, true to their faith in a Crucified Redeemer, and a sanctifying Spirit, and the claims of conscience, and the imminence of a world beyond the grave,—these have been the real soul of the Church, the root from which new saplings

[a] Milman, *Lat. Christ*. ii. 451, Bk. v. c. 11.

and shoots would spring. And in their life of faith and hope, whatever might be the load of distress and discouragement, there has reigned all along the profound conviction that the faith and life of Christendom would not perish; that the Church still might say, "I shall not die, but live, and declare the works of the Lord."

Good men always feel strongly the evils of their own day; it is their business to recognise and to combat them. But in doing so they are sometimes led to think that no previous age has been so weighted with energetic mischief as their own. Here there is a risk of losing a true sense of proportion; of not merely exaggerating the evils of present as compared with those of past times, but of forgetting the Divine resources upon which the Church of Christ may always fall back, and which are more than equal to her needs. Let us be sure that to believe that Christ has risen is to know that, come what may, His Church will not die, but live, and declare the works of the Lord.

III.

But, once more, in these words we have the true language of the individual Christian soul, whether in recovery from illness, or face to face with death.

And, first, this is the language of the convalescent.

Most of us who have reached middle life have seen some one in an extreme stage of illness. The patient has been given up. The doctors say that the case is hopeless. The relations are making up their minds to the separation, the wrench, the sorrow, the blank, the many forms of trouble that lie before them. It is said to be a question, at most, of days, perhaps only of hours. The sufferer cannot move, cannot speak, rarely opens his eyes, is supposed to be insensible to all that is passing. Perhaps he is keenly alive to every word that is said; but he thinks of himself as despondingly as do others. Hezekiah has described his thoughts in like circumstances :—

> "I said, in the cutting off of my days,
> I shall go to the gates of the grave :
> I am deprived of the residue of my years.
>
> . . . . .
>
> Mine age is departed,
> And is removed from me as a shepherd's tent :
> I have cut off like a weaver my life :
> He will cut me off with pining sickness :
> From day even to night wilt Thou make an end of me."[a]

All seems to be virtually over: and yet—the end does not come. Why this pause before the gates of death? Why this delay, when it needs but a convulsion, or a sigh, and all will have ended? Surely there is something more than hesitation to die; there is a faint sense of increased vitality; there is a surmise, which becomes a hope, a hope which becomes a conviction, that recovery is possible. At last the sufferer murmurs, "I shall not die, but live."

It is a wonderful experience—this resumption of that which had been so solemnly taken leave of; this recovery of a sense of power and possession, when, as it seemed, all had been for ever resigned. One by one they come back,—the use of each deadened sense; the power to wield each languid limb; the free and buoyant exercise of first this and then that faculty of the mind which had sympathised so deeply with the weakness of the failing body. "I remember," says one,[b] not long since taken from us, who when ill was wont to pass the hours of weariness

---

[a] Isa. xxxviii. 10, 12.
[b] Rev. E. B. Pusey, D.D., who described this experience to the author.

and pain in repeating the Hebrew Psalms, "I remember how, in recovering from an illness, I could just say, 'Thou shalt purge me with hyssop.'ᵃ I could not possibly recall the next words. A day later, 'and I shall be clean' flashed on me. Then I knew that I was better."

Convalescence! it is like a renewal of youth, when its strength is developed and its freshness has not yet passed. It is like a bright day in October re-animating, in the gloom of the falling year, the sense of recovered sunshine and life which belongs to spring. Convalescence! yes, it soon passes; its first vigour and freshness die away into the experiences of average life; but, meanwhile, what has it done for us? Is it nothing, think you, to have been thus face to face with death, to have surveyed from this Pisgah the plains of the land of promise; to have touched the very gate of the grave, and felt the powers of the world to come playing around us; to have had experiences which come to most men only once—when they have set out on that journey from which none return? Is it nothing to have been the object of those anxieties, those forebodings, those watchings, those prayers; to have been taken leave of by friends on earth; to have been waited for perhaps by evil spirits, perhaps by the blessed intelligences in Paradise? The legend that the risen Lazarus was never seen to smile expresses the sense of mankind as to what beseems him who has passed the threshold of the other world; and surely a new and peculiar seriousness is due from those who have all but passed it, and have returned to life by little less than a resurrection. Of what remains of life the motto should surely be, "I shall not die, but live, and declare the works of the Lord." Surely such a life must be consecrated; it is not thus paradoxically restored that it may forthwith be wasted; it must, by

ᵃ Ps. li. 7.

word and deed, by precept and example, be a living exposition of the Unseen; like the Risen Jesus, and in virtue of His Resurrection power, it must declare the works of the Lord.

But further, these words should express the feeling of every Christian soul, in the prospect of death and eternity.

We all of us have to die. There are many contingencies in life: but death is not a contingency. Everything indeed relating to it is uncertain; its date, its manner, its attendant circumstances. But death itself is, in the case of every human being, a certainty. It is appointed unto all men once to die.* But there are two very different estimates of death. Is it the end of all things to us? Or is it a passing experience, an episode, in a vastly extended, nay, unending existence?

Nothing is more pathetic than the study of efforts which for thousands of years the human mind has made to answer this question; straining thought and fancy, and often what it believed to be experience, if only it might see the outline of that land which lies beyond the grave. Certainly it is impossible to read the dialogues in which great heathens, like Plato in one age and Cicero in another, endeavoured to satisfy themselves of the spirituality and survival of the soul, without sympathy and admiration for their anxious reaching after higher truth, their cautious, reverent, although at times necessarily mistaken endeavour to grasp the realities which are so familiar to Christians. For them immortality was a guess, rising, according to the temper of different minds, upwards towards certainty; they hoped rather than knew that the immaterial principle in man would survive the grave. Something more is needed to enable Christians to say, as we do, each of us,

* Heb. ix. 27.

say, if we are Christians indeed, 'When my body is laid in the dust, I shall not die; my true self, my personal being, will live, and, through Christ's grace, will declare His redeeming work to all eternity.'

Jesus Christ our Lord has brought life and immortality to light.[a] Again and again He has in words taught us that there is a life beyond the grave; as when He says, "He that loseth his life for My sake shall find it."[b] But He has done more: He has made recovery from death even of the body palpable to the senses. He has, by His Resurrection, transferred the question of man's future from the region of speculation to that of experience, from the invisible world to the world of sight and touch. It is not for us Christians to say, 'Man may survive death.' We should know that he will. It is not for us to say, 'Man may be reunited to the material form which has been so intimately associated here with his life of consciousness and resolve.' We should know that this reunion is a certainty. Jesus Christ surely has not risen that we should live on in the twilight of conjecture as to the destiny that awaits us. He has risen, for this end among others, that He may one day "change our vile body, that it be fashioned like unto His glorious Body, according to the mighty working whereby He is able even to subdue all things unto Himself."[c]

Do not let us confuse the fact of our survival after what we call death with our consciousness of it. The fact is as independent of human consciousness as the sun in the heavens. The sun is there whether we recognise him or not. The supersensuous realities are what they are, whatever be our mental attitude towards them; the world of fact does not dance attendance upon the petty, fitful, uncertain world of human thought. But what we

[a] 2 Tim. i. 10.   [b] St. Matt. x. 39.   [c] Phil. iii. 21.

think habitually on the subject is to each one of us a matter of the greatest moment, since our fitness for the inevitable future depends upon the preparation which is being made for it by our minds and hearts and wills in our present state of existence.

With thousands of men there is no speculative difficulty as to the future life. The real speculative difficulty would be to suppose that such a force as the human mind could possibly be extinguished by the dissolution of the human body. And the Resurrection of the human body is not more wonderful, because it is more unfamiliar, than its birth. But men who admit this still say, 'How am I to acquire, and carry about with me, and act upon, this practical conviction, this ever-present sense of the future that awaits me? How am I to turn a speculative conclusion into a persuasion that shall sway, and mould, and completely influence my life? How am I to learn, in this sense to say, "I shall not die, but live, and declare the works of the Lord"?'

The answer must be: Give your conviction a chance of growing. A conviction of a working kind depends less upon exact processes of the intellect than upon loyalty of the heart and will. If a man knows that a great earthly future is before him upon which he has not yet entered, he dwells on it in his leisure moments, and, though his life be a busy one, he makes time to prepare for it. If you would have the Christian sense of living for Eternity, allow time for it in your present life. We have spoken of Germany in the last century; it offers few more interesting characters than Haller, the great naturalist, who made physiology a science. Haller was professor at Göttingen, but his reputation and his activity were European; the Universities of Berlin, Stockholm, Copenhagen, St. Petersburg, Paris, Florence, Bologna, Padua, accounted it an honour to reckon him among their members; not merely German princes, but the Emperor Joseph the Second eagerly sought his friendship. After his death a private diary was found, which shows how on every day in this busiest of lives, so constantly devoted to the scientific investigation of matter, time was made for communion with the Unseen, and for meditation on the Future. "Enable me to think," these are his words, "in this still hour, on eternity, and prize at their true worth the poor joys of this fleeting life." "May I not only know, but feel, that, if I have not peace with Thee my God, I have nothing; and that the most enjoyable of such lives is but a sad dream, which eternity will end."[a]

If a man has a serious conviction, he makes ventures on the strength of it, and these ventures in return strengthen, deepen, broaden the conviction. Act as men who have Eternity before you, and you will soon have no doubts about its reality. Especially is the sense of the future world strengthened and deepened by our accompanying the dying, so far as we may, on their journey towards it. The poet of the *Christian Year* notes this effect of joining in Communion with the sick, in lines which are not easily forgotten, when once attention has been called to them :—

> "O soothe us, haunt us, night and day,
> Ye gentle spirits far away,
> With whom we shared the cup of grace,
> Then parted;—ye to Christ's embrace,
> We to the lonesome world again—
> Yet mindful of the unearthly strain
> Practised with you at Eden's door,
> To be sung on, where angels soar,
> With blended voices, evermore."[b]

---

[a] Quoted in Hagenbach's *Germ. Rationalism.*
[b] *The Christian Year :* Visitation of the Sick.

All this will seem easy and natural, if, in the Apostle's words, we have "risen with Christ." The sense of immortality will be enfeebled and die away, should we constantly live as though this world alone were real, and the other only a shadowy and distant uncertainty. But if, escaping from the grave of sense as well as the grave of sin, we retire like our Risen Lord from the sight of men, for communion with the Unseen; if, by His grace, we have the heart to turn away from the finite and the perishing to the Imperishable and the Infinite, we shall learn the lessons of eternity even during the hours of time, and shall know as others cannot know, that, whenever or however death may await us, we shall not die, but live, and shall hereafter, as now, declare the works of the Lord.

SERMON X.

THE LIVING NOT AMONG THE DEAD.

St. Luke xxiv. 5, 6.

Why seek ye the living among the dead? He is not here, but is risen.

THESE were the words of the two angels at the sepulchre to the Holy Women, who had gone very early in the morning of Easter Day, bringing spices to "anoint" the Body of Jesus. Greatly to their surprise they found the stone rolled away from the sepulchre. They entered in and found not the Body of the Lord Jesus. They were shocked at this: as they had made sure of finding Him; when suddenly, in their perplexity and distress, they found that they were not alone. Two men—St. John explains that they were two angels—stood beside them in shining garments. They were frightened at being so visibly close to beings who belonged to another world. They were afraid, and bowed down their faces to the earth; and then the angels addressed them in the words before us: "Why seek ye the living among the dead? He is not here, but is risen."

We have here a gentle remonstrance, and the announcement of a fact. The fact is the certainty of the Resurrection: "He is not here, but is risen." The remonstrance is, "Why seek ye the living among the dead?"

I.

The fact announced by the angel is, as we can see when we look back on it, among the best attested in human history. For forty days the Apostles continually saw Jesus Christ Risen; touched Him, spoke with Him, ate and drank with Him as before His death. They staked everything upon this fact. It was to them a fact of experience. They put it in the forefront; they made it almost the staple of their teaching. They died—most of them—rather than disown their belief in it, and the larger faith which was based on it. St. Paul, writing some twenty-six years after the event, says that there were still alive more than two hundred and fifty people who had seen the Risen Jesus.

The experience of the Apostles and disciples is confirmed by the convictions of the eight thousand converts who were received into the Church of Christ by St. Peter, on preaching his two sermons, fifty days after the Resurrection. These converts were upon the spot where all had taken place: the event was much nearer to them in point of time than last Christmas is to us. They might have made any inquiries they liked; they might have cross-questioned the Apostolic witnesses; they might have examined the tomb; they might have asked the Roman guards to recall their exact impressions; they might have entered into the reasons which the Jews alleged for disbelieving the fact. And in a matter of such vital moment, when a change of religion was in question, when the new Christians might soon have to seal their convictions with their blood, they would naturally have done this. They would have made sure that they were not running serious risks for a baseless dream, that, in language of the day, they were not "following cunningly devised fables."*

It is said, I know, that the critical faculty in those days was not so keen and exacting as it is in ours; that men were contented with evidence which we should deem insufficient to establish their conclusion; that we cannot therefore accept their convictions without revising the grounds on which they rest. Now there is truth in this observation, if we apply it to certain departments of literary evidence; the authorship of a book, for example, or the value of a local tradition. But there is no truth in it as applied to a fact attested as was the Resurrection of Jesus Christ; a broad public fact of the highest possible interest. The Resurrection of Jesus Christ either did take place or it did not. The first converts were at least as interested as we are in ascertaining the truth. And the common-sense methods of finding out whether a fact of this kind is true do not vary every one, or five hundred years: they are always the same. And if we find a number of witnesses in their senses asserting that they saw, touched, heard a living man, it is not reasonable to say that they only saw a corpse or a phantom, and that fancy did the rest. One or two people may be hallucinated: but not a multitude. A large number of people will not easily be so swayed by a single interest or a single passion as to believe simultaneously in a story that has no foundation in fact.

* * * *

[Here follows a passage which traverses ground already occupied in Sermon V.]

II.

The fact of the Resurrection is the ground of the remonstrance of the angels with the Holy Women,—" Why seek

* 2 St. Pet. i. 16.

ye the living among the dead?" But is this question applicable only to them during that pause when they felt the shock of the empty tomb? Let us consider.

First of all, then, it would seem that we may literally seek the Living among the dead if we seek Christ in a Christianity, so termed, which denies the Resurrection. Strange to say, there are men in our day who deny the true Resurrection of Jesus, yet still cling to the Christian name. They make much of the moral teaching of Jesus; of His precepts about self-knowledge and self-conquest; of His marvellous example. When the French Protestant Synod met last year in Paris, this idea of Christianity without a Risen Christ, which has its exponents nearer home, found public expression. It was urged on behalf of the advanced school of unbelief in the Synod, that denial of the Resurrection did not really much matter. "We agree with you," said a representative of that school to their believing opponents, led by M. Guizot, "we agree with you in valuing the moral teaching of Jesus; why should we quarrel about His corpse?"* But if St. Paul had been there he certainly would have held that this question about the "corpse" of Jesus Christ is vital. If His Body never left the grave, if it has somewhere mingled with the dust of earth; then, however we may be attracted by His moral teaching, we have no ground for hoping in Him as our Redeemer: there is nothing to prove that He was the Son of God in the way He pointed out, or that He has established any new relation between earth and

---

* M. Colani said in this Synod, of our Lord's Crucified Body, "le cadavre qui a été mis en terre . . . reste en terre et s'y décompose," and he even asserted that this was St. Paul's belief.—Bersier, *Histoire du Synode Général de l'Église Réformée de France*, i. 279. He was effectively answered by M. Bois.—*Ibid.* p. 311.

heaven. "If Christ be not risen, then is our preaching vain, and your faith is also vain."[a] "Ye are yet in your sins: then they also which are fallen asleep in Christ are perished."[b] That is St. Paul's estimate of the question; and it is in keeping with the earnestness with which he and the other first heralds of the Gospel made the Resurrection of Jesus the main subject of their teaching. No! wherever the pulse of Christian faith beats ever so faintly, we hear, at the tomb of the Redeemer, as the very first truth to which it clings, its confession of the precious, invigorating words, "He is not here; He is risen." And wherever Christ's true Resurrection from the tomb is denied, though genius and eloquence should do their best to disguise the aching void, there, depend upon it, Christ is not. And if souls are ever to be awakened from this dreary caricature of His religion, it will be by some voice, Divine or human, heard in the depths of the conscience, "Why seek ye the living among the dead?"

But nearly the same thing may happen, in cases where the Resurrection is not denied, but nevertheless men fail to see what habits of thought about our Lord it involves. How many, who would not think of denying the Resurrection, yet think of Jesus Christ our Lord habitually only or chiefly as one of the greatest men in the past history of the world! That He was at least this would be admitted by any educated and sensible heathen; the French infidels generally rank Him with Socrates, Confucius, and other great moralists and teachers of the past. Even if it be admitted that He is, as a teacher, on a totally distinct level from any of these; that He is incomparably the greatest teacher who has ever appeared upon the scene of human life, still if we think of Him only in this way,

[a] 1 Cor. xv. 14. [b] 1 Cor. xv. 17, 18.

we are seeking the living among the dead. Those other teachers whom I have named, and such as they, where are they now? They have given an impulse to human thought: they have been the founders of institutions; they have created literatures; they have shaped large masses of feeling and conviction which to this hour are powers in the world. They live, in their works, in their influence, in the minds which reproduce them; they live as names honourably attached to great causes, great convictions, great organisations. But where are they themselves? Somewhere, we know not where, under conditions we know not what, they live, as undying spirits in another world of being, awaiting the great account. But they have no personal present concern in this our world. And in estimating their influence we refer only to what they said and did, hundreds of years, or a few years, ago: we do not for a moment suppose that their action among men goes on still as a continuous though unseen force.

Now, a real believer in Jesus never thinks of Him in this way only or chiefly; as a mighty power in the past history of the world; as he might think of the great teachers and writers in question. He is not, as they are, in any sense among the dead. He has left to the tomb nothing but His winding-sheet. He is not only, as they are, one of the great influences of the past; He lives now as a pervading energetic influence among men. True, we do not see Him, as He was seen eighteen hundred years ago in the villages and on the hill-sides of Galilee. But for all that, it is the work of the Holy Spirit to make us feel Him present among us; present in this world as a living power, just as truly as He was present then. His life is continued on among us; only its conditions are changed. "Lo, I am with you alway, even unto the end of the world."ᵃ And the fact, external to himself, upon which the Christian falls back when he would remind himself of this, is the solid, unalterable, unyielding fact of the Resurrection; the fact by which Jesus made it plain to the senses of men that He had passed for ever from the realm of death; the fact which He proclaims, as from the throne of heaven, so in the inmost Christian consciousness, "I am He that liveth, and was dead; and, behold, I am alive for evermore."ᵇ To think of Him as only one of the great teachers of the world, who have come and disappeared, is to lose sight of the significance of His Resurrection from the grave: it is to rank Him in thought with men whose eminence has not saved them from the lot of mortality, and whose dust has long since mouldered in the tomb. It is to lose sight of the line which parts the superhuman from the human. It is to seek the living among the dead.

Yet more literally do we seek the living among the dead, if without formally rejecting Christianity we give the best of our thought, of our heart, of our enthusiasm, to systems of thought, or to modes of feeling, which Jesus Christ has set aside. The love of change, which is so deeply implanted in human nature, is constantly leading men, in one form or another, to do this. True, if they did but know it, this love of change itself should attach them indissolubly to Jesus. For what is the love of change, the thirst for novelty? It proceeds from the noblest distinction of the human soul, from man's appetite for That Infinite Being Who made us for Himself, and will not allow us lastingly to rest in any but Himself. This love of something new is man's witness in himself, and to himself, that nothing finite, nothing perishable, nothing

ᵃ St. Matt. xxviii. 20. ᵇ Rev. i. 18.

created, can really satisfy him. And Christianity in all earnest and thorough souls does satisfy this want: men find in it that repose to give which is the prerogative of the Divine;—" Lord," they say, " to whom shall we go ? Thou hast the words of eternal life." * But in every age a large percentage of Christians look at Christianity only on the surface; dwell only on its human characteristics; miss its Divinity. The seed falls by the wayside and on the rock, as well as elsewhere; and so old modes of thought and feeling, which might have been supposed to be for ever discredited, regain something of their power.

The Renaissance of the fifteenth century was a great example of this: it was a reaction in the direction of pure Paganism. For nearly a hundred years all over Europe educated men and women tried to write, feel, and live, as had the Romans and Greeks in the old Pagan days. And some of them succeeded remarkably well, to the enrichment undoubtedly of certain departments of art and literature, but at the serious cost of fundamental morality. The Reformation, on the Continent at least, was on one side a protest against the Paganism of the Renaissance. The Renaissance was in Christendom what the craving for the flesh-pots of Egypt had been in Jewish history; what the folly of the Galatian Christian, in attempting to reimpose circumcision, had been in early Apostolic history. The life of Christendom is Christ; and for the Christian nations to throw themselves back into the thoughts and feelings of the old Pagan world, in the hope of renewing their youth by contact with its moral and mental life, is to seek the living among the dead.

This holds equally good of the enthusiasm for some materialistic explanations of the theory of the Uni-

* St. John vi. 68.

verse, which are very popular just now, as being put forward by very able men, who can write very good English. The idea that force and matter are either or both of them eternal, and that all life, not excepting its highest forms, is the product of their fated action upon each other, is by no means, at least in its fundamental features, a novelty. The old world of Greece and Rome was familiar with it. Yet to suppose that the true life of humanity, that all that can raise man above sense, above passion, above selfishness, to the level of those higher aspirations of which he is conscious, is to be discovered in the tomb of matter, is an infatuation of which none have spoken more strongly than spiritualist thinkers who are not Christians. We Christians know that the only permanent safeguard for spirituality of aim, of thought and life, is to be found in Christianity, and particularly in faith in Christ's Resurrection. Here is the mystery which bids the imperious laws of matter subserve the interests of man's higher nature. To seek man's true life, in any materialistic system, is to seek life among the dead.

We may not be tempted, in these ways, to seek the living among the dead teachers or dead elements of old or untrustworthy ways of thinking. But there is a risk of our doing so, certainly not less serious and very much more common, to which we are all exposed. As you know, my Christian friends, our Lord's Resurrection is a moral as well as an intellectual power. While it convinces us of the truth of Christianity it creates in us the Christian life. We are risen with Christ. Just as we die with Him to our old nature, we rise with Him in newness of life. Just as we have shared His tomb, we share, even here and now, His victory. This is not the language of a recondite mysticism. It is the constant language of that most practical of men, St. Paul. The moral resurrection of Christians is a fact of experience. Resurrection from the grip of bad habits, from the charnel-house of bad passions; resurrection from the enervation, corruption, and decay of bad thoughts, bad words, bad deeds, to a new life with Christ, to the life of warm and pure affections, the life of a ready and vigorous will, of a firm and buoyant hope, of a clear strong faith, of a wide and tender charity. St. Paul says that the germ of this life is given us in baptism:[a] we then rise from the grave with Jesus Christ. And the one point which the Apostle would have us recollect is that "Christ being raised from the dead, dieth no more; death hath no more dominion over Him. For in that He died, He died unto sin once, but in that He liveth, He liveth unto God."[b] We are therefore to reckon ourselves "to be dead indeed unto sin, but alive unto God, through Jesus Christ our Lord."[c]

But, as a matter of fact, how do we risen Christians really act? We fall back, willingly or wilfully, into the very habits we have renounced. Our repentance is too often like the Lent of Louis the Fourteenth; it is a paroxysm, followed, almost as a matter of course, by the relapse of Easter. To do the great French monarch justice, he did not expect to find Christ's presence in sin and worldliness: as do they who complain of the intellectual difficulties of faith and prayer, while their lives are disposed of in such a manner, that it would be wonderful indeed if faith and prayer could escape suffocation, in that chaos of everything save the things which suggest God.

Surely Easter has its warnings as well as Lent: its warnings as well as its joys. It dictates to conscience the continuous cry,—Why seek the living among the

[a] Rom. vi. 4; Gal. iii. 27. [b] Rom. vi. 9, 10. [c] Rom. vi. 11.

dead? Over the tomb of worldliness and of sin, angels read the legend: "He is not here; He is risen." He is not to be found in this home of refined sensuality, in that atmosphere of frivolity and levity, in this clever but profane writing, in that brilliant but insincere society, in those haunts, those manners, that language, those sympathies. Excitement, yes! you may find that, such as it is; the surface excitement, which cannot drown the deep wail of restless misery that is heard in the depths of the soul. But life, true life,—the life of illuminated, enfranchised, invigorated men,—never. It is to be found only by those who do not lose the precious moments of existence in seeking the living among the dead. One great lesson of Easter is permanent elevation of aim. Jesus has left the tomb for good: we must do so too. We are surrounded in this life, by little else than by the chambers of the dead; and the painted imagery which decorates their walls, as of yore the tombs of Egyptian monarchs, might for a moment make us think that they are other than they are. Our true wisdom is to know that life is travestied in these sepulchres of thought, these sepulchres of morality; and that the life of emancipated souls is to be found only with the Risen and Eternal Christ, Who came down indeed among us, to visit us in our errors and our sins, but Whose angels have traced over all faiths but one, all rules of life but one, the motto which proclaims His triumph and our duty: "He is not here; He is risen."

SERMON XI.

THE POWER OF THE RESURRECTION.

PHIL. III. 10.

That I may know Him, and the power of His Resurrection.

THE power of Christ's Resurrection! Here is one of those phrases which we only understand when we remember that it is in tacit contrast to another phrase which suggests it. "Power" seems here to be contrasted with "fact." In every occurrence, whether great or unimportant, there are to be considered, first, the fact, or, that which actually occurred, and secondly, its consequences, actual or possible, or, what St. Paul calls its power. We know the fact of an occurrence when we have handled the proofs which show that it really took place; when we know how it has been described, what were its several aspects, near or distant, seen from without or from within. We know the fact when we have mastered its scene, its mechanism, its dimensions. But we know the power of an occurrence when we can trace what its effects have been, or what, but for disturbing or interrupting causes, they might have been, or might be, whether in the world at large, or upon individuals, whether upon others or upon ourselves. It is easier to apprehend a fact than to take the measure of its consequences, its practical meaning, its power. If I throw a stone as far as I can, I can ascertain without much difficulty the weight of the stone, the moment at which it leaves my hand, the distance of the spot at which it touches the ground from the spot on which I am standing. So much for the fact. But what is hard to ascertain is the effect of the stone's passage through the air; the thousands or millions of insects instantaneously disabled or destroyed by it; the radiation of disturbance caused by the displacement of the atmosphere, and extending, it may be, into regions which defy or escape calculation.

All of us understand, more or less, at least, the general outline and succession of recent events in Egypt, but what will be, in the course of years, their import and influence upon the condition and history of our own country and of the world who shall say? This is a matter much less easy to determine: it needs the lapse of time, observation, reflection, very varied experience, in order to do so with any approach to accuracy. So on Good Friday morning we were all of us startled by hearing that a great lawyer and statesman had passed away:[a] and it is not necessary to subscribe to all of Lord Cairns's opinions in order to do justice to the great ability and to the fearless conscientiousness which have throughout marked his career. But what will be the effect, or as St. Paul would say the "power," of the withdrawal of so prominent a figure from the public life of our country, and at such a time as the present? This question also can only be answered some months, perhaps some years, hence; and even then, the influence of a single mind upon those with whom he acts, or upon men in general, is not easy to measure with anything like exactness. You see, my hearers, to

[a] Earl Cairns died at Bournemouth, April 2, 1885.

apprehend a fact is one thing; it is quite another to understand its power.

When then St. Paul utters his earnest prayer that he may know the power of Christ's Resurrection, he implies that he already has knowledge of the fact. He had indeed no sort of doubt about it. Here perhaps some of you may recall ground over which, at this sacred season, we have travelled together in former years; I mean the nature and vigour of the witness which St. Paul in particular bears to the fact of the Resurrection, and by which accordingly he unveils before our eyes the basis of his own conviction. St. Paul wrote his first Epistle to the Corinthians before any of the Gospels had been written; and that Epistle is one of the only four books in the New Testament against the genuineness and authenticity of which unbelieving criticism has found absolutely nothing to allege. There is, in fact, in a purely sceptical judgment, no more reason for doubting that St. Paul wrote that Epistle than for doubting that Sir Walter Scott wrote *Waverley*. And what does St. Paul tell the Corinthians about our Lord's Resurrection? He tells them that, while he was writing, there were more than two hundred and fifty persons still living who had seen our Saviour on one occasion after His rising from the dead. "He was seen of five hundred brethren at once; of whom the greater part remain unto this present."[*] Now here was an assertion which the Corinthians might, if they would, verify for themselves. There was intercourse enough between Greece and the coast of Syria; and any Corinthian who thought that St. Paul was too impetuous, or too credulous, or anything else of the kind, had only to investigate the accuracy of his statement by paying a visit to some of the two hundred and fifty

[*] 1 Cor. xv. 6.

survivors, and cross-questioning them for himself. St. Paul's statement was itself a challenge to do so. And if, so far as we know, the challenge was not accepted, this would only have been because men felt that unless the Apostle had been quite sure of his ground, the statement would never have been made. Even those who do not, with the Church, venerate in St. Paul a glorious Saint and Apostle, enthroned, now that his life of toil and suffering is over, not far from the very Throne of Christ in heaven—even they must, and do, gather from his writings that he was a remarkably clever man, and a man of shrewd common-sense. And as such, putting for the moment his inspiration out of sight, he never, we may be sure, would have made an assertion like that before us had he believed it to be liable to be disputed upon examination; had he been less than certain of its literal and severe accuracy. St. Paul was convinced that Christ had risen, for other reasons, as we know, but also because more than two hundred and fifty people were still living who, if questioned, would say that they had seen Him.

And St. Paul, being thus sure of the fact of the Resurrection, was not embarrassed by any *a priori* doctrine bidding him ignore it; he was not like those schoolmen whom Lord Bacon condemned, and who, instead of learning what to think about nature from the facts of nature, endeavoured to persuade themselves that the facts of nature corresponded to what they already thought about it. If a man says that miracle is impossible or incredible, no amount of proof that the Resurrection actually occurred is likely to satisfy him. When some early navigators, of whom Herodotus tells us, coasted round Africa, and returned with the story that they had reached a region at which their shadows at noonday pointed toward the south, their report was treated as ludicrous by the inhabitants of the Mediterranean seaboard, and among them, by the great historian himself; since the constant experience of their own neighbourhood furnished them, as they thought, with ample reason for thinking that nothing of the kind was possible. When asserting the fact of the Resurrection, St. Paul planted his foot upon the rock of experience; he was proof against the seductions of the idols whether of the den or of the cave. He had no need to pray, as have many in our time, that he might be assured of the fact of Christ's Resurrection. What he did pray for was that he might increasingly know its power.

Now, we may be sure we can trace only very partially the range of power which attaches to such an event as the Resurrection of our Lord. But let us do what we may within such narrow spheres as are the thought and life of man.

I.

The power of Christ's Resurrection, then, may be observed, first of all, and generally, in the way in which a true belief in it enables us to realise habitually the moral government of the world by God.

Our age has many characteristics which honourably distinguish it from earlier times, and which will be pointed to hereafter by historians. But it is not an age in which men believe, as they believed in the past, that, whatever happens or is permitted, all is overruled by a Being Who is perfectly Good and perfectly Wise.

When people are not deliberately and consciously sceptical about this, they often believe it only in a languid, hesitating way. They feel the doubt which floats in the intellectual air around them, and which enervates their mental grasp of the truth. We may perhaps flatter ourselves that this weakened hold on elementary truths is the result of a wider mental culture than was enjoyed by our fathers; of greater readiness to welcome new impressions; of a more judicial and balanced habit of mind. In this manner disbelief in an overruling Providence may assume in our eyes the colours of a distinction, if not of a virtue. And it is only when we find ourselves at one of the sterner crises in life, and the heavens seem as brass above our heads, and we cry, and there is, we think, none to answer, that we understand the extent and the misery of our loss.

And when some man,[*] not a clergyman, appears on the scene of our public life, to whom the Divine government of the world is as certain and as obvious as the action and language of his friends, or of the members of his family; a man to whom prayer is the most natural form of conversation, and the Bible and the imitation of Christ the rule of conduct;—we experience almost a new sensation, as at the presence of a striking and original apparition. Yet if we knew more of the days that have preceded us, we should know that the type which for the moment so fascinates and astonishes us, has been heretofore even the prevailing type among the sincere worshippers of Jesus Christ.

There are circumstances, no doubt, in the modern world which make belief in the Divine government harder for us than it was for our ancestors. One such circumstance is our wider outlook. Thanks to the press, the railway, the telegraph, we know a great deal more of what is going on all over the world, at the same time, than has any previous generation of men. And one consequence is that human life presents itself to many

[*] The late General Gordon, killed at Khartoum, January 1885.

minds as a much more tangled and inexplicable thing than it ever did before. The picture which is brought before us is so complex, so blurred; the details are so much more importunate than any obviously presiding and ruling principle; the disappointments in store for the conscience which is searching for clear traces of a law of right vigorously asserting itself are so frequent and so great, that men lose heart where heart and purpose are especially needful. They lazily acquiesce in some indistinct conception of the world which treats it as an unexplored and inexplicable moral chaos, amid the confusions of which it is vain to look for any clear note of a Reign of Righteousness maintained behind the veil.

Now here the certainty that Jesus Christ rose from the dead asserts what St. Paul calls its power. For when Jesus Christ was crucified, it might have seemed, it did seem, that the sun of God's justice had gone down behind thick clouds; and that a moral darkness, of which that in the sky was but a shadow, had settled on the earth. It might have seemed that while all the vices were being crowned and feasted in Rome, all the virtues could be crucified, and crucified with impunity, in Jerusalem. It might have seemed that we lived in a world where nothing was more surely at a discount than moral beauty, and nothing more certain of the future than physical and brute force.

And when He burst forth from the grave in which they laid Him under seal and stone, He proclaimed to men's senses, as well as to their consciences, that the real law which rules the world is moral, not material law; and that if the sun of God's righteousness is at times overclouded in human history, it is sure to reappear. To know that Jesus Christ rose from the dead is to know that, whatever may be the perplexities of the moment or of the age, the world is really swayed by God's most holy and overruling Providence.

II.

Next, the power of the Resurrection of Christ is seen in the firm persuasion which it should create, in our own days as in those of the Apostles, that the Christian Creed is true; true as a whole, and in its several parts. Thus the Resurrection of Christ has a twofold aspect. It is at once a proof that the Christian Creed is true, and a truth of the Christian Creed.

There are many truths of Christianity which do not contribute anything to prove its general truth, although they could not be lost sight of or denied without fatally impairing its integrity. Take for an example the truth of our Lord's perpetual intercession in heaven. Nothing tells more powerfully upon the life and conscience of a believing Christian than the knowledge that our living but unseen Saviour is ever engaged in one ceaseless act of self-oblation on high on behalf of His members and servants here on earth; on behalf of all and of each of them. "He ever liveth to make intercession for us."[a] But this truth does not attest the truth of any other part of our Creed; although it is, if we may reverently say so, their inevitable complement. We believe in our Lord's intercession because His Apostles have so taught us. We do not believe in the Creed as a whole because we believe in His intercession.

It is otherwise with the Resurrection, which, as I have said, is not only an article of the Christian faith, but a proof that the Christian faith is true as a whole. It is this because it is the certificate of our Lord's mis-

[a] Heb. vii. 25.

sion from heaven, to which He Himself pointed as the warrant of His claims. He laid this stress on His coming Resurrection on two occasions especially: in His saying about the destruction and rebuilding of the temple, and in His saying about the sign of the Prophet Jonah.[a] His words came in effect to this: 'You Jews doubt whether I have any right to teach you, and to proclaim Myself as I do. Very well; wait a short while, and an event will take place which will prove that your misgivings or doubts are unwarranted. I shall be put to death, and then I shall rise from the dead on the third day. This will be a countersign of My mission from heaven: if it does not take place, reject; if it does, believe Me.'

It is a mistake to say that our Lord referred to His Resurrection only on rare occasions, and that it had no such place in His mind as in the teaching of His Apostles. For it is plain from the Gospels that He was constantly dwelling on it. Thus He alluded to it, at least by implication, in the synagogue of Capernaum, when He spoke of the Son of Man ascending up where He was before.[b] He foretold both His Death and Resurrection explicitly after the confession of His Divinity by Simon Peter at Cæsarea Philippi.[c] While coming down from the Mount of the Transfiguration, He bade the disciples who had been with Him tell no man what they had seen until the Son of Man was risen from the dead.[d] After healing the demoniac, He is crossing Galilee, and He explains to His disciples that He will be delivered into the hands of men, and that they will kill Him, and the third day He will rise.[e] Still more striking is the saying that in dying He does not submit to the irresistible; that no man takes His life from Him;

[a] St. John ii. 19; St. Matt. xii. 39, 40.
[b] St. John vi. 62.   [c] St. Matt. xvii. 9; St. Mark ix. 9, 10.
[d] St. Matt. xvi. 21.   [e] St. Matt. xvii. 23.

that He has power to lay it down, and has power to take it again.[a] In going up to Jerusalem He repeats the prediction about dying and rising with great detail and precision;[b] and in the Upper Chamber the gracious promise, "A little while and ye shall see Me,"[c] certainly points to the Resurrection. Even on the road to Gethsemane, when the little company had left the Upper Chamber, and had sung a hymn, He assures them, "After I am risen again, I will go before you into Galilee."[d]

The Resurrection was thus constantly before His mind, because it was to be the warrant of His mission. And when He did rise, He redeemed the pledge which He had given to His disciples and to the world. The first preachers of Christianity understood this. The Resurrection was the proof to which they constantly pointed that our Lord was really what He claimed to be. "Jesus and the Resurrection" was the popular name at Athens for the Gospel as taught by St. Paul.[e] "This Jesus, Whom ye have crucified, hath God raised up," had been the keynote to the early teaching of St. Peter.[f] The Resurrection was the truth which filled the early Church with its first converts. The Resurrection was the decisive proof that Christianity was from God.

Let us ask, more precisely, What is the true value of the fact that our Lord rose from the dead among the credentials of Christianity? what is the measure of its evidential power?

Here, it would seem, there are two opposite mistakes to be avoided.

There is the mistake which was made nearly a century

---

[a] St. John x. 18.
[b] St. Matt. xx. 17-19; St. Mark x. 32-34; St. Luke xviii. 31-33.
[c] St. John xvi. 16.   [d] St. Matt. xxvi. 32.
[e] Acts xvii. 18.   [f] Acts ii. 22-24, 32.

ago by a writer of genius, who was, however, unduly influenced by the wish to simplify questions which are not always really simple,—I mean, Archdeacon Paley. Paley wanted to put the evidence of the truth of Christianity, as the phrase goes, in a nut-shell; and, in his well-known *Evidences*, he makes the whole case of Christianity rest upon the fact that the Resurrection was so certain to its first preachers that they willingly gave their lives to attest it. Paley's mistake lay, not in insisting upon this fact, which is indeed of the first importance as an evidence of Christianity, but in insisting on it, as if it stood alone, and would, of itself and unsupported, prove to all minds the truth of the Christian Creed. The consequence has been that, in many minds of our own and two preceding generations, Paley's book has failed to create or to reinforce the convictions which its author was anxious to serve; men have felt that more stress has been laid on a single line of evidence than it will properly bear. The truth is, that the evidences of Christianity are not one and simple, but many and complex. Their strength lies in their convergence; and the conviction of the truth of the Resurrection which was held by the Apostles is only one of several lines of argument which point towards a single and central truth, although of these it is the most important. And when this is overlooked, there is always risk of a catastrophe: the fabric which its Divine Architect meant to rest upon a group of pillars cannot be safely rested by us on one.

The other mistake is of later date, and much more serious. From saying that the Resurrection alone proves Christianity to be true, men have, in some instances, come of late to say that it is of no value whatever as an evidence of Christianity. Christianity is said to be recommended solely by the moral character of Christ. The supernatural incidents of His earthly life, and notably His Resurrection, are treated as an embarrassing addition to what else would be a simple and convincing exhibition of moral excellence. We believe the Resurrection, men have said, if we do believe it, for the sake of the religion which seems to warrant it; we do not believe in Christianity for the sake of the Resurrection.

Enough has already been said to show that this estimate of the evidential value of the Resurrection is altogether opposed to the mind of our Lord and His Apostles. They did not mean the Resurrection to stand alone, but they assigned to it a high, nay the highest place, among the facts which go to show that Christianity is true. The real value of the Resurrection, as an evidence of Christianity, would seem to be that it is a countersign in the world of nature to the teaching of our Lord in the court of conscience. The outward miracle assures us, through the senses, that the Being Who is the Author of nature is the same Being as He Who speaks to conscience in the Moral Law, in the Beatitudes, in the Sermon on the Mount, in the Last Discourse, in the whole character and teaching of Jesus Christ. If we heard the inward verdict of conscience alone, we might doubt whether there was anything external to ourselves which really warranted it. If we witnessed the outward miracle alone, we might see in it a mere wonder, with no moral significance, with no ascertainable relation to the inward and the spiritual. But when the Teacher Whose voice pierces, rouses, quickens conscience, is accredited by an interference with, or a suspension of, the observed course of nature, the combined evidence is reasonably overwhelming: deep answers to deep, sphere to sphere, the moral and the material are in felt harmony, and the combination is more than sufficient to warrant that assent of the mind and heart which we call faith. And in this way a persuasion of the literal certainty of the Resurrection is at the present day, as of old, a power which has weight with the most well-informed and thoughtful minds, as decisively attesting the claims of Christianity.

III.

And thirdly, the power of the Resurrection should be traced and felt in the spiritual and moral life of Christians.

Let us remind ourselves that our Lord Jesus Christ is not merely our one authoritative Teacher, not merely our Redeemer from sin and death, but also, and especially, through real union with us, the Author of a new life in us. He gives us a new nature, which is indeed His Own. St. Paul teaches us this truth again and again, and by a great variety of expressions. Sometimes he speaks of our Lord as though He were a sphere of being within which the Christian lives: "If any man be in Christ, he is a new creation: old things are passed away; behold, all things are become new."[a] Sometimes he speaks of Him as of an inhabitant of the Christian soul. "Christ in you," he says to the Colossians, "the Hope of Glory."[b] This union is not in St. Paul's mouth the language of metaphor; it is to him just as real a thing as eating or walking, or reading or preaching, or going to Athens or to Jerusalem. It is an actual experience of which he is certain. It began with him when he was baptized by Ananias; for "as many as have been baptized into Christ have put on Christ."[c] It was deepened and strengthened in many ways, but especially by the reception of that other Holy Sacrament, in which, unlike the careless Corinthians, he really "dis-

[a] 2 Cor. v. 17.   [b] Col. i. 27.   [c] Gal. iii. 27.

cerned the Lord's Body,"ᵃ and knew that he was admitted to the closest contact with the Source of his highest life.

Let none think that, in insisting on the presence of Christ in the bodies and souls of Christians, we are forgetting the office of the Holy Spirit, or confounding the work of the Spirit and the Son. The office of the Spirit is to convey Christ's nature and to interpret His teaching to Christians. This is one of the reasons for His being so constantly termed in the New Testament the Spirit of Christ. "He shall take of Mine, and shall show it unto you,"ᵇ was our Lord's description of His office. And thus He is the Agent Who makes the Christian Sacraments effectual in conveying Christ's Human Nature to Christians. The baptized puts on Christ,ᶜ but he is born of water and of the Spirit;ᵈ the communicant eats the Body and drinks the Blood of Christ,ᵉ but it is the Spirit that quickenethᶠ the dead elements, and makes them veils and vehicles of the unseen Gift. Our Lord then dwells in Christians; their bodies and souls are temples of His Presence;ᵍ His Incarnation is perpetuated in His living Church.ʰ And, as a consequence, the New Testament teaches us that the mysteries of His earthly life are reproduced, after a measure, in the Christian soul. If Christ is born supernaturally of a Virgin Mother, the Christian is made God's child by adoption and grace,ⁱ and Apostles are in travail until Christ be formed in their converts.ᵏ If Christ is crucified on Mount Calvary, the Christian, too, has a Calvary within, where he is crucified with Christ,ˡ where he crucifies the flesh with the affections and lusts.ᵐ If Christ, while His disciples behold, is taken

---

ᵃ 1 Cor. xi. 29.   ᵇ St. John xvi. 14.   ᶜ Gal. iii. 27.
ᵈ St. John iii. 5.   ᵉ St. John vi. 53.   ᶠ St. John vi. 63.
ᵍ 1 Cor. vi. 19, 20.   ʰ 1 Cor. xii. 12.   ⁱ Rom. viii. 15.
ᵏ Gal. iv. 19.   ˡ Gal. ii. 20; vi. 14.   ᵐ Gal. v. 24.

up into heaven, and sits at the Right Hand of God, the Christian in heart and mind with Him ascends, and with Him continually dwells;[a] nay, he is, as St. Paul says, made to sit together with Him in heavenly places.[b] And in like manner, if Christ rose from the dead the third day, according to the Scriptures, the Christian also has experience of an inward resurrection. As at a primitive baptism the adult neophyte was plunged beneath the waters, and then lifted up amid prayers and benedictions, so in this Sacrament Christians are still buried with Christ, and raised to newness of life.[c] And if the baptismal gift be impaired or forfeited, a second putting forth of the Resurrection power becomes necessary. A resurrection in penitence is a new effort of the power of recovery from sin and death, issuing from contact with the Risen Redeemer.

All this seems to be the language of metaphor, or the language of mysticism, until it has been discovered to be the record of an experience. St. Paul knew that it meant, or might mean, a solemn reality. It was this inward power of Christ's Resurrection, in its ever-increasing fulness, that he chiefly desired to know. Of this power of Christ's Resurrection lodged in the recesses of the Christian soul, of this moral and spiritual resurrection which issues from, and corresponds with, the literal Resurrection of Jesus Christ from His grave, there are three leading characteristics.

1. Our Lord rose really. It was not a phantom that haunted the Upper Chamber, or the road to Emmaus, or the shores of the Sea of Galilee; the Apostles had but to handle Him, and see, for a phantom had no such flesh and bones as they might see He had. And an Easter resurrection from sin should be no less real, will be no

[a] Col. iii. 1-3.   [b] Eph. ii. 6.   [c] Rom. vi. 3, 4.

less real, if it is His power by which we are rising. The flesh and bones, the actual substance of recovered life, true prayers, true confessions, true resolutions, truth in thought and word and act, are indispensable. To have a name that we live again, and yet to be dead,[a] is only too easy: it is scarcely less easy to impose upon ourselves than upon others with false appearances of life. Little indeed will a phantom-resurrection avail us here or hereafter; let us pray for that first mark of Christ's Resurrection power,—reality.

2. Our Lord really rose, but He rose to lead, for the most part, a hidden life. On the day of His Resurrection He appeared five times, but rarely afterwards during the forty days that preceded the Ascension. So it is with the risen life of the soul. It is not constantly flaunted before the eyes of men; it seeks retirement, solitude, and the sincerities which these insure. They whose religious life is perpetually displayed to the public eye may have risen really. But at least they are very unlike our Risen Lord. "If ye then be risen with Christ, seek those things that are above, where Christ sitteth at the right hand of God. . . . For . . . your life is hid with Christ in God. When Christ, Who is your life, shall appear, then shall ye also appear with Him in glory."[b] Reserve in speaking about ourselves may make heavy demands upon buoyant and impetuous natures. Frequent retirement for communion with God is not natural to flesh and blood: it fails to satisfy the demands for excitement and human sympathy, which enter so largely into much of our modern religion. But let us be sure that it is a true note of the presence of Christ's Resurrection power, that we should be thankful to be often alone with God.

[a] Rev. iii. 1.   [b] Col. iii. 1-4.

3. And thirdly, our Lord "being raised from the dead dieth no more; death hath no more dominion over Him. For in that He died, He died unto sin once: but in that He liveth, He liveth unto God."[a] His Resurrection power does not lend itself to the perpetual alternations of relapse and recovery, which mark the lives of so many Christians: "Christ, being raised from the dead, dieth no more." It is sad work when Easter is only reached to forfeit by relaxation what little may have been gained in Lent and Passion-tide. We may sink into the grave of sin once too often. Surely we should pray with the Ancient Church—

> "O Jesus, from the death of sin
> Keep us, we pray; so shalt Thou be
> The everlasting Paschal joy
> Of all the souls new-born to Thee."

God grant to all of us that St. Paul's desire may be fulfilled, alike in our convictions and in our lives; and that we may know something of what the power of Christ's Resurrection really is. As the years go by, our natural forces become sensibly weaker; they will fail altogether at the approach of death. But here is a Power which death cannot extinguish or arrest, since it is itself the conquest and repudiation of death; a Power which may enable the weakest of us to feel that, while his bodily strength decays, he is enriched with a new energy that comes from heaven.

[a] Rom. vi. 9, 10.

SERMON XII.

EASTER HOPES.

1 ST. PETER I. 3.

Blessed be the God and Father of our Lord Jesus Christ, Which according to His abundant mercy hath begotten us again unto a lively hope by the Resurrection of Jesus Christ from the dead.

ST. PETER addresses his Epistle, not, as St. Paul's manner is, to some particular Church, but to Christians scattered over a wide extent of territory throughout Pontus, Galatia, Cappadocia, Asia Minor, and Bithynia. It is true that these districts join on to each other; that they are all comprised between the Black Sea and the Gulf of Cyprus; and that the cruel yoke of the Turk has, in the course of four centuries and a half, reduced them to a dead level of barbarism, obliterating the sharp provincial distinctions which still existed in antiquity. But when St. Peter wrote, although the Roman power was established throughout all these districts, the Empire was still young, and it was wisely tolerant of provincial characteristics. As a consequence, the people to whom St. Peter wrote differed not less widely than do the inhabitants of the various states of Europe at the present day. Doubtless the "strangers" would have been mainly although not exclusively, converts from Judaism; since of these converts St. Peter had particular care, after the division of labour between the leading Apostles which St. Paul mentions in writing to the Galatians.[a] They would have had for the most part the blood of Abraham in their veins; and yet, notwithstanding this sense of a common descent, which since their conversion had lost its religious value, they would have shared, in many respects, the divergent provincial sympathies of the populations around them. They would have been parted by different customs, different walks in life, different commercial interests, different relations with the various local governments, very different ideas upon a great many subjects which form the staple of interest in ordinary lives. But as St. Peter thought over these scattered strangers, with all their manifold divergencies from each other, he felt that they had one thing in common. They were, as he expresses it, "sanctified by the Spirit, unto obedience and sprinkling of the Blood of Jesus Christ."[b] And this implied a great deal beyond itself. It meant that the horizons of their lives were greatly enlarged, that they were living, not for this world merely, but for a world beyond it. And therefore the Apostle bursts forth in a hymn of praise, which the genius of Dr. Wesley has made familiar to us at this season in our Cathedral service; "Blessed be God, even the Father of our Lord Jesus Christ, Which according to His abundant mercy hath begotten us again unto a lively hope by the Resurrection of Jesus Christ from the dead, unto an inheritance incorruptible, and undefiled, and that fadeth not away, reserved in heaven for you."[c]

To the question, "What has the Resurrection of Jesus Christ from the grave done for us Christians?" a great many answers may be given. Of these, the answer which Christ's Own Apostles would have given, is that, by

[a] Gal. ii. 9.   [b] 1 St. Pet. i. 2.   [c] Ib. 3, 4.

rising from the dead, Jesus Christ proved that He had a right to speak about God, about the old religion of His countrymen, about the religious conduct of the influential classes among them, above all, about Himself. When He was asked to give a sign, which might be accepted as evidence of the commission which He had from above, He said, that just as the old prophet Jonah had been buried out of sight in the whale, and yet restored to his ministry and his countrymen, so He Himself, stricken by the pangs of death, would be laid in the darkness of the tomb, in the very heart of the earth, and yet would burst the fetters of the grave, and " rise again."[a] And accordingly when this prediction had been realised, the fact was appealed to, as we see from the Acts of the Apostles, by the earliest preachers of Christianity in almost every sermon. It evidently did their work in compelling men to listen to what they had to say about their Lord, better than any other topic they could urge. And St. Paul, to cite no other illustrations, begins his great Epistle to the Romans by saying, " that Jesus had been declared to be the Son of God by the Resurrection from the dead."[b]

But the Resurrection has done other things for us besides this its great evidential achievement; and upon one of these other results of it, I desire to dwell this afternoon. It has endowed Christians, who treat it as a serious matter of fact, with the great grace of hope. St. Peter feels the preciousness of this when he exclaims, " Blessed be the God and Father of our Lord Jesus Christ, Which according to His abundant mercy hath begotten us again unto a lively hope by the Resurrection of Jesus Christ from the dead."

[a] St. Matt. xii. 40; xx. 19.   [b] Rom. i. 4.

I.

To say that we cannot get on without hope is a truism. But as truisms are more apt to be lost sight of than paradoxes, it is a truism which will bear repeating. Hope is not the salt, it is the sinew of man's moral life. Explain it as we may, there is no doubt about the fact that the human mind must, to a certain extent, live in and for the future. The brute is content with the present: he feeds, fights, gambols, sleeps, and makes the most of each successive sensation, because his attention is not diverted from it by forecasts about a coming time: he apprehends nothing, until the experience of his senses, appealing to a faculty of association, forces the apprehended danger right in upon him. He has no view or theory of his life, of his place in creation, of his relation to other living creatures around him, of his capacity for and title to a coming destiny of any sort. And herein the brute differs from man; because man is so little content with and occupied or exhausted by the thoughts, sensations, and interests of the present moment, that he cannot but look forward, whether to a nearer or to a more remote future. His capacity for excellence is exactly proportioned to his power of throwing himself onward into a future, which is as yet beyond his reach, and which may even be always beyond it.

This truth holds good whether we look at man as an individual or as a member of society. What is the true object of education? Is it merely to teach a boy so much writing and arithmetic, so much history and geography, so much natural science and humane literature, so much of political or of mathematical truth? No, it is much more than this. The great object of a wise educator is to set before the boy whom he is teaching some future to which he may aspire, and which may fire his best enthusiasms;

some future which may supply him with a strong motive for making the most of his present opportunities; some future upon which, during the drudgery and toil of his earlier tasks, his eye may rest, as upon the prize which will reward him, the object of his hope. It is, of course, a difficult and delicate thing to do this without developing in the boy the vice of a purely selfish ambition. But it can be done; and if education is to be vigorous and thorough, it must be done. What becomes of a boy whose every lesson, every exercise, every effort to remember, to understand, to think, to compose, is strictly without an object; only sterile and isolated labour having no end beyond itself, or none beyond that of avoiding certain consequences of neglect? And does not the same rule hold in later life? The boy becomes a man, the father of a family, and he transfers to his children some of the hope which he cherished for himself. He thinks less of what they are than of what it is probable that they will be a few years hence. He thinks over their characters, their tastes, their dispositions, the evidence they have given of fitness for a particular work in life; and he enters upon a calculation of probabilities; he tries to picture to himself their various positions and occupations in after years. So strong and penetrating is his sympathy, that in them he lives his own boyhood over again, only with the larger experience and wider horizon of his manhood. He may, God only knows, be destined to a terrible disappointment. But he lives in hope; and this hope enables him to work hard for his children, and to deny himself lawful enjoyments for them, and to put up cheerfully with ingratitude or worrying, or dulness or perversity, on the part of these objects of his strongest affections, in a manner which would be impossible, had his hopes not been strongly engaged.

Nor is this less true of a professional work in life: hope is ever the motive principle of the exertions which command success. The statesman, the artist, the man of letters, the great chemist or engineer, all look forward. Minds of a lower type look forward to the reputation which will be won by success; minds of a higher order look forward to the happiness of doing work for God by rendering some real service to their generation or to posterity. And it is this hope which sustains them under all the discouragements of weak health, of unfriendly criticism, of unfruitful efforts to mould intractable materials, of conscious present inability to compass and express the ideal of excellence which has floated before their mind's eye, and which originally roused them to exertion.

Nor is hope less essential to associations of men than to man in his individual capacity. An institution, a society, a nation which has no future before it, is already doomed. It may still exist; but its life is a thing of the past. An army is never thoroughly demoralised until the hope of victory is gone. A nation is not ruined until it has reached a point at which it remarks that it can make out for itself no prospect of expansion, development, progress, in coming years; a point at which it turns regretfully back upon itself, confessing to itself that it has exhausted its destiny, and has only to await the onset from without or the collapse from within, which will seal the doom of which it has already felt the terrible presentiment.

And as hope is thus necessary to the temporary wellbeing of societies of men, and of individual men, so is it essential to the highest wellbeing of man as man. The hope upon which states, institutions, artists, painters, military men, politicians, rest is directed to objects within the sphere of sense and time. But man, as man, must look beyond sense and time. For man is confronted everywhere with the barrier which arrests or dissolves all earthly hopes; he sees death ever before him. Does all end with death? That is the question of questions; the greatest question that confronts man when he sets himself to think seriously about his place in the universe, about his real being, about his destiny. It is impossible altogether to put off the consideration of a point like this; it rises to life whenever there is a resurrection of serious thought. It is as fresh, as interesting, as full of unspeakable importance for this generation as it was for the last: it will be as much so for the next generation as for this. Science does not solve it; a materialised civilisation cannot bury it out of sight; time does not tell upon it: there it is,—this awful question awaiting us each and all—Whither am I going?

"What are you going to do?" said an elderly friend to a young man who was just entering upon life. "I hope," was the answer, "to complete my education at the University." "And what then?" "I shall learn a profession, and devote myself to it." "And what then?" "I shall marry as soon as I can afford it." "And what then?" "No doubt I shall have enough to do in educating and providing for my family." "And what then?" "Well, of course, in time I shall grow to be an old man." "And what then?" asked his questioner. "In time, I suppose, . . . I shall die." "And what then?" There was silence: the young man had never looked so far ahead as that.

Man needs an answer to that question, if the deepest springs of his being are to be really moved. And if we cast our eyes upon the forms of opinion which lie outside the Christian Church, what do we find?

There is, of course, the Materialist answer that all does

end with death; that man's higher being is but the vitality of his animal frame, and perishes with it, perishes utterly and for ever. But this answer does not really satisfy men in their better and more thoughtful moods. Why should they be haunted, possessed, as they are, by the idea, the instinct of a coming immortality? why should this idea be so general, so importunate, as, upon the whole, it is? If Descartes was right in arguing that the world-wide idea of God in the soul of man could only be explained by the fact of God's existence, is it not equally reasonable to argue that the idea of immortality, which is so general, points equally to the fact of our immortality as human beings? How else are we to explain it? Why should such a hope or apprehension, as the case may be, of existence after death, be so deep, so well-nigh universal? A superstition which has no basis in fact has its limits in time and territorial sway. But whenever man has risen above the lowest stages of animalised life, the idea of a future, in some indistinct way, has dawned upon him, if only as a correlative of the idea of God. As our own Addison makes Cato in his soliloquy say:—

> "It must be so : Plato, thou reasonest well,
> Else whence this pleasing hope, this fond desire,
> This longing after immortality ?
> Or whence this secret dread and inward horror
> Of falling into nought ? Why shrinks the soul
> Back on herself, and startles at destruction ?
> 'Tis the Divinity that stirs within us,
> 'Tis Heaven itself that points out an hereafter,
> And intimates eternity to man."

This general impression or instinct of immortality has been taken to pieces. It has been traced sometimes to the idea that the soul is of itself indestructible, as being an uncompounded essence; sometimes, as by Goethe, to the profound conviction that mental and moral activity which has lasted up to the moment of dissolution, cannot be arrested by the death of man's outward husk, and must continue in some other form and sphere beyond it; sometimes to the sense of justice, which refuses to believe that a Moral Governor of the world will not provide a future in which to redress the terrible inequalities of our present state of being. But so long as the conviction does not rest upon some fact which is independent of our varying and shifting moods of thought and feeling, it is scarcely strong enough to govern conduct, and restrain passion, and invigorate the sense of duty, and make men embark in serious ventures. For this reason such convictions are only found in the old Pagan world, in any tolerable degree of distinctness, among the cultivated classes. They scarcely influenced the great mass of persons, or they produced that depressed view of life of which we find traces in the literature which abounded in parts of Europe, simultaneously with the great outbreak of infidel opinion at the end of the last century. Life was failure: to have lived was a misfortune: moral apathy was common sense: moral or spiritual enthusiasm was abject fanaticism. Over such a generation the Psalmist's sentence might be written: "They lie in the hell like sheep, death gnaweth upon them, and the righteous shall have domination over them in the morning: their beauty shall consume in the sepulchre out of their dwelling."[a]

The man who has no clear belief in a future life may undoubtedly have, within some very restricted limits, a strong sense of duty. He may even persuade himself that this sense of duty is all the better and purer from

[a] Ps. xlix. 14.

not being bribed by the prospect of a future reward, or stimulated, as he would say, unhealthily, by the dread of future punishment. But, for all that, his moral life is fatally impoverished. It is not merely that he has fewer and feebler motives to right action: it is that he has a false estimate of his real place in the universe. He has forfeited, in the legitimate sense of the term, his true title to self-respect. He has divested himself of the bearing, the instincts, the sense of noble birth and high destiny which properly belongs to him. He is like an heir to a throne who is bent on forgetting his lineage and his responsibilities in self-sought degradation. Man cannot, if he would, live with impunity only as a more accomplished kind of animal than the creatures around him. He is a child of eternity; and he cannot unmake himself. He cannot take up a position that abdicates or ignores his highest prerogatives without sooner or later sinking into degradations, which are in themselves his punishment.

II.

Man then needs a hope, resting on something beyond this scene of sense and time. And God has given him one, by the Resurrection of Jesus Christ from the dead. Our Lord indeed taught, in the plainest language, the reality of a future life. "In My Father's house are many mansions: I go to prepare a place for you."[a] "Lay up for yourselves treasure in heaven, where neither moth nor rust doth corrupt, and where thieves do not break through and steal."[b] "These shall go away into everlasting punishment: but the righteous unto life eternal."[c] "God is not the God of the dead, but of the living: for all live unto Him."[d]

[a] St. John xiv. 2.
[b] St. Matt. vi. 20.
[c] St. Matt. xxv. 46.
[d] St. Luke xx. 38.

Passages of this kind from among the very words of Christ might be multiplied: but in teaching that man would live after death, our Lord was only teaching what, with various degrees of distinctness, Pagans and Jews had taught before Him. He contributed to the establishment of this truth in the deepest convictions of men, not merely many lessons taught in words, but a fact, palpable to the senses. When, after saying that He would rise from the grave, He rose, He broke the spell of the law of death. He made it plain, within the precincts of the visible world, that a world unseen and eternal awaits us hereafter. His Resurrection converted hopes, surmises, speculations, trains of inference, into strong certainties. "Because I live ye shall live also"* was a saying which faith, under the guidance of reason, would henceforth inscribe upon Christ's empty grave. For that He had risen was not a secret whispered to a few: it was a fact verified by the senses of five hundred witnesses: and established, in face of a jealous and implacable criticism, which would fain have silenced its eloquent protestation that there is a world beyond the grave, in which Christ is King.

Not that the fact of Christ's Resurrection could force itself upon reluctant minds, or rather upon reluctant wills. In the earliest ages, as now, there were expedients for evading its force. It was a trick of the disciples; or it was a phantom apparition; or it was the product of a woman's excited imagination; or it was a prosaic transfer to the history of an individual of that which was true, but only true of the deathless ideas which He taught to men. The Evangelical narrative, the convictions of the earliest Church, the moral strength of the Church, advancing through blood and suffering to the heights of a worldwide empire, resist these expedients, as inconsistent with

* St. John xiv. 19.

fact, inconsistent with reason. St. Paul's argument that "if Christ be not risen, our labour is vain, your faith is also vain,"* is really an appeal to common sense. Is it probable, the Apostle suggests, that we Apostles should have ventured everything, that we should have surrendered everything, that we should be prepared to endure everything, for the sake of a faith, without having been careful to assure ourselves of the truth of the central fact on which it rests?

There are at least three forms of interest which might be accorded to such a fact as the Resurrection. The first, the interest of curiosity in a wonder, altogether at variance with the observed course of nature. This interest may exist in a high degree; observing and registering the fact, yet never for one moment getting beyond it. The second, the interest of active reason, which is satisfied that such a fact must have consequences and is anxious to trace them. This interest may lead a man to see that the Resurrection does prove the truth of Christianity; even though he may know nothing of the power of Christ's Blood and of Christ's Life, as a matter of experience. A third kind of interest is practical and moral. It is an effort to answer the question, What does the Resurrection of Christ say to me, mean for me? If it is true, if Christianity is true, what ought to be the effect on my thoughts, my feelings, my life? Now St. Peter answers that all should be invigorated by a living Hope. But then this absorbing moral interest does not come of ordinary powers of observation and reason, like the two earlier forms of interest. We are, says St. Peter, "begotten" unto it. It is no outcome of our original stock of common sense, though it does not contradict that common sense; it is the product of a Divine Breath

* 1 Cor. xv. 14.

playing upon the soul, and giving it a new birth, a new capacity for life. Of this birth, the Father of souls is the Author, and His Eternal Spirit the instrument, and union with Christ the essence or effect. It does much else for us; but it does this among other things, and not least among them: it endows us with a living hope. Looking to the Rising Christ, we Christians live in the future even more than in the present: it is part of our new nature to do so, just as surely as it is natural to a Pagan to be entirely engrossed with things of sense and time.

III.

St. Peter calls this "hope" a lively, or living, one. What does he mean by this? There are within many a soul traces of powers, ideas, feelings, which once lived, but which have died away. We investigate them from time to time, like the buried ruins of Pompeii or Herculaneum. Every man in later life finds the soil of his mind more or less strewn with the husks of hopes which have ceased to live. Time and disappointment do their work: and we bury our earlier enthusiasms quietly away, as, one after another, they cease to burn within us. But a Christian's hope endures. Earthly disappointments do but force us to make more of it. The lapse of time does but bring us nearer to its object. It is not subject to those laws of decay which tell upon the strength and vitality of a merely human enthusiasm. The vigour of its life is in an inverse proportion to that of the decaying frame upon which years have done their work, and which is drawing onwards in its course towards the portals of the grave.

Surely, we can ask ourselves few questions so important as "Have I this hope?" If not, what is the real value of any other hopes I may have? They do not reach beyond the frontiers of time. They must fail, when the end draws near; they must be buried, utterly and for ever, in my grave. "He shall carry nothing away with him when he dieth: neither shall his pomp follow him."[a] A hope worth having is, as the Apostle says, "an anchor of the soul, sure and steadfast, that entereth within the veil."[b] Its object is throned beyond the narrow frontiers of this life; beyond the kingdom of change and death. Not to have this hope is to be living at random; it is to be drifting on towards eternity without a chart in hand, or a harbour in view. No cry for help can be too earnest, too piercing, if such is our case: nor, if we do cry, will it be in vain. And if we humbly trust that we have this hope, what are the tests of our possessing it?

A first test is that earthly things sit easily upon us. We are not uninterested in them: far from it. We know how much depends on our way of dealing with them. But, also, we are not enslaved by them. To have caught a real glimpse of the eternal is to have lost heart and relish for the things of time. To have the imperishable clearly in view is to perceive the insignificance of that which passes. A living hope of an inheritance incorruptible and undefiled, enables a Christian to understand life in its real proportions: what things were once a gain to him, those he accounts loss for Christ.[c]

A second test of our having this hope is a willingness to make sacrifices for it. We do not really cherish it till we have asked ourselves the question, 'What difference do my hopes of another world make in my daily life? What am I doing, what do I leave undone, that I should

[a] Ps. xlix. 17.   [b] Heb. vi. 19.   [c] Phil. iii. 7.

not leave undone or do, if I believed that all really ended at death ? What changes would be made in my habits, occupations, daily modes of thought and feeling, if—to put a horrible supposition—I could awake to-morrow morning and find that Christ's conquest of the eternal world for me was a fable ?' Depend upon it, Christians, the sincerity of our hopes may be exactly measured by the sacrifices which we have made, or which God knows us to be prepared to make, on behalf of them. He who ventures little hopes for little. He who has a heaven in view where neither moth nor rust doth corrupt, and where thieves break not through or steal, lays up treasures in it,[a] and that he may do so, surrenders all that need be surrendered here, in order to secure them. He cuts off the right hand, he plucks out the right eye,[b] which offend him; that, albeit maimed and with one eye, he may yet enter heaven.

A third test is progressive efforts to prepare for the future life. "Every man that hath this hope in Him," says St. John, "purifieth himself, even as Christ is pure."[c] Heaven too, the home to which hope looks forward, has its atmosphere, its manners, its interests, its language; and they must be learnt, at least to a certain extent, by its future inhabitants, on earth. Worship is of such vast importance in the Christian life, because it is a continuous preparation for the future state revealed to hope; because it forms in us those habits, interests, enthusiasms, desires, which will then be not occasional but continuous. When we enter this Cathedral for prayer, we do well to say deliberately to ourselves: 'Now I am going to exercise a living hope; I am going to speak to God, as I hope to speak to Him unceasingly hereafter.'

[a] St. Matt. vi. 20. [b] St. Matt. v. 29, 30. [c] 1 St. John iii. 3.

A last test is inward peace, and its accompaniment, habitual outward cheerfulness. A Christian may have his full share of anxieties, but at bottom he is always lighthearted. His soul has found its anchorage in Christ Crucified, Risen, Ascended, Glorified, Interceding. He wants no more. The events of life may tell hardly upon him: but they do not touch his real self, any more than the storm on the surface of the ocean can agitate the depths below. "Thou wilt keep him in perfect peace whose mind is stayed on Thee, because he trusteth in Thee."[a]

Eternal Jesus, Who when Thou hadst overcome the sharpness of death, didst open the kingdom of heaven to all believers, fix our eyes, we pray Thee, on our great inheritance, that, washed in Thy Blood, and sanctified by Thy Spirit, we may live indeed for that world whence we shall hereafter look back upon death as the gate of an existence which is really life.

[a] Isa. xxvi. 3.

SERMON XIII.

EASTER JOY.

PSALM XXX. 12.

Thou hast turned my heaviness into joy: Thou hast put off my sackcloth, and girded me with gladness.

HERE is described a change, complete, and more or less sudden, from sadness to joy. David has escaped a danger which had brought him very near to death; and now he is thankful and exultant. His words are in keeping with what Christians feel, as they pass from the last days of Holy Week into the first hours of Easter. If Easter is associated predominantly with any one emotion, it is with that of joy. When Mary Magdalene and the other Marys had heard the words of the angel of the Lord, "they departed quickly from the sepulchre, with fear and great joy."[a] When, on the evening of Easter Day, Jesus stood in the midst of the assembled disciples, and showed them His Hands and His Feet, their joy was too great for the steady exercise of their understanding: "they believed not for joy, and wondered."[b] In these first hours of ecstatic bewilderment, as St. John says, "the disciples were glad when they saw the Lord."[c]

[a] St. Matt. xxviii. 8.   [b] St. Luke xxiv. 40, 41.
[c] St. John xx. 20.

Easter Joy.

Was it not His Own promise of a joy which would be beyond the reach of outward circumstance, that had now become true? "Verily, verily, I say unto you, That ye shall weep and lament, but the world shall rejoice"—that was the hour of Calvary—" and ye shall be sorrowful, but your sorrow shall be turned into joy"[a]—that was to be the radiance of Easter. "A woman when she is in travail hath sorrow, because her hour is come: but as soon as she is delivered of the child, she remembereth no more the anguish, for joy that a man is born into the world. And ye now therefore have sorrow; but I will see you again, and your heart shall rejoice, and your joy no man taketh from you."[b] And thus, ever since, the Church of Christ has laboured to make the Easter festival, beyond all others, the feast of Christian joy. All that nature and art could furnish has been summoned to express, so far as outward things may, this overmastering emotion of Christian souls worshipping at the tomb of their Risen Lord. All the deliverances of God's ancient people, from Egypt, from Assyria, from Babylon, are but rehearsals of the great deliverance of all on the Resurrection morning; and each prophet and psalmist that heralds any of them, sounds in Christian ears some separate note of the Resurrection Hymn. "Sing unto the Lord, for He hath triumphed gloriously;"[c] or, "He hath broken the gates of brass, and smitten the bars of iron in sunder;"[d] or, "The Lord awaked as one out of sleep, and like a giant refreshed with wine;"[e] or, "This is the day which the Lord hath made, we will rejoice and be glad in it;"[f]—these, and many other passages, referred originally to some event in Jewish history, and yet are felt to receive their highest fulfilment and interpretation when they are uttered by

[a] St. John xvi. 20. [b] St. John xvi. 21, 22. [c] Exod. xv. 21.
[d] Ps. cvii. 16. [e] Ps. lxxviii. 65. [f] Ps. cxviii. 24.

Christian hearts on the Easter festival. And this, the joy which fills the soul of the believing Church on Easter Day, has some sort of echo in the world outside; so that those who sit loosely to our faith and hope, and who worship rarely, if ever, before our altars, yet feel that good spirits are somehow in order on Easter morning. For their sakes, as for our own, let us try to take the emotion to pieces, as we find it in a Christian soul; let us ask why it is so natural for Christians to say, this day, with David, "Thou hast turned my heaviness into joy: Thou hast put off my sackcloth, and girded me with gladness."

I.

The first reason, then, for this Easter joy is the triumph and satisfaction enjoyed by our Lord Himself. Certainly it is now more than eighteen hundred years since He died and rose. But we Christians are well assured that He is alive; that He is reigning on His throne in heaven, yet also invisibly with us on earth, and perfectly well aware of all that is passing both within our souls and without them. Yes! eighteen centuries have gone; yet, year by year, we follow Him, step by step, through all the stages of His sufferings and death. We sympathise reverently with the awful sorrows of our Adorable Lord and Friend; and thus we enter, in some far-off way, into the sense of triumph, unspeakable and sublime, which follows beyond it. It is His triumph; that is the first consideration; His triumph, Who was but now so cruelly insulted and tortured; His, Whom they buffeted and spat upon, and mocked and derided, and nailed to the wood, and laid in the sepulchre. It is all over now; His enemies have done their best or their worst; and He has swept it all aside, since, now that the hour has come, by a single motion of His Majestic Will, He is risen. And we, as we kneel before Him, think, first of all, of Him. It is His joy which inspires ours; it turns our heaviness into joy, and puts off our sorrow and girds us with gladness.

Do I say, This is the case? Perhaps it were more prudent to say, that it ought to be. For in truth the habit of getting out of and forgetting our miserable selves in the absorbing sense of the beauty and magnificence of God, belongs rather to ancient than to modern Christianity. Few things are more striking in the early Christian mind, taken as a whole, than its power of escaping from self into the thought and presence of God. To these old Christians God was all, man nothing, or wellnigh nothing. They delighted to dwell on everything that He had told them about Himself, about each one of His Attributes, each one of His acts, simply because it was His, and without reference to the question whether it had any or what bearing upon their own lives and needs. Theirs was a disinterested interest in God; and to them our Lord's Resurrection was, in the first place, of commanding moment, because it meant His glory and triumph, whatever else it might mean for them.

With us moderns the case is somewhat otherwise. We value God, if the truth must be spoken, at least in many cases, not for His Own sake, but for ours. Perhaps, without knowing it, we have drunk deeply into the subjective temper, as it is called, of our time; the temper which assumes that truth only exists so far as we can measure it, or as it exists for us; the temper which practically, like the old sophist in Plato, makes man the measure of all things. With us of to-day it is too often assumed that the human mind is the centre, not merely of human thought, but of universal being. And thus God, the one self-existent Cause of all that is, is banished to a distant point on the circumference of our imaginary universe. Men carry this temper unconsciously into their religion. And thus our first question, in presence of a great Truth like the Resurrection, is too often, not, What is its intrinsic importance? but, What interest has it for me? Look at a modern hymn: it is, as a rule, full of man; full of his wants, his aspirations, his anticipations, his hopes, his fears; full of his religious self, if you will, but still of himself. But read an ancient hymn: it is, as a rule, full of God, of His awful Nature; of His wonderful Attributes; full of the Eternal Son, of His Acts, His Sufferings, His Triumph, His Majesty. Certainly ancient Christianity did justice to the needs and moods of the soul; just as in the Psalms we find the soul's several moods of hope and fear, of penitence and exultation, so abundantly provided for. But we often hear even religious people express something like impatience with the great Psalms, which describe God's relations with Nature, or His dealings with His people Israel; an impatience grounded on the fact that they think those Psalms only of real interest which enable them to say something to God about themselves. Surely, my friends, we moderns have lost something, nay much, in this matter, by comparison with the early Church of Christ; and thus I may have said too much just now, when I took it for granted that the joy of our Lord would be our first reason for rejoicing on Easter Day. Be it yours to show that my misgiving is unwarranted. You know that pure sympathy with an earthly friend's happiness leaves altogether out of consideration the question whether it contributes anything to your own; and in like manner endeavour to say to-day to your Heavenly Friend: 'It is because Thou, Lord Jesus, hast vanquished Thine enemies, hast overcome death, and hast entered into Thy glory, that Thou hast turned my Lenten "heaviness into joy, and put off my sackcloth, and girded me with gladness."'

II.

But, having said this, note, secondly, that Easter joy is inspired by the sense of confidence with which Christ's Resurrection from the dead invigorates our grasp of Christian truth.

The understanding, be sure, has its joy, no less than the heart; and a keen sense of intellectual joy is experienced when we succeed in resting truth, or any part of it, on a secure basis. This is what the old Roman poet meant by saying that the man was really happy who had attained to know the causes of things. And no one who has been thrown into close relations with men engaged in the eager pursuit of any branch of knowledge, can mistake the depth and reality of this kind of satisfaction. The chemist who has at last explained the known effect of a particular drug, by laying bare, upon analysis, an hitherto undiscovered property in it; the historian who has been enabled to show that the conjecture of years rests on the evidence of a trustworthy document; the mathematician on whom has flashed the formula which solves some problem that has long haunted and eluded him; the anatomist who has been able to refer what he had hitherto regarded as an abnormal occurrence to the operation of a recognised law;—these men know what joy is. This joy of the understanding at coming into felt contact with some truth underlying that which it has hitherto grasped, wins for it a new vigour and buoyancy, enhances its present sense of life, and is full of hope and promise for the time to come.

Now, akin to the joy of students and workers is the satisfaction of a Christian when he steadily dwells on the Resurrection of our Lord Jesus Christ. During large tracts of time we Christians think naturally and mainly of truths or duties, which, however important, are not the foundations of other truths. The Christian Creed is like a tower which rears towards heaven its windows and pinnacles in successive stages of increasing gracefulness. We lavish our admiration first on this detail of it, and then on that; and, while we thus study and admire, we dwell continuously in its upper stories, till at last perhaps a grave question occurs or is suggested to us. What does it all rest upon? What is the foundation-fact on which this structure has been reared in all its audacious and fascinating beauty? What is the fact, if there be any, the removal of which would be fatal to the edifice? And the answer is that our Lord's Resurrection from the dead is one such fact. It is a foundation on which all truth in the Christian Creed, that is distinctively Christian, and not merely Theistic, really rests. Our Lord pointed to it as the certificate of His mission. He rebuked indeed the temper which made men ask whether He could show a sign of having a mission from above: but He granted the request. The prophet Jonah was the type of the Son of Man: "As Jonah was three days and three nights in the whale's belly, so would the Son of Man be three days and three nights in the heart of the earth."[a] And the earliest sermons of the Apostles were almost entirely concerned with Christ's Resurrection. As we read them in the Acts it might seem that the Resurrection was the only Christian doctrine. The prophecies which it fulfilled; the consequences to which it pointed; above all, the reality of the fact itself, of which those first preachers

[a] St. Matt. xii. 40.

were witnesses: this was the subject of the earliest preaching of the Apostles of Christ. And why did they dwell so persistently on the Resurrection? Why did they not say more about our Lord's Atoning Death, or the power of His example, or the drift and character of His moral teaching, or the means of grace with which He has endowed His Church? Why, but because, before building the superstructure in the hearts of believers, it was necessary to lay the foundation deep and firm. If it was true that Christ had risen, then the faith of Christendom, in all its vast significance, would be seen, step by step, but surely, to follow; whereas, "if Christ be not risen," as said one of themselves, "our preaching is vain, your faith is also vain."[a]

*   *   *   *

[Here followed a passage substantially identical with part of Sermon V.]

Here, then, in the Resurrection of Christ, we have a solid fact on which the Christian Faith securely rests, both as a whole, and in its most vital parts. Does our Lord say that hereafter we shall see the Son of Man sitting on the right hand of power, and coming in the clouds of heaven?[b] If the speaker were a being whose life is conditioned as our own, such language could, at best, be regarded as an extravagant illusion. But if He really rose from the dead, He evidently is a Being of another order than we, and this and much more is possible. Does He speak of giving His life as a ransom for many;[c] of His Blood being shed for the remission of sins?[d] This, again, would be unintelligible or intolerable in an ordinary man; but it is clear that the death of One Who resumed His

[a] 1 Cor. xv. 14. [b] St. Mark xiv. 62.
[c] St. Matt. xx. 28. [d] St. Matt. xxvi. 28.

life after His life had been wrung out of Him by a death of torture, may well have consequences beyond our calculation. Does He say that He and the Father are one thing;[a] that to have seen Him is to have seen the Father;[b] that all men should honour the Son—that is, Himself—even as they honour the Father;[c] that unless men would eat His Flesh and drink His Blood, they would have no true life in them?[d] Ah! what must have been the verdict of the human conscience upon such language as this, if the speaker, after an ignominious execution, had rotted in his grave? Whereas, in view of the considerations which we have had before us, an Apostle exclaims that Christ was "declared to be the Son of God with power, by the Resurrection from the dead."[e]

Yes; it is here, beside the empty tomb of the Risen Jesus, that Christian faith feels itself on the hard rock of fact; here we break through the tyranny of matter and sense, and rise with Christ into the immaterial world; here we put a term to the enervating alternation of guesses and doubts which prevails elsewhere, and we reach the frontier of the absolutely certain; here, as we kneel in deep thankfulness, and the Christian Creed in all its beauty and in all its coherent truth opens out before us, we hear, it may be, as did His beloved Apostle, His Voice from heaven, "I am He that liveth, and was dead, and behold, I am alive for evermore, and have the keys of hell and of death."[f] And we can but answer, Truly, Lord Jesus, by Thy Resurrection Thou hast turned my heaviness into joy: Thou hast put off my sackcloth, and girded me with gladness.

[a] St. John x. 30.   [b] St. John xiv. 9.   [c] St. John v. 23.
[d] St. John vi. 53. [e] Rom. i. 4.   [f] Rev. i. 18.

III.

But there is a third reason for Easter joy, which must be briefly touched on, before we close.

As a man gets on in life, he finds his deepest human interests transferred, one after another, to a sphere beyond that of sense and time. One after another they are withdrawn, the friends of our childhood, the friends of our manhood, the friends of our riper years. One after another they reach the brink; there is hesitation, it may be, perhaps, for a moment; it seems that they might return. But the hour strikes; and they part. One such[a] we cannot but call to mind to-day, since he was with us last Easter, and even at our last great festival in this Cathedral. And, indeed, he had been engaged in its service for a much longer period than any of us, his colleagues and brethren; for some half-century at the least. Never again in this life shall we see that well-known form, bowed down of late by advancing years and weakness; never again shall we meet that perfectly courteous and kindly welcome which betokened so many a high Christian grace of soul and character. Long will he live in the affectionate memory of his brethren, and of many who worshipped constantly before this altar; but he has joined —with how many others—the great company of the dead. The company of the dead! All here remains as it was, at least for a while; the home in which they dwelt, the haunts they frequented, the enterprises in which they were engaged, the faces they loved. All these remain; but they—they are gone. They have disappeared beyond recall; their bodies indeed, we know, lie beneath the

[a] The Rev. J. V. Povah, Minor Canon of St. Paul's, and Rector of St. Anne and St. Agnes.

sod, a prey to corruption and the worm; but their souls, their spirits, themselves, that which flashed through the eye, that which was felt in the manner, in the tone of the voice, as well as in the thought and action,—where is it? Has it then become absorbed into some sea of life, in which all personality, and with it all consciousness, perishes? Or has it sunk back, after a momentary flicker, into an abyss of nothing, now that the material framework, whose energy it was, is withdrawn?

There is no occasion here to review the arguments by which wise and good men, living in Pagan darkness, but making the most of such light as reason and conscience could give them, have attained to belief in the immortality of the soul. We know that their guess or speculation, whichever we deem it, is a solemn certainty. But we know also that it is only half the truth. Man is not merely a spiritual being; he is also an animal organism: and if his spiritual part were to be isolated for an eternity; wrenched away for ever from the senses and framework, in which it has been lodged since the first moment of its existence; then man would be no longer the same being; he would be unrecognisable even by himself. For the spirit strikes its roots deep into the animal organism; indeed this intimate relation between them is the element of truth on which materialism fixes, that it may thence infer its degrading falsehood that man has no purely spiritual being at all. And thus it is that when the Gospel brought life and immortality to light,[a] it did this thoroughly. It unveiled the immortality of man in his completeness; the immortality of his spiritualised but still-existing body, as well as the immortality of his soul.

We may then hope to meet our friends, those whom we have loved long since and lost a while not as formless,

[a] 2 Tim. i. 10.

unrecognisable shades, but with the features, the expressions which they wore on earth. "For if we believe that Jesus died, and rose again, even so them also which sleep in Jesus shall God bring with Him."[a] His Resurrection is the model as well as the warrant of our own. Nay more: "All men shall rise with their bodies."[b] In that future world there will, we know, be shadows, dark, unpenetrable, unchanging. But there will also be joy unspeakable and full of glory.[c] And if they whom we call the dead know anything of what is passing here on earth; if, as has been supposed by great Christian divines, they see in the Eternal Word, as in a mirror, the reflection of all that happens in this world of sense, from which they have been separated by death, then we may believe that the Easter Festival is for them too, in whatever measure, an occasion of rejoicing, and that the happiness of the Church on earth is responded to from beyond the veil. To them, at any rate, our thoughts involuntarily turn, in these moments of rare and thankful joy; they live again now in our memories, though years should have passed since they were withdrawn from our sight; and, as we look forward to the hour when we, unworthy but repentant, through redeeming grace and mercy, shall join them; and beneath the throne of our Risen Lord shall again behold the features which we have loved best on earth, can we but exclaim, with deep thankfulness, 'Thou, O Jesus, hast by Thy Resurrection "turned my heaviness into joy: Thou hast put off my sackcloth, and girded me with gladness"?'

[a] 1 Thess. iv. 14.   [b] Athan. Creed.   [c] 1 St. Pet. i. 8.

SERMON XIV.

THE UNDYING ONE.

ROM. VI. 9.

Christ being raised from the dead dieth no more.

EASTER Day is a day on which the best Christians are hardly in a mood for sermons. Their hearts are full of joy, and they come to church, as they would go to a wedding; to make their congratulations; to utter their hymns of joy and praise to the King of kings on the anniversary of His great victory. Their hearts say more to them than any fellow-man can possibly say; and much of what their hearts tell them cannot well be rendered into human language. They wish to be left alone with their joy: sermons, they say, are very well in seasons and on days of penitence: but when the heart is bursting with triumphant emotion, sermons either lag behind our feelings or are out of harmony with them. And for this kind of reason, I suppose, it has been said that a sermon on Easter Day requires an apology.

It is not my business to dispute the existence of a state of mind such as this. There are Christians, no doubt, who in some sort, in varying degrees, even while here on earth, anticipate heaven. They know what may be known about invisible things; about God, about conscience, about the future. They enjoy not merely light, but love. They feel as angels feel rather than as men; and human voices or human experiences can do, for such as they are, little or nothing. We need not doubt that such Christians exist; but the immense majority of us, you and I, are on a very different level. We are the children of time all over; at least as yet. We are entangled in difficulties, greater or less; we have to battle with weakness in our wills and with darkness in our understandings. For us, too, in our measure, Easter is a day of joy: we catch the inspiration which moves higher and brighter souls around us; we keep pace, as we can, with the loftier feeling of the time. But, at least for us, it is a great help to have definite points to fall back upon as the reasons for our joy: and, with a view to this, we cannot do better than place ourselves under St. Paul's guidance this afternoon, in those words which are so familiar to us from childhood, as forming part of the Easter anthem, " Christ being raised from the dead dieth no more."

In these words are two assertions which lie at the bottom of all Easter satisfaction. First, The reality of the Resurrection: " Christ being raised from the dead." Secondly, The perpetuity of Christ's risen life: " Christ being raised from the dead dieth no more."

I.

The Resurrection then asserts a truth which is by no means always written legibly for all men on the face of Nature. It tells us that the spiritual is higher than the material; that in this universe spirit counts for more than matter. There are no doubt abstract arguments which go to show that this is the case. But the Resurrection is a palpable fact, which assures us that the ordinary laws of animal existence may be altogether set aside in obedience to a higher spiritual interest. It was, we all know, no natural force like that of growth which raised our Lord Jesus Christ from His grave. And such a fact as this is worth much more than abstract arguments. It can always be fallen back upon, when we are in no mood for speculative thought; and it leaves less room for mistake or self-deception.

"Christ being raised from the dead." The Resurrection is not merely an article of the Creed: it is a fact in human history. That our Lord Jesus Christ was begotten of the Father before all worlds is also an article of the Christian faith. But it has nothing to do with human history, and it cannot be shown to have taken place, like any event, say in the life of Julius Cæsar, by the reputed testimony of eye-witnesses. It belongs to another sphere; it is believed on account of the proved trustworthiness of Him Who has taught us this truth about His Own Eternal Person. But that Christ rose from the dead is a fact which depends on the same sort of testimony as any event in the life of Cæsar; with this difference, that no one ever thought it worth while to risk his life in order to maintain that Cæsar defeated Vercingetorix or Pompey. Our Lord, as you know, was seen five times on the day that He rose from the dead. Mary Magdalene saw Him in the garden.[a] She saw Him again, with the other Mary and Salome, when He allowed them to hold Him by the feet, and to worship Him.[b] At a later hour in the day He appeared to Peter.[c] In the afternoon He discovered Himself to Cleopas and another disciple who were walking on the Emmaus road.[d] In the evening He was

[a] St. Mark xvi. 9; St. John xx. 11-18. [b] St. Matt. xxviii. 9, 10.
[c] St. Luke xxiv. 34.   [d] St. Luke xxiv. 13-35.

with the Apostles, excepting Thomas.^a He showed them His hands and His feet, as those of the Crucified; He ate before them; He gave them the power of remitting and retaining sins. And after this first day, six separate appearances are recorded; while it is implied that they were only a few of those which actually occurred. After the interval of a week, He appeared again to the Eleven. Thomas then was with them; and He convinced Thomas that He was really risen.^b On another occasion they saw Him on a mountain in Galilee.^c On another He was seen by five hundred persons, more than one half of whom were still living when St. Paul described the fact to the Corinthians.^d On another He appeared to St. Peter, St. Thomas, St. Bartholomew, St. James the Great, and St. John, with two others, on the shore of the Lake of Tiberias.^e On another He had a private interview with St. James the Less.^f Once more, He was with all the Apostles at Jerusalem, before He led them out to Bethany, gave them His last promises and benediction, and went up to heaven before their eyes.^g

And when He was gone, His Apostles went forth to do and teach, no doubt, a great deal else, but especially, they went forth as "witnesses of His Resurrection."^h That was a fact of which they were certain; they were prepared to attest its truth, if need were, with their blood. We learn from the Acts of the Apostles that the earliest Christian preaching was a constant assertion that Christ had really risen. The reality of His Resurrection was so certain that it emboldened and indeed forced His followers to address themselves to the conversion of the

---

^a St. Luke xxiv. 36-43; St. John xx. 19-25.
^b St. John xx. 26-31.   ^c St. Matt. xxviii. 16-20.
^d 1 Cor. xv. 6.   ^e St. John xxi. 1, 2.   ^f 1 Cor. xv. 7.
^g St. Luke xxiv. 50, 51.   ^h Acts i. 22; iv. 33.

world. "We cannot but speak the things," they said, "which we have seen and heard."[*]

If the testimony which can be produced in proof of the Resurrection concerned only a political occurrence, or a fact of natural history witnessed eighteen centuries ago, nobody would think of denying its cogency. Those who do reject the truth of the Resurrection quarrel, for the most part, not with the proof that the Resurrection occurred, but with the supposition that such a thing could happen under any circumstances. No proof would satisfy them; because they have made up their minds that the thing cannot be. Certainly, on the face of it, the Resurrection is a miracle; nay, we may well say, it is the greatest of Christian miracles. As such it is unwelcome to those who make their limited personal experience of the physical world the measure of all spiritual as well as physical truth. Look, they say, at the fixed order of Nature: day after day, year after year, it is what, within our memories, it always has been. The day waxes and wanes; the seasons follow each other; the apparent caprices of Nature are, upon closer observation, more and more easily referred to the empire of law; the life of every animal obeys a fixed order from birth to death; and man, he too, however he may flatter himself, is no exception to the general rule; he too obeys this universal order; whether he will or no, he obeys, alike in life and in death, those physical laws which govern the course of animal existence. So that, when man dies, he lies down to mingle his body with the dust for good and all; he does not, so far as we see, break the bonds of death. It is the fixed order of Nature.

The fixed order of Nature! Surely, brethren, we in this age are, at least as much as our less scientific forefathers,

[*] Acts iv. 20.

the slaves of phrases! The fixed order of Nature, you say. Fixed, I ask, by whom or by what? By some fated necessity, do you say? But you yourselves, out of the experience of that existence which minute by minute you enjoy, can dispose of this phrase about a fixed order. You know that you can speak, move, act, or refrain from acting, moving, speaking, as, minute by minute, you will, and without any allegiance whatever to a supposed necessity. This is a fact within your experience: and what you know about yourselves to be experimentally true, you reasonably think may well be true, on a much greater scale, of beings higher than yourselves, of the highest Being of all. For that such a Being exists, as the Cause of all else, Nature itself assures you by its existence; and that He is not a mindless cause, but an ordering and disposing Intelligence—I do not forget recent attempts to set aside the argument from design—the order and symmetry of Nature assure you too. If then you believe in God, you confess that the order of Nature is fixed not by a necessity or a fate, but by a Will which can at pleasure innovate upon or reverse it. He Who made life and Nature what they are, could have made, and can make them otherwise. The power to work miracles is implied in the Power Which created Nature. Miracles, to say the least, are not antecedently incredible for any rational believer in God.

'God can work them,' you say; 'but will He? Are not miracles a libel upon the wisdom and far-sightedness of God? How should the All-providing Mind have to supply deficiencies? How should the Perfect Wisdom consent to break in upon the settled order of His work? God in creation is the Supreme Engineer: it is only the unskilful workman who, having set his machine in motion, has to thrust in his hand in order to correct some defect, or to communicate some new impulse for which no provision was made originally.'

Here you run a risk of manufacturing argument out of mere metaphor. To say that God, in creation, is an Engineer or an Artist, is a very pardonable phrase. Within certain narrow limits it expresses a truth about His relation to the Universe. It reminds us that all the resources and provisions of Nature are due to His contriving Mind. But such an expression must not be pressed so as to obscure or deny other, and higher, truths about God, and about His work. The Universe is something more than a machine: since it contains not merely matter but minds; not merely inanimate masses, governed by rules which they unconsciously obey, but free spirits, able consciously to yield or to refuse obedience to the true law of their being. And God is much greater than a Supreme Engineer. He is, before all things, a Moral Governor; He is a Father. His first care is for His intelligent offspring: and the Universe of matter was framed not for its own sake, but for the rational beings who were to tenant it. If no such being as man had been created, miracle might have been superfluous. The Universe might then well have been nothing more than a perfect machine, admitting of no interference, for any cause whatever, with its ordinary working. But if the education, the improvement, the rescuing from darkness and from evil, of a created rational mind or soul be God's noblest purpose in creation, then, if we believe Him to be Wise and Good, as well as Almighty, we shall expect Him to make the world of matter instruct and improve us, by deviating, if need be, from its accustomed order, as well as by observing it. No one who considers carefully what a mind endowed with freedom of choice is, and how various is the discipline and teaching which it needs, will say lightly that it needs no lights or aids to its true perfection and development, but such as an unvarying order of Nature can supply.

We may indeed go further than this. The order which is observable in the natural world teaches no doubt a great and precious lesson to the man who already has a firm faith in the Living God; it teaches him that order is a law of the Divine Mind. But for thousands upon thousands of human beings, who have indistinct and fluctuating ideas of God, in all countries and in all generations, and not by any means least in our own, the order of Nature paralyses the spiritual sense. Perhaps, if it were possible to watch a fellow-creature continuing undeviatingly a single movement during a period of twenty years, we should come to look at him also as a machine which worked unconsciously, instead of as a free agent who might at any moment hold his hand. And undoubtedly men whose minds, or rather whose imaginations, are controlled mainly by impressions derived from sense; who mark how regular God's work is, how undeviating; and who instinctively presume that it must always be what it has hitherto been;—such men gradually come to think of this visible scene of things as the whole universe of being. They drop out of mind that more wonderful world beyond it; they forget Him Who is the King of this world as well as of that. Nay; let us own that there are times in the lives of many of us when the physical world lies like a weight, or like a nightmare, heavy upon our thoughts; when we long for some higher promise of blessedness and perfection than any which a fixed order of Nature can give; when we would fain rise in spirit beyond this material sphere,—

"But still the wall impassable
Bars us around with sensual bond;

> In vain we dive for that beyond ;
> Yet traverse o'er and o'er the bound
> Walking on the unseen profound.
> Like flies, which on my window pane
> Pace up and down, again, again,
> And though they fain would break away
> Into th' expanse of open day,
> They know not why, are travelling still
> On the glass fence invisible :
> So dwell our thoughts with the unseen
> Yet cannot pass the bourne between."*

This, then, is the happiness, which is bestowed on many a human mind by the fact of Christ's Resurrection. It breaks down the iron wall of uniformity which goes so far to shut out God. It tells us that matter, and the orderly arrangement of matter, is not the governing principle of the Universe. It assures us that matter is controlled by Mind; that there is a Being, a Will, to Which matter can offer no effective resistance; that He is not bound by the laws of the Universe; that He is their master. God had said this before to men who had ears to hear and eyes to see. But He never said it so clearly as in the Resurrection of our Lord. If ever there was a case which might be expected to warrant summary interference with the common order of the world on the part of a moral God, here was one. When Jesus died on Calvary, the purest of lives seemed to the eye of sense to have ceased to be. The holiest of doctrines appeared to have died away upon the air, amid the blasphemies which raged at the foot of the Cross. Apart from the question who the Sufferer was, there was the question whether a righteous God did really reign on earth and in heaven. And the Resurrection was an answer to that question. It was the finger of God visibly thrust down amid the

* Williams's *Baptistery*, vol. i. p. 161.

things of sense; disturbing their usual order; bidding matter bend itself to proclaim the supremacy of spirit; bidding brute human force, as well as physical order, own the superiority of goodness; bidding us men know and feel that the truths which Christ has taught us about God and about the soul are higher and deeper than any which are written on the face of Nature. Christ has risen. "This is the day which the Lord hath made: let us rejoice and be glad in it."*

II.

But to-day's festival is also significant as commemorating the beginning of an Undying Life. The Resurrection was not an isolated miracle, done and over, leaving things as they had been before. The Risen Christ is not like Lazarus; marked off from others by having visited the realms of death, but knowing that he must again ere long be a tenant of the grave. Christ rises for eternity: "Christ being raised from the dead dieth no more." His Risen Body is made up of flesh, bones, and all things appertaining to the perfection of man's nature. But It has superadded qualities. It is so spiritual that It can pass through closed doors without collision or disturbance. It is beyond the reach of those causes which slowly or swiftly bring down our bodies to the dust. Throned in the heavens now, as during the forty days on earth, It is endowed with the beauty and glory of an eternal youth;—"Christ being raised from the dead dieth no more."

Nor is this, in itself, a new miracle. The real miracle, perhaps, was that the sinless Christ should have died at all. Death was an innovation upon the true conditions of

* Ps. cxviii. 24.

His existence; and the Resurrection was but a return to His rightful and normal immortality. Let us recall the truth which, within our limited range of experience, we may verify for ourselves, namely, that bodily pain, disease, death, came at first, as they often come now, to man in the train of the disease and death of man's spiritual nature. Adam died, because he sinned.[a] If Adam had not sinned, he would not have died. Men point, I know, to the presence of disease and death among the lower creatures. But, not to enter upon the difficult question of their relation to the Fall, who shall say that these creatures too may not be under the same law of pain following upon such a measure of wrong-doing as their natures are capable of? And if we are told of fossil human remains, of a much higher antiquity than that of the Adam of Genesis, it may be observed that, supposing the fact to be certain, it is consistent with the Revealed Account to hold that, between the original act of creation, and the present outfit of this our planet, ages upon ages may have elapsed during which the earth may have been peopled by races like our own, who had their period of probation, and finally passed away in some great geological catastrophe. In any case, what we say is that "by one man," of our present race, "sin entered into the world, and death by sin, and so death passed upon all men, for that all have sinned."[b] But when the Second Head of our race appeared, cut off from the entail of corruption by His supernatural birth of a Virgin Mother, and exhibiting in His life absolute conformity to eternal Moral Law, He was, by the terms of His Nature, exempt from the law of death. Therefore He died, not as a matter of course, but by violence. He consented, for the sake of others, to undergo the violence which was to kill Him. In His

[a] Gen. ii. 17; iii. 17-19; Rom. v. 12; 1 Cor. xv. 21. [b] Rom. v. 12.

case, death was a momentary innovation upon the true law of being. "I am," He says, "the Living One, and I became dead, and behold, I am alive for evermore."[a] God loosed the pains of death, because it was impossible that He should be holden of it.[b] And therefore when He had paid the mighty debt which the human family, represented by because impersonated in Him, owed to the deeply-wronged Righteousness of God, Life resumed its suspended sway in Him as in its Prince and Fountain. "Christ being raised from the dead dieth no more."

Now observe how the perpetuity of the Life of the Risen Jesus is the guarantee of the perpetuity of the Christian Church. Alone among all forms of society which bind men together, the Church of Christ is insured against utter dissolution. When our Lord was born, the civilised world was almost entirely comprised within the Roman Empire. That vast social power might well have appeared, as it did appear to the men of our Lord's day, destined to last for ever. Since then the Roman Empire has as completely vanished from the earth as if it never had been. Other kingdoms and dynasties have risen up and have in turn gone their way. Nor is there any warrant or probability that any one of the states or forms of civil government which exist at present will always last. And there are men who tell us that the Kingdom of Christ is no exception to the rule; that it too has seen its best days and is passing. We Christians know that they are wrong; that whatever else may happen, one thing is impossible; the complete effacement of the Church of Jesus Christ. And what is our reason for this confidence? It is because we Christians know that Christ's Church, although having likeness to civil societies of men in her outward form and mien, is

[a] Rev. i. 18.   [b] Acts ii. 24.

unlike them inwardly and really. She strikes her roots far and deep into the World Invisible. She draws strength from sources which cannot be tested by our political or social experience. Like her Lord, she has meat to eat that men know not of.[a] For indeed she is endowed with the presence of Christ's Own Undying Life. "Lo, I am with you alway, even unto the end of the world."[b] Christ's superiority to the assaults of death is the secret of His Church's immortality: our confidence in the perpetuity of the Church is only one form of our faith in the unfailing Life of the Risen Jesus.

Certainly, although the Church of Christ is insured against dissolution, she is not insured against vicissitudes, not even against corruption, more or less extensive. Her Lord is Divine: but the beings who compose her are human. She has not always triumphed: she has through weakness fallen back before an impure fanaticism like Mohammedanism, as in North Africa and Western Asia. She has been corrupted, as we know too well, sometimes by large and unwarranted additions to the original Creed of Christendom; sometimes by forgetfulness of truths which were constantly on the lips of Apostles and Martyrs. And upon corruption, division has followed, so that she no longer presents a united front to the powers of evil. And there have been times when it has seemed as if the world was right, and the Church was on the point of disappearance from among men; so great has been the weakness or the corruption of her representatives. To say that she would perish would have been reasonable if she had been only a human society, founded by some human genius, who had passed away. That which is so striking in her history, making it unlike that of any other society whatever, is the power of self-restoration—so men term it—which she has

[a] St. John iv. 32.   [b] St. Matt. xxviii. 20.

again and again developed, partially or as a whole. The tendency to dissolution has clearly been arrested by an inward Influence against which ordinary circumstances and causes could not prevail. What is this but the presence of Him Who, being raised from the dead, dieth no more? And who shall forecast the future? She may or may not, here or elsewhere, enjoy the friendship of civil governments; she may be welcomed in high places or persecuted in catacombs. This only is certain:—she will exist while the world shall last. "God is in the midst of her, therefore shall she not be removed: God shall help her, and that right early. The heathen make much ado, and the kingdoms are moved: but God hath showed His voice, and the earth shall melt away."[a]

It may indeed be said, 'Why should I rejoice on Easter Day in the perpetuity of the Church? Why should I grieve at her failure, if my personal Christian life remained? To me Christianity is not a political or ecclesiastical, but a personal matter; and I cannot affect such enthusiasm for the institution which only embodies and transmits it.' My brethren, if you hold this language, you do not yet know what it is, in the fulness and reality of the term, to be a Christian. Your isolated, or as you call it, your "personal" Christianity, is not the Christianity of the New Testament. If one thing is clear in that blessed Book, it is that Christ came to found a Divine Society, and that the life of Christians comprises duties to, and privileges intimately bound up with that Society. What! is it nothing to be welcomed into a vast association of souls, extending through so many centuries, so many countries, reaching up into the world invisible, reaching from our homes and hearths to the very throne of Christ? Is it nothing to have a home

[a] Ps. xlvi. 5, 6.

and refuge for the solitary spirit, where we again find father and mother, and brother and child, who in the order of nature may have passed away? Is the endurance of this Church of God a matter of indifference to any who have felt its place in the Divine counsels; to any who have known what it is to have come unto Mount Sion, and to the city of the Living God, and to an innumerable company of angels, and to the general assembly and Church of the firstborn, and to Jesus?[a] I trow not. Glorious things are spoken of thee, thou city of God; because thou art the home of saints, the home of angels, the home—so an Apostle teaches—of the Living Christ; because, as in thy chequered story of shame and honour, of failure and victory, thou traversest the centuries, thou dost always bear with thee, in thy assured and indestructible vitality, the certificate of thy Lord's deathless Life.

III.

Lastly, the great event of this day reveals the secret, as it displays the model, of perseverance in the life of godliness. Christ risen from death, Who dieth no more, is the model of our new life in grace. I do not mean that absolute sinlessness is attainable by any Christian. "If we say that we have no sin, we deceive ourselves, and the truth is not in us."[b] But at least faithfulness in our intentions; avoidance of known sources of danger; escape from presumptuous sins; innocence, as the Psalmist has it, of the great offence:[c] these things are possible. And they are necessary. Lives which are made up of alternate recovery and relapse: recovery perhaps during Lent, and swift relapse after Easter; or even lives lived, as it were, with one foot in the

[a] Heb. xii. 22-24.   [b] 1 St. John i. 8.   [c] Ps. xix. 13.

grave, without any strong vitality, with feeble prayers, with half-indulged inclinations, with weaknesses which may be physical, but which a regenerate will should away with; lives risen from the dead, yet without any seeming promise of endurance, what would St. Paul say of them? "Christ being raised from the dead dieth no more." Just as He left His tomb on Easter morning, once for all, so should the soul, once risen, be dead indeed unto sin. There must be no hovering about the sepulchre, no treasuring the grave-clothes, no secret hankering after the scent and atmosphere of the guilty past. If any of you who hear me humbly hope that you have by God's grace during this Lent attained to a spiritual resurrection; if in your case the words have been fulfilled, "The hour is coming, and now is, when the dead shall hear the voice of the Son of Man, and they that hear shall live;"[a] then, be well assured that you have great need to see that you persistently set your affections on things above; that you desire passionately to live as those who are alive from the dead, "yielding your members as instruments of righteousness unto God."[b]

Depend on it, Christians, the Risen Life of Jesus tells us what our own new life should be. Not that God, having by His grace raised us from death, forces us whether we will or no to live on continuously. That great company of associated souls, which we call the Church, has indeed received from the King of kings a charter of perpetuity. But to no mere section of the Universal Body, and much more to no single soul on this side the grave, is it said that "the gates of hell shall not prevail against" it. Judas, after sharing that Divine companionship, may sell his Master if he wills to do so.[c] Demas, after his friendship with St. Paul, may forsake him at pleasure, through

[a] St. John v. 25. [b] Rom. vi. 13. [c] St. Matt. xxvi. 14, 15.

love of this present world.[a] The Galatians, among whom Christ has been evidently set forth crucified, may yet be bewitched by the fascinations of a plausible falsehood.[b] Paul himself may for a moment tremble, lest having preached to others, he himself should be a castaway.[c]

No force is put upon us; no man is carried up to heaven mechanically if he prefers to go downwards, or even does not sincerely desire to ascend. God allows us to employ that freedom of choice, in which our peril and our dignity as men consists, against ourselves, against Himself, if we choose to do so.

But how, you ask, can we rejoice in our Risen Lord, if we are so capable, in our weakness, of being untrue to His example? I answer, because that Life is the strength as well as the model of our own. "If the Spirit of Him that raised up Jesus from the dead dwell in you, He that raised up Christ from the dead shall likewise quicken your mortal bodies, by His Spirit that dwelleth in you."[d] The Risen Christ in us is "the hope of glory."[e] And God gives us His grace, not to withdraw it, but to continue it to us, if we will not resist Him and sin it away. "If any man love Me, My Father will love him, and We will come unto him, and make Our abode with him."[f] "He that eateth My Flesh, and drinketh My Blood, dwelleth in Me, and I in him."[g] "No man," says our Lord of the elect, "is able to pluck them out of My Father's Hand."[h] "Who," asks St. Paul, "shall separate us from the love of Christ?"[i] Plainly God desires our salvation; He gives us, in and for the sake of His Blessed Son, all necessary grace: but it is for us to say whether we will respond to His bounty.

[a] 2 Tim. iv. 10.   [b] Gal. iii. 1.   [c] 1 Cor. ix. 27.
[d] Rom. viii. 11.   [e] Col. i. 27.   [f] St. John xiv. 23.
[g] St. John vi. 56.   [h] St. John x. 29.   [i] Rom. viii. 35.

Pray to-day, brethren, then, in the spirit of this text, that at least you may persevere, in anything you have learnt of the life of God. Perseverance is a grace, just as much as faith, or hope, or charity. The secret strength of perseverance, is a share in the Glorified Life of Jesus. Perseverance may be, it will be, won by prayer for union with our Risen Saviour. Say to yourselves with the Psalmist, "It is good for me to hold me fast by God."[a] Cling to the Risen Lord, by entreaties which twine themselves round His Person; by Sacraments, the revealed points of vital contact with His Human Nature;[b] by obedience and works of mercy, through which, as He says Himself, you abide in His love.[c] Invigorate your feeble life, again and again, by that Divine Manhood which, reigning on the Throne of Heaven, can never more sink into the grave; and then, not in your own strength, but in His, "likewise reckon ye also yourselves to be dead indeed unto sin, but alive unto God through Jesus Christ our Lord.[d]

[a] Ps. lxxiii. 27.
[c] St. John xv. 8-10.
[b] St. John vi. 56, 57.
[d] Rom. vi. 11.

SERMON XV.

THE DAY OF DAYS.

PSALM CXVIII. 24.

This is the day which the Lord hath made: we will rejoice and be glad in it.

WHAT is the high day to which the author of this verse refers? It is hard to say, at least with certainty. Possibly it was the day on which the foundation stone of the new Temple was laid, after the return from Babylon. More probably it was the day on which this new Temple was consecrated to the service of God. Less probably it was the Feast of Tabernacles. In any case, it was a great historical occasion, or a festival of the first class of importance.

In our Lord's time the whole of the hundred and eighteenth Psalm was applied to the Messiah by the Jewish interpreters. Christ was the Stone, refused by the builders of Israel, but afterwards made the Head of the corner.[a] His was the welcome, " Blessed is He that cometh in the Name of the Lord ; " to Him was addressed the prayer, " Hosanna, save, I pray,"[b] as on Palm Sunday, by the Jewish multitude. Thus it was very natural for

[a] St. Matt. xxi. 42 ; cf. Ps. cxviii. 22.
[b] St. Matt. xxi. 9 ; cf. Ps. cxviii. 25.

the Christian Church to find in the words, "This is the day which the Lord hath made: we will rejoice and be glad in it," an application to our Lord Jesus Christ. What was the day in His life which He made His Own, beyond all others? Not His Birthday; for that meant His entrance on a life of sorrows. Not His Ascension day; for that was the closing scene of a triumph already achieved. Not His Transfiguration day; it was a momentary flash of glory in a career of pain. Not the day of His Crucifixion; it was a great day for a ruined world, but for Him it marked the lowest stage of humiliation and of woe. The Day of days in the life of Christ was the day of His Resurrection. It reflected a new glory on the day of His Birth. It witnessed a triumph of which the Ascension was but a completion. It was to the Transfiguration what the sunrise is to the earliest dawn. It poured a flood of light and meaning on Calvary itself; and showed that what took place there was not simply the death-scene of an innocent Sufferer, but a Sacrifice which would have power with God to the end of time.

Something of this kind is what was felt by the old Christians about Easter Day; and as it was the greatest day in the life of Jesus Christ, so for them it was the greatest day in the whole year. It was the day of days; it was the Lord's Own Day; it was the queen of festivals. Every Lord's Day in the year was a weekly feast of Christ's rising from the dead; on Easter Day, the force and meaning of all these Lord's Days was gathered into one consummate expression of joy and praise. "This is the day which the Lord hath made: we will rejoice and be glad in it." Easter should provoke a joy in Christian hearts, greater than any event in our private lives; greater than any in the world's public history; greater than any other even in the life of our Lord Himself. This is the immemorial feeling and sense of Christendom; but why should it be so? why has Easter, why has the Resurrection, this extraordinary claim on the buoyancy of the Christian heart?

I.

The joy of Easter, then, first of all, is the joy of a great reaction; a reaction from anxiety and sorrow. So it was at the time of Christ's Resurrection. The Apostles had been crushed by the sufferings and death of Jesus Christ. They could not have imagined beforehand that One so popular, so powerful, so gifted, would die like a malefactor, amid the execrations of the populace, and be buried away out of sight. They had "trusted that it was He Who should have redeemed Israel."[a] Their disappointment, their despondency, their anguish, were exactly proportioned to their earlier hopes. And, as is the case in the life of feeling, one deep answered to another. When He was in His grave, all seemed over; and when He appeared, first to one, and then to another, on the day of His Resurrection, they could not keep their feelings of welcome and delight,—traversed though these were by a sense of wondering awe,—within anything like bounds. "Then were the disciples glad when they saw the Lord."[b] It is not often that we are able to picture to ourselves what that joy of theirs must have been. But let us try to do so, by imagining a case which may easily suggest itself just now. Let us suppose that it were consistent with the present Will of God that any of those brave men who sank beneath the waves just a month ago, in the *Eurydice*, could, instead of waiting for the general Resurrection, rise now from their watery shrouds; that they could

[a] St. Luke xxiv. 21.   [b] St. John xx. 20.

enter the homes which were awaiting their return, and which are now plunged in sorrow; that they could speak to a wife, to a mother, to a sister, some words of reassurance and peace. What would be the measure of the joy of such a meeting as that? It would be exactly proportioned to the anguish which followed the first announcement that the vessel had been lost; an anguish which has been deepening ever since. It would be an exulting rebound of feeling to which nothing in ordinary life is at all parallel. Yet it would be only a distant likeness of the joy which the Apostles experienced on Easter Day. No one, whom his friends mourn as among the brave men who died on that Sunday afternoon, can have been, to those who mourn him, what Jesus was to the Twelve, or to the Marys, or to His Own Blessed Mother; they knew that He had died by a death of studied pain and shame, to which nothing in the sudden sinking of a vessel at sea is in any way comparable. Their joy at seeing Him corresponded to the agony which had preceded it; the rebound was proportioned to the recoil. For them, assuredly, in words which the Church applies to Easter, "the winter is past; the rain is over and gone; the flowers appear on the earth; the time of the singing of the birds is come."[a] Nature, in her yearly resurrection from the grave of winter, might fitly reflect the exulting joy with which Nature's Lord was greeted by His servants on His return from the realms of death.

And this joy of the first disciples is repeated every year in the greatest feast of the Christian Church. Those who have felt the sorrow feel the joy. Those who have entered into Christ's sufferings, and their own sins as the cause of these sufferings, can rise with glad hearts, if we may not say to the heights of Apostolic exultation,

[a] Cant. ii. 11, 12. Easter Monday, Even-song—1st Lesson.

yet to a level of tranquil delight which offers to our Risen Saviour a sincere greeting on the Day of His Resurrection. Year by year we Christians accompany our Divine Lord, as it were, over again, to the Garden of the Agony, to the Hall of Judgment, to the Way of Sorrows, to the Hill of the Crucifixion. Year by year we stand by, in spirit, while Joseph of Arimathæa and Nicodemus lay Him in His grave; and the tension of sincere feeling, of sympathetic sorrow, of penitence and contrition which this implies, is followed by a corresponding reaction on Easter morning. Yes! across the interval of eighteen centuries, we rejoice over again, in our poor way, with the company of the first disciples. We say over to ourselves, again and again, without comprehending all its meaning: "The Lord is risen indeed, and hath appeared unto Simon."* We lay ourselves open to the strong impulse of reactionary delight which has followed upon the desolation and the misery; and we cry, "This is the day which the Lord hath made: we will rejoice and be glad in it."

II.

The joy of Easter, secondly, is the joy of a great certainty. The Resurrection of our Saviour is the fact which makes an intelligent Christian certain of the truth of his Creed. And in this way it satisfies a real mental want, and it occasions keen enjoyment by giving this satisfaction. The human mind has its own joys no less truly than the human heart. The human mind craves for truth not less truly than does the human heart for an object of affection, or than the human body for nourishment. In debased natures this original appe-

* St. Luke xxiv. 34.

tite for truth may have been killed out, but in every healthy mind, whether Christian or not, it is a lasting, and, indeed, in some sense, an insatiable appetite. It is insatiable, because its only adequate object is the Infinite Being. Well, this appetite for truth demands first of al an answer to certain questions of the very first importance to every thinking man: Whence do I come? Why am I here? What is the destiny, if any, which awaits me after death? Christ our Lord has answered these questions. He has told us authoritatively what is our true origin, what our work, and what our destiny, and how we may be secured against failure, through what He Himself has done for us. But then the question occurs, How are we to know that He really had authority to teach, as He did, on these great subjects? He may have had it, but what is the proof *to us?* what is the fact about Him upon which we can lay our fingers and say that it proves His right to speak as He did? The answer is: He "was crucified, dead, and buried, and then He rose again the third day from the dead." He had said that He would rise. And He did rise. He had pointed to this coming Resurrection when the Jews asked Him for a sign of His mission. The old Hebrew prophet Jonah had been three days and three nights in the belly of the fish.[a] The Son of Man, to Whom this prophet, and all else that was great and noble in Hebrew history, pointed on, would be also three days in the heart of the earth.[b] His Resurrection would prove His right to speak as from God; to speak as compelling the allegiance of men; to speak as the organ of the highest truth on the highest subjects that could interest human beings. The Apostles accordingly entered on their work with one conviction, prominent beyond all

[a] Jonah i. 17.   [b] St. Matt. xii. 40.

others. It was that the truth of Christianity, and its claims upon the minds and hearts of men, mainly depended upon the fact of the Resurrection of Christ from the dead. Within a few weeks of the occurrence, and amidst a population passionately interested in denying the truth of what they said, they took every opportunity of virtually saying—" Christianity is true; it is true because Christ has risen from death." They could not have ventured to do this unless they had been sure of the fact upon which they were so ready to risk everything, even life itself; sure, with that sort of certainty which comes from actual experience. On every occasion, before every opponent, almost in every sermon, they put forward the Resurrection as their reason for being where they were and for saying what they did. Read the first chapters of the book of their Acts; see how their first discourses were full of the Resurrection; how they preached it as the sum and substance of the Gospel; almost as if it were the whole of the Christian Creed. So did Peter in Jerusalem;[a] so did Paul in Antioch,[b] and Athens,[c] and Corinth.[d] For these men the Resurrection was practically Christianity, nay, the whole of Christianity, in so far as Christianity as a whole rested on it as the proof-fact of its having come from heaven. Here was the fact which showed that the Gospel was not one Creed among many, all having some truth and some falsehood in their composition; but that it was The Truth, the one absolute Truth, the real unveiling of the mind of God to His reasonable and immortal creatures. This is what the first Christians felt; of the truth of their Faith " God had given an assurance unto all men, in that He had raised Jesus from the dead."[e] Therefore did the

[a] Acts ii. 22-36; iii. 12-16; iv. 10-12; v. 29-32.
[b] Acts xiii. 14, 16-37.   [c] Acts xvii. 22-31.
[d] Acts xviii. 1-5.   [e] Acts xvii. 31.

Resurrection inspire them with such fervent joy. It was the event which riveted their grasp on the Truth which they prized above all else in life. Without the Resurrection, what was Christianity? Possibly a beautiful thought; possibly a new and fresh life of feeling; a social enterprise for improving the race; a passionate regret for a departed friend; the highest love of humankind; the enthusiasm of humanity. Without the Resurrection, what was Christianity? A human system, or at least a system uncertificated by God; destined like other human systems to have its day, its day perchance of ascendency, but also its day of decline; destined " to have its day and cease to be." Without the Resurrection, what was Christianity? On the whole, it was a failure. Had Jesus been crucified, buried, and then subjected to the decay of death, His human life,—we must dare to say it,—would have been a splendid mistake. His miracles would have reckoned for successful juggleries. His strongest claims on the love and allegiance of men would have been resented as the language of a presumptuous self-assertion. His clearest predictions about Himself would have been set aside as the reveries of a dreamer. His death, if men still held it to be undeserved, would have only illustrated the triumph of might over a cause that was partly right. His bones might perchance have been gathered by a distant generation, and reverently laid up in a shrine more ornate than any which has covered the relics of later men who have owned His Name. But St. Paul would still have written, " If Christ be not risen, our preaching is vain, your faith is also vain."[a] Other miracles of His might conceivably have been omitted; Christianity might still be Christianity, if the five thousand had not been fed, if the demoniacs had been uncured, if

[a] 1 Cor. xv. 14.

Lazarus had not been raised from death. But deny a literal Resurrection of Jesus from the grave, and you take the spring out of the year; you remove the keystone from the arch. All else in our Creed depends on the Resurrection of Christ; and to-day when we remind ourselves of its historical certainty, which is scarcely less illustrated by the apparent contradictions than by the collective and direct force of the accounts which have come down to us, we experience a mental delight at the freshening touch of truth, and cry, "This is the day which the Lord hath made: we will rejoice and be glad in it."

III.

Thirdly, the joy of Easter is inspired by the hope which Easter warrants and quickens. Hope and Joy are twin sisters. Joy best enters the human soul, when leaning on the arm of Hope. As the Apostle says, "We rejoice in the hope of the glory of God."[a] What is this hope which Easter most distinctly puts before us? and how does it spring from our Saviour's Resurrection? The great hope which Easter sets before us is the completeness of our life after death. If Christ had never risen from the dead, there still would have been much to urge, on grounds of natural reason, in favour of the immortality of the human soul. Great thinkers, who were not Christians, have done this; and we, with the light of faith streaming on us from heaven, may well pronounce their names with affectionate reverence. But, after all, what is the exact result of their efforts? Does it approach the confines of certainty? Is it anything better than a reasonable anticipation? And, even if the immortality of the soul were certain, would it assure us of enjoying

[a] Rom. v. 2.

hereafter more than a mutilated existence; the existence of a soul divorced from that body which had been for so long its companion and its instrument, and with which, since the moment of its creation, its every act had been until death so intimately associated? The Jews felt that immortality must be something more than the immortality of the soul; they had, in their later history, as especially in the Maccabee period,[a] a certain faith in the resurrection of the body. But this faith was confined to sects and places; it was perhaps less of a faith than an opinion. When our Lord came, the complete future life of man was revealed, by being taken as a matter of course. Our Lord referred to it as He referred to the objects around Him, as a thing obvious to any soul that had eyes to see. Sometimes under figures, sometimes literally, He treated the future life as a continuance of the life which men lead here and now. The very furniture and plan of heaven: its many mansions;[b] the thrones[c] on which the disciples would sit; the effulgence of the blessed;[d] the new fellowship in which men and women would consort, while yet neither marrying nor giving in marriage, but being as the angels of God;[e] the presence of the venerable Patriarchs, living on from age to age, because God is their God, and He is not the God of the dead, but of the living;[f]—in this way or that the Great Future was constantly on His lips. Especially did He insist that "all in the graves would hear the voice of the Son of Man, and would come forth."[g] Man's future life would be the life of man; of a being consisting of body and soul; of a body, no doubt, spiritualised and invigorated by new properties, but still a body, continuing under new conditions the life which it had lived on earth.

[a] 2 Macc. vii. 9, 14. [b] St. John xiv. 2. [c] St. Matt. xix. 28.
[d] St. Matt. xiii. 43. [e] St. Matt. xxii. 30. [f] St. Matt. xxii. 32.
[g] St. John v. 28, 29.

How was this teaching to be brought home to the minds of men, as being something more than a religious reverie, as a literal and solemn truth? If men were to be convinced of the reality of the future life, it was necessary to grapple with the main difficulty which they feel in treating it as being what it is,—a certainty. That difficulty, as I have hinted, is not suggested by the reason. Reason, left to itself, and deliberately examining the powers and instincts of the human mind, always has leant, always will lean, to the side of belief in a future after death. In all ages of the world, the best men, in their best moments, have believed in their immortality. The difficulty of believing in a future life is due, not to the reason, but to the imagination as controlled by the senses. Who of us has not made this discovery, in some one of those dark hours, which sooner or later visit every human life? Who of us has not stood by the open coffin, and felt himself, or marked how others feel, the terrific empire of sense in the presence of death? The form which was once full of life, quivering with expressiveness, with thought, with feeling, now lies before us cold and motionless, like a plaster cast of its former self. Perhaps the traces of what must follow are already discernible; and forthwith the imagination surrenders itself, like a docile pupil, to the guidance of the senses. It follows the corpse into the grave which awaits it; it pictures to itself the gradual advances of an inevitable decay; it ponders over the chemistry of dissolution; it dwells, with affectionate but misplaced sympathy, on the surrender, first of this and then of that feature, so well loved in life, to the gnawing agencies of decomposition and ruin; it lives,—this imagination,— not merely, like the demoniac whom our Lord exorcised, among the tombs, but inside them; and it ends by proclaiming the victory of death; a victory too clear, too complete, too unquestionable, to allow reason or Revelation to raise their voices in favour of any sort of life that can possibly survive it. At such a moment the most modest anticipations of reason are deemed an unsubstantial guess: the clear teaching of Revelation a solemn fancy; the mind's sceptre has passed to the imagination and the senses, and they decide that all ends with death, and that the grim secrets of the grave are the measure of man's impotent aspirations after a future existence.

Now it was to deal with this specific difficulty that our Lord willed to die, and then, by a literal bodily resurrection, to rise from the grave. He would grapple with the imperious urgency of the senses and the imagination on their own ground. He would beat down by an act, palpable to the senses, and attested by evidence which should warrant its reality for all time, the tyrant power which sought to shut out from man the hope of an immortal life. When the disciples saw that the Risen Being before them was their Lord; when they noted His pierced hands, His feet, His side;[a] when they conversed with Him,[b] ate with Him,[c] listened to Him,[d] followed Him much as of old;[e] then they knew that the Master Who had been killed upon the Cross by a protracted agony, and committed to the grave as a bleeding and mangled corpse, had really risen from death, and had opened a new era of hope for the human race.

And for us, in a distant age, this fact that Christ rose from death is not less full of precious hope and joy than

[a] St. John xx. 26, 27; St. Luke xxiv. 40.
[b] St. Luke xxiv. 32.
[c] St. Luke xxiv. 30, 43; St. John xxi. 12, 13.
[d] St. Luke xxiv. 44-48; St. John xxi. 15-22.
[e] St. Luke xxiv. 50; St. John xxi. 12-14; Acts i. 3, 4.

for our first forefathers in the Faith. In our day there has been another res rrection; a resurrection of doubt. And the gloomy uncertainties about the future which were dissipated by Christ again threaten to overshadow sections of Christendom with little less than a Pagan darkness. But while negative speculation is ever active, the broad facts of human life remain what they always have been. Death claims, year by year, month by month, its victims from every household; science and thought, it may be, reluctantly bow their heads at the presence of death. They confess his power; they can suggest nothing to relieve the gloom which surrounds his empire. Only beside the empty Tomb of Jesus Christ can this generation, or those who will succeed us, recover any true hope in the destinies of man; for "Christ is risen from the dead,-and become the Firstfruits of them that slept. For since by man came death, by Man came also the Resurrection from the dead. For as in Adam all die, even so in Christ shall all be made alive." [*]

It is this invigorating and joyous hope which Easter bestows on us. Unbelief once wrote at the entrance of a cemetery the word *Fuerunt*, "They have been." Faith always writes over the gate of a churchyard, "I am the Resurrection and the Life." To unbelief the dead are but memories; memories of beings who have ceased to be. To faith the dead are living, working, praying friends, whom nothing but the dulness of sense hides from sight. They are not yet what they will be; but they are there—

> "The dead! They have become
> Like guardian angels to us;
> And distant heaven, like home,
> Through them begins to woo us:

[*] 1 Cor. xv. 20-22.

> Love, that was earthly, wings
> Its flight to holier places:
> The dead are sacred things
> That multiply our graces."[a]

The Resurrection of Christ has done its work: it has quickened our perceptions of the unseen and the future. The hope of meeting those whom we have loved and lost; of renewing, in a brighter atmosphere, all that was worth keeping in the intercourse of earthly life; above all, the hope of seeing and being welcomed by Him, their Lord and ours, Who in His Human Body is set at God's Right Hand in heavenly places; this hope, glorious and inspiring, springs directly from Easter Day. Truly we may exclaim with the Apostle, that God "hath begotten us again unto a lively hope through the Resurrection of Jesus Christ from the dead,"[b] and with the Psalmist, that "this is the day which the Lord hath made: let us rejoice and be glad in it."

Yes; Easter Day is not a day for protracted argument: it is a day for Christian joy. Of this joy the outward signs are around us. Nature and art are here; the flowers from the garden and the music of the choir; each contributes its best to the honour of our Risen Lord. May He grant that outward tokens of joy may be for us all in keeping with an inward experience. The reality of a man's Easter joy is a fair test of his Christian sincerity. If we have at all felt sympathy with Christ in His sufferings, we must rejoice at the triumph which has ended them. If we do account our Christian faith as indeed the pearl of great price, we must rejoice at the event, which, more than any other, demonstrates its value. If we have staked our all upon the eternal future, our hearts must indeed bound with delight at the

[a] Faber, *Hymns*, No. 134.   [b] 1 St. Pet. i. 3.

memory of that majestic Fact which shows that we have not wasted our efforts on an unsubstantial fancy. May Christ our Lord vouchsafe to deepen in us this joy in His Blessed Resurrection; to give it more and more practical expression in our lives; and to satisfy it perfectly hereafter, in that world where, through His Death and Resurrection, we shall be like Him, and shall see Him as He is.

* 1 St. John iii. 2.

SERMON XVI.

EASTER CONSOLATIONS.

St. Luke xxiv. 17.

And He said unto them, What manner of communications are these that ye have one to another, as ye walk, and are sad?

IT will be in your recollection, my brethren, that our Lord asked this question of the two disciples, whom He joined, as they were walking along the road from Jerusalem to Emmaus, on the evening of the day of His Resurrection from the dead.

Of these two disciples we know very little. One of them is named Cleopas; but he is not to be confounded with the Cleophas or Clopas, the husband of one of the Marys who stood beneath the Cross.[a] The other is not named, except in later Church traditions of doubtful value. All that we know is that they both belonged to the company of our Lord's disciples, while neither of them was an Apostle: since when they returned later in the evening to Jerusalem they found the eleven Apostles gathered together.[b] Notice here what is well worth our grateful attention. Although these two men belonged to the outer circle of the earliest company of Christ's people, and were in no way distinguished as leaders or teachers

[a] St. John xix. 25. [b] St. Luke xxiv. 33.

of the rest, they were selected, on the very day of the Resurrection, for an extraordinary distinction, which has made them famous in the kingdom of God to the end of time. Truly we may perceive, with St. Peter, that "God is no respecter of persons,"[a] and that the lowliest of His subjects is as truly an object of His loving care as are the princes of His Church; even though these last sit on thrones, judging the twelve tribes of Israel.[b]

St. Luke's narrative makes it probable that Emmaus was the home of one, if not of both, of these disciples. Emmaus was a village which could be reached from Jerusalem by a journey of from two to three hours. When we are told that the disciples were leaving Jerusalem on "the very same day," the expression seems to imply that they had made up their minds pretty well that the claim of Jesus of Nazareth to be the Messiah must be given up. They were in the position of men who had gone through a period of religious enthusiasm, and then fancied themselves to have found out that they had been mistaken. They had tried the Galilean prophet, and now they were disillusionised. In this spirit they were leaving Jerusalem, to return to their ordinary occupations at Emmaus: but while this was their general conclusion, the recent past had still far too strong a hold on them to allow them to think, as yet, of much else. Thus as they walked along the road, they "talked together of all these things that had happened."[c] The word which St. Luke employs implies that they did not altogether agree; much of their conversation was argument, however friendly. And, as their discussion proceeded, Jesus drew near. It is natural to ask, From what quarter? Did He meet them, by coming along the road from an opposite direction?

---

[a] Acts x. 34.   [b] St. Matt. xix. 28.
[c] St. Luke xxiv. 14.

Did He overtake them from behind, and, as one writer suggests, place Himself between them? We are not told. One moment they were apparently alone: another—and He was there. There was no approach to be measured by distance and by the lapse of time. The thin air around them had yielded His Form, just as it did in the upper chamber when the doors were shut. Now in His Resurrection Life, His Body was spiritual. It had qualities which do not belong to our grosser flesh and blood. It was not ubiquitous, but It was not subject to the conditions which make movement from place to place slow, difficult, palpable to sense. He was there; walking side by side with them. But, disciples of His though they were, and with minds and hearts quite full of Him, they did not know Him. St. Mark implies that the reason was an outward one: He appeared "in another form"[a] than that to which they had been accustomed. St. Luke says that the cause was internal: "their eyes were holden."[b] There is no contradiction: doubtless the two causes conspired to produce the result. He was there, and they did not recognise Him. Then followed His question, "What manner of communications are these that ye have one to another, as ye walk, and are sad?" It was the language, not of reproof, but of sympathy. Something like reproof came later on: but as yet He can think only of their sadness. Their sadness was written, so the original word implies, in their countenances; but He of course saw deeper. And whether the allusion to the sadness formed part of His question, or belongs, as is probable, to the Evangelist's description, does not really matter: the drift of the early part of His question was plain enough.

[a] St. Mark xvi. 12. [b] St. Luke xxiv. 16.

I.

What was at the bottom of the sadness of the two disciples?

It was, first of all, the sadness of a bereavement. They had been with Jesus, we know not how long; they had seen and heard Him: He had conquered a great place in their hearts. They had seen Him arrested, insulted, crucified, dead, buried. So far their sadness was that of the Magdalene, when she asked the supposed gardener where they had laid the Sacred Body. We most of us know something of the heartache of a great bereavement.

But, then, secondly, the sadness of the disciples was also caused by mental perplexity. Here, as elsewhere in the Gospels, we see the different bearing of men and women in the hour of sorrow. A woman is most distressed when her heart has lost its accustomed object. A man is by no means insensible to this source of sorrow; but he commonly feels a distress, which a woman does not feel, at least equally, when his intelligence, his sense of truth, is perplexed. These disciples were profoundly troubled at their inability to reconcile what had actually happened with all that Jesus had led them to expect. "We trusted that it had been He Which should have redeemed Israel."[a] They were still chiefly thinking of a political Redeemer, and, of course, they were disappointed. But in this disappointment lay the painful problem of the apparent untrustworthiness of a loved and trusted Friend. How were they to reconcile what had happened with what had been promised? How were they to escape from the misgivings which seemed to be only too well warranted by the facts?

[a] St. Luke xxiv. 21.

Once more, theirs was the sadness of a forfeited object in life, of a shattered career. They had, as they thought, given themselves to Jesus, to His cause and work, for good and all. They had embarked all the energy and resolve of life in that service, in that companionship, so full, as it seemed, of coming blessing and triumph: when lo! as it appeared, all had collapsed. He was in His grave; slain by the very influences which He should first have won, and then have led to victory. There were rumours of His being alive; but only, as they thought, empty rumours. Practically all looked dark. And they were leaving Jerusalem, for good and all, and retiring to their old homes and occupations at Emmaus.

Those of you will sympathise with them who may, as young men, have embarked hope and energy in some task, which you had dared to hope would be your work for life, and then, all at once, through some unforeseen event, have been thrown out of it, stranded, wrecked. Men who never carry much heart and purpose into anything might pass through an occasion of this kind easily enough. Men who do with all their might whatsoever their hand findeth to do, and who suddenly are forced to throw up their life-work, are often thus plunged, heart and soul, into a condition, which is very imperfectly described as "sadness." "What manner of communications are these that ye have one to another as ye walk, and are sad?" Our Lord's question compels an answer. And in the answer there is something of displeasure as well as of surprise. How could He be ignorant of the subject which is filling their thoughts and hearts? How could He not be aware that this is the cause of the sorrow that weighs them down? Cleopas answering said unto Him, "Art Thou only a stranger in Jerusalem, and hast not known the things which are come to pass there in these days?"ᵃ They thought that He must be one of the guests who had come to Jerusalem from a distance for the Paschal festival, and that He must have been living alone, in that great crowd, and so have missed seeing all that had happened; nay, He could not have heard of it. Otherwise they could not account for His strange ignorance. And He, in His tender condescension to their narrow and mistaken judgment, will not rudely set them right. He does not indeed affirm that He was one of the strangers at the feast; nor does He deny that He knew what had happened during the three preceding days. He does not ask for information; but He would lead them to express what they feel, that He might instruct them the better afterwards. "He said unto them, What things?" They said unto Him, "Concerning Jesus of Nazareth, Which was a Prophet mighty in deed and word before God and the people: and how the chief priests and our rulers delivered Him to be condemned to death, and have crucified Him. But we trusted that it had been He Which should have redeemed Israel: and beside all this, to-day is the third day since these things were done."ᵇ How pathetic is this confession! First, their warm acknowledgment of the greatness of the Prophet of Nazareth: next, the shock they had experienced at His ignominious arrest and crucifixion: then the implied confession that their trust in His power of redeeming Israel from slavery and shame was no longer what it had been: and lastly, the gentle reference to a "third day," on which He had promised —they remembered without saying it—a decisive event of some kind, a Resurrection. Thus far their words breathe darkness and failure: yet in the gloom there were perplexing rays of light. "Certain women of our

ᵃ St. Luke xxiv. 18.   ᵇ St. Luke xxiv. 19-21.

XVI]   *Easter Consolations.*   247

company made us astonished, which were early at the sepulchre; and when they found not His Body, they came, saying, that they had also seen a vision of angels, which said that He was alive. And certain of them which were with us went to the sepulchre, and found it even as the women had said: but Him they saw not."ᵃ

Yes! They said out all this before His very Face; this story of mingled despair and hope, of hope overmastered on the whole by despair. And He—He does not emerge from the disguise, whatever it was, of His "other form,"ᵇ nor does He at once enlighten their holden eyes. Their last word is despair. "Him they saw not." They evidently thought that the sights of that early morning were a beautiful but passing illusion.

And now it was His turn to speak: it was for them to listen. He turns their thoughts away from the dark perplexities of the passing time to the ancient Scriptures of the Jewish Church. He does not ask them to trust the women, or the angels, or Peter and John: He simply asks, "Ought not the Christ to have suffered those things, and to enter into His glory?"ᶜ And then, "beginning at Moses and all the prophets, He expounded unto them in all the scriptures the things concerning Himself."ᵈ They were familiar with the letter of the Jewish Bible: He set before them the idea which unveiled its unity, its drift, its spirit. Then it was that their hearts burned within them, while He talked to them by the way, and opened to them the Scriptures:ᵉ and the Revelation of Truth which was begun by the exposition of Scripture on the road was completed at the sacred Eucharistic feast which followed. Their eyes were opened, and they knew Him, and He vanished out of their sight.ᶠ He had done His work. To

ᵃ St. Luke xxiv. 22-24.   ᵇ St. Mark xvi. 12.
ᶜ St. Luke xxiv. 26.   ᵈ *Ib.* 27.   ᵉ *Ib.* 32.   ᶠ *Ib.* 31.

their hearts He had restored the old object of affection. Their understandings He had relieved of their sore perplexity. And they had re-entered on the purpose in life which seemed to have been altogether forfeited. He was living after all, and they could still, with absolute simplicity of purpose, live and work for Him.

II.

In our modern world are to be seen, not seldom, disciples of Christ in name, downcast and saddened, who are leaving Jerusalem, as if on the point of giving Him up. And He, as of old, joins them in "another form," so that their eyes are holden, and they do not know Him. He comes to them in His Church, which is in their eyes only a human institution; or in His Scriptures, which seem to them but a human literature; or in His Sacraments, in which they can discern nothing more than outward ceremonies. Yet He has a question to put to them, and a word of comfort to address to them, if they will but listen. For they are sad; sad for nearly the same reasons as were the two disciples on the Emmaus road.

a. First of all, there is the sadness of mental perplexity. The understanding has its fashions as well as the heart; its fashions of distress as well as its fashions of enjoyment. In our day, many men, who have not wholly renounced the name of Christ, are oppressed by what they call, not unreasonably, the mystery of existence. They see around them a world of nature, and a human world too. Each in a thousand ways creates perplexity and disappointment.

Whence comes the natural world? If we lose sight of what faith teaches as to the creation of all things out of nothing by God, all is at once wrapped in darkness. We may be told that the world comes from itself: that it has formed itself, by the aid of forces within it, into the world which we see; that it is what it is because it was what it has been. But then, whence came that which it has been? If all is from chaos, whence comes chaos? if all from an atom, whence the atom? And how is it governed? By moral laws? by arbitrary laws? or by a fated necessity? Above all, for what end does the world exist? why is existence at all remarkable? what is the end, the purpose, the destiny of existing things? It is folly to say that these questions should not be asked. They must and will be asked. To cease to ask them, at least in the secret recesses of the mind, is to cease to think.

Man himself too is not less a puzzle to himself than is the Universe around him. Face to face with Nature, man is at once conscious of insignificance and conscious of superiority. He is a mere speck in this vast expanse of heaving matter and force, and yet he is greater than it; for he is aware of his own existence. In like manner he is controlled by material forces around him at every point of his life, while he is also conscious of being endowed with a sense of freedom. Pascal has developed this contradiction in the finest chapter of his *Thoughts;* that on the "Grandeur and Misery of Man."[a] In the same manner, the contrast between man's longing for goodness and moral freedom, and his practical subjection to the habits and weaknesses of nature; between his craving for happiness and his failure ordinarily to attain it; between his desire for truth and his being surrounded by uncertainties, are contradictions which weigh him down. "We are always groping at problems," said Goethe. "I have spent just eleven happy days in my life," said Byron. "I

[a] ii. 79, etc.

was sitting yesterday," says the Christian Father, St. Gregory Nazianzen, "under the shady side of a hedge. My soul was inwardly agitated, I was plunged in grief. The questions, What have I been? what am I now? what will become of me? deeply disturbed me. I do not know. A wiser than I does not know. I wander about surrounded with obscurity. What I was has escaped me. What shall I be to-morrow if I still exist?"[a]

If these sad perplexities were not unknown to ancient Christians, we cannot be surprised at their being felt in our modern world, which, whatever its achievements and advantages in the realms of secular knowledge, does not always think or know more of Christ our Lord than did our forefathers. And our Risen Lord offers us the true solution to these perplexities. That God made the Universe; that everything exists to promote His glory; that He rules everything, yet on principles of order which we apprehend as law; that in the visible world man is incomparably the most important object, and that man's soul is the most important part of man; that the contradictions in man's intellect, his affections, and his will, are not permanent, and do but illustrate his period of trial and probation, all this we know, directly or indirectly, on our Lord's authority. And that He can speak with authority on such subjects we know, because He has given a pledge to the world of His right to speak, by first dying publicly in the full daylight of history, and then raising Himself from the dead.

β. Next, there is the sadness of the conscience. Where distinct acts of wrong-doing are not constantly and vividly present to the memory, there is a moral cloud brooding over the soul, from whose shadow escape is rarely possible.

[a] *Carm. de Hum. Nat.* i. 3. 14, quoted by Luthardt.

In order to feel this a man need not be a Christian, or recognise the beauty and obligation of the moral law of Jesus Christ. Heathens have felt it. Wherever there is the recognition of an inward law, however imperfect; wherever there is a conscience at work, however feebly and intermittently, there is the sense of sin. This sense of sin is not merely the recollection of definite acts, but the perception of a moral atmosphere at variance with the Will of God. This atmosphere is not merely discoloured by the misdeeds of the soul which perceives it; it inherits some of its discolouring ingredients, just as each human body inherits its vigour or its weakness from a remote past.

"It has often been remarked," says Professor Lassaulx of Munich, when he is discussing the spirit of ancient Greek poetry, "that in the majority of genuine national songs, there is a prevalence of the melancholy, the plaintive, and the aspiring. Aspiration is an innate feeling in man, inseparable from his inmost nature. Man's aspirations have been mingled with a feeling of sadness for the loss of innocence; and these two radical feelings of the human heart, aspiration and sadness, have ever pervaded all genuine national poetry." "So universal a lament over the loss and ruin of the original beauty of life must," the Professor argues, "date from a time antecedent to that of the history of individual nations: it can but be the echo of a feeling which has possessed, not this or that nation, but the human race. This note of sadness is the keynote of the earliest history, and runs in various forms through the oldest national traditions."[a]

This original sense of moral failure is of course largely aggravated by individual shortcomings. We instinctively feel sin to be what the common Greek word for it means; a missing the true aim of human conduct and life. And

[a] Quoted by Luthardt, *Apologet. Vorlesungen.*

thus the sadness which it inspires is not an artificial propriety, but a primary and natural instinct of the soul: nor does it exist the less truly because men endeavour to suppress it by noisy merriment or gross indulgence. These disguises last only for a while. The suppressed sorrow only gathers strength and volume, until at last it bursts out irresistibly, " My confusion is daily before me, and the shame of my face hath covered me.[a] . . . My sins have taken such hold upon me that I am not able to look up, and my heart hath failed me."[b]

Our Risen Lord reveals Himself to those who are weighed down by sin, as pardoning and blotting it out. He bare our sins in His Own Body on the tree;[c] and it is the Blood of Jesus Christ which cleanses us from all sin.[d] But what is it that gives His Death this power? It is that the worth and merits of His Person are incalculable, since He is the Everlasting Son of God. And what is the proof of this which He Himself offered to His disciples and to the world? It is His Resurrection from the dead. Deny the Resurrection of Christ, and there is no reason for believing in the atoning virtue of His Death. Recognise the historical fact, that He did rise from the dead, and the virtue of His Death, as taught by His Apostles, is credible enough. For He is plainly One Whose relation to God and to mankind altogether transcends the ordinary measures of human life.

γ. Thirdly, there is that sadness of the soul which arises from the want of an object in life; an object to be grasped by the affections, to be aimed at by the will. This is a kind of melancholy which is common enough among persons who have all the advantages which money and position

[a] Ps. xliv. 16. [b] Ps. xl. 15.
[c] 1 St. Pet. ii. 24. [d] 1 St. John i. 7.

can secure: they do not know what to do with themselves. They devote themselves to expedients for diminishing the lassitude of existence; they apply first to this excitement, then to that: they spend their lives in trying to "kill time." What a disclosure of the hopeless misuse of life lies in that expression, "killing time"! Time, that most precious gift, which is given once and not again; time, which escapes us as we think of it; time, for every minute of which we must give an account; time, in which all must be done, if anything is done, that will really last when it has ceased to be; time, in which a Christian has to work out his salvation with fear and trembling,[a] redeeming the time, because the days are evil;[b]—that time should be treated as a burden and a trouble, how surely does this mean that a life has woefully missed its object! They who work, either with the hands or with the brain, from early morning until late hours at night, are apt to think that for them the lot of life is hard, and to look with envy upon the wealthy who, as the phrase goes, have nothing to do but to enjoy themselves. How little do they dream that there is a misery of the soul, of whose approach they have never felt the first symptoms; the misery which it experiences, when, sated, jaded with that which can never satisfy, it turns back with deep unexpressible heart-sickness upon its weary self. As a well-known German poet has put it:—

> "Vain emptiness where'er my glances stray,
> Life; but a tedious journey towards no shore:
> A fruitless chase from this to that,—no more;—
> We lose our little strength upon the way."[c]

To persons who are thus living without an object, Christ our Lord appears, once it may be at least; to teach them that there is something worth living for; the known Will

[a] Phil. ii. 12.   [b] Eph. v. 16.   [c] Lenau, qu. by Luthardt, *ub. sup.*

of the Eternal God. And He in His Resurrection glory can speak on this too with authority: for He was declared to be the Son of God with power, by the Resurrection.[a] It was His Resurrection which proved His Divinity: and so it warrants us in living for Him, and in devoting the exercise of our best powers to Him as to the supreme Object of life. Thus His Resurrection rescues us from the misery of an aimless existence; in which men, like children playing at marbles on the edge of a precipice, risk the loss of all while they laboriously trifle with the priceless gifts of time and life.

For the main result of our Lord's Resurrection from the dead is the certainty with which it invests the life beyond the grave. Before He rose, the existence of that life was a speculation, based no doubt on some presumptions of the greatest weight, but still a speculation. Our Lord has made it a certainty. Yet for many of us, who own His Blessed Name, the future life is, during long tracts of time in this, only very faintly apprehended as certain; it is borne in upon us, on two kinds of occasions more particularly, when some very near relation, or some great public character, sinks into the grave. Then it is that thought involuntarily strains to explore, if it may be, the secrets of that other sphere of being; then it is that, during a lucid interval, we take a more accurate measure than usual of the relative insignificance of this.

My brethren, since last Sunday a great blank has been created in our national life, by the disappearance from among us of a prominent and remarkable figure, who beyond question filled all but the greatest place in the public eye.[b] This is not the time or the place for touching,

[a] Rom. i. 4.
[b] Referring to Lord Beaconsfield's death. *Ob.* Easter Tuesday, April 19, 1881.

even remotely, upon the many questions suggested by his career; questions which have already been largely and variously discussed by the public press, and which will continue, no doubt, to be matters of controversy for some time to come. It is little to say that his abilities were of the very highest order; that his rise to the foremost position in public life is almost, if not quite, without a parallel in our history; and that he has left his mark upon our country, and indeed upon Europe, traced in characters which will not readily be effaced. If he had ceased to exist, it would be natural only to reconsider, again and again, those years of incessant and brilliant effort which closed with Tuesday last; but here, in the Temple of Truth, we may not thus ignore the reality. None, as we know, ceases to exist at death. But when a human mind, up to the hour of dissolution, gives evidence of many-sided and vigorous power, we seem to have before us a sensible basis for the independent conviction, that it lives on beyond the catastrophe which has rent it from the body; that still, as before, it is eagerly surveying the past, the present, and the future, but in the light of a new state of existence, which is beyond not only our experience but our imagination. Assuredly the only important question is, not what any of the departed have been in the sight of men, but what and where they are now. While we can seldom answer that question with certainty, we must follow those who have left us with our hopes and prayers. The question itself is infinitely more important than any other that can be raised in connection with a human life. Our great concern is, not what we are called here, or what the world has said about us, for good or evil; but what we are. God, the Perfect Moral Being, God alone is great; and that, that only, in His creatures which resembles Him will be deemed great hereafter.

SERMON XVII.

THE EMMAUS ROAD.

St. Luke xxiv. 32.

Did not our heart burn within us, while He talked to us by the way, and while He opened to us the scriptures?

THIS was the reflection of the two disciples whom our Lord joined as they were walking along the Emmaus road on the day of His rising from the dead. These disciples were neither of them Apostles: they were among the less prominent members of the little community which followed our Lord, and which fifty days afterwards would, on the descent of the Holy Ghost, become His Church. In the confusion and dismay which followed upon the Crucifixion,—unable as they were to share the counsels of the Eleven—they may have thought it better to retire for a time from the Holy City. So on the afternoon of Easter Day they set out for Emmaus; talking to each other as they walked along; talking incessantly, as was natural, about the occurrences which, to the exclusion of everything else, had filled their minds and hearts.[a] While thus engaged they scarcely observed that they had been joined by a Stranger. The Stranger walked on at their side, and listened, and at last broke in on the conversation. What was the

[a] St. Luke xxiv. 13, 14.

subject they were discussing so earnestly? They were for a moment too sad to reply; but at last one of them, Cleopas, expressed his surprise that the Stranger—Whom he supposed to have come up as a pilgrim from the country to the Paschal festival,—could have been staying in Jerusalem without hearing of what had happened.[a] He told the Stranger of the greatness of the prophet Jesus of Nazareth, of the fate which had befallen Him at the hands of the High Priests and Rulers, and of their own deep disappointment; since they had hoped that this Crucified Prophet would have redeemed Israel from its enslavement to the Romans. Nor was this all. This was the third day since the tragedy, and wild rumours were in the air. Some pious women of their community had visited the tomb early that morning, but the Body had disappeared. And the women said that they had seen some heavenly beings, who told them that the Prophet was alive. Since then, others had visited the spot. They confirmed the report of the women so far as it went: but they had seen nothing of Him Whose death had wrung their hearts with sorrow, and the disappearance of Whose Body from His grave had filled them with wondering dismay.[b]

The Stranger listened, and then, when Cleopas had ceased, He burst into grave and earnest reproaches of the speaker and his companion. Why had they not believed the report of the women? Was it the head or the heart that was at fault? Were not the sufferings of a Prophet Who claimed to be the true Messiah certainly necessary, if His claim was justifiable? Was not the promised Christ, after suffering, to enter upon a glorious existence, such as the report of the women seemed to hint at? And then, passing from rebuke to demonstration, the

[a] St. Luke xxiv. 15-18.   [b] Ib. 19-24.

Stranger explained everything in the Old Testament that referred to the hope of a Deliverer, suffering yet triumphant.[a] He passed from Genesis to Malachi, touching with authoritative clearness upon type and symbol, upon separate passages, upon the general tenor and drift of books, upon each feature of the Hebrew Scriptures that illustrated the position and work of the Christ. To do this was to show that all which was happening in Jerusalem had already been anticipated, and indeed was only what was to be expected by instructed faith.

What must it not have been, we think, to listen to such an exposition, from such Lips, at such a time? What an experience! to hear Him comment on the sacrifice of Isaac, or on the ceremonies of the Day of Atonement, or on the fifty-third chapter of Isaiah, or on the second, or twenty-second, or forty-fifth, or seventy-second Psalms!

The time went quickly by; but the subject was a large one; and the exposition lasted until they were close to Emmaus. The Stranger would have left them, and passed on: He was saying farewell to them, in the usual way.[b] But they could not part with One to Whom, they already felt, they owed so much. The sun was already sinking in the west at that late hour, and He must stay in the humble home which one of them owned at Emmaus. "Abide with us," they cried, "for it is towards evening, and the day is far spent."[c] He consented; and they took their places at a table on which a simple supper of bread and wine was laid. Then, not waiting as a guest to be served, but exerting an authority which was gentle, irresistible, beyond dispute, He took the bread and blessed it, and gave It to them. Some Apostle would have told them of what had passed in the awful supper-room. And as they ate That which He gave them, a flood of light was poured

[a] St. Luke xxiv. 25-27.   [b] *Ib.* 28.   [c] *Ib.* 29.

within their souls.* It was indeed the Prophet. But how much more! How glorious, how majestic! They gazed at Him; and as they gazed, the outline of His Form became fainter. No door was opened; there was no visible movement, no observed retreat; they stretched forth their hands, and, lo! where only just now He had sat, there was vacancy. He had given them Himself, yet He had vanished from sight. And then it was that, before returning to Jerusalem to make their report to the Apostles, they thought over what had passed; and they asked themselves the question, "Did not our heart burn within us, while He talked to us by the way, and while He opened to us the scriptures?"

Now this is a very suggestive question; and we may profitably occupy ourselves this afternoon with some of the points which it raises.

I.

It suggests, first of all, the difficulty which we commonly have in understanding the real importance of many incidents in our lives at the time of their occurrence. These two disciples cared about nothing so much as their relation to their Crucified Master. Yet it seems they could be in His company for a considerable time, and hear Him explaining the Old Testament in its relations to Himself, without understanding their extraordinary privilege.

They recognised neither His voice nor His manner. But He discovered Himself to them in administering the Holy Sacrament. Then He vanished: and they knew what had taken place. At the time all had seemed to belong to the range of ordinary experience. He might be only a country Rabbi come up to the festival. They

* St. Luke xxiv. 30, 31.

had no idea that any one of the Apostles who had remained in the city, was not, religiously speaking, far better off than they were.

This illustrates, I say, the difficulty we have in understanding at the time the relative importance of events in our lives, and especially of the religious events in them. We are naturally disposed to think that the important events must be striking; that they must address themselves powerfully to the imagination; that they must stand out, in obvious prominence, from among surrounding occurrences. Whereas it may very well happen that what is most important in reality, that is to say, in its bearing on our prospects in the Future Life, is in appearance commonplace and trivial.

The owner of the ass on which our Lord sat when He entered Jerusalem, had, we may be sure, very little idea of what was meant by the message, "The Lord hath need of him."[a] Pilate would have been astonished had he been told at the time that nothing in his whole public and official life could distantly compare in point of real significance with his trial of the Prisoner Who was placed side by side with Barabbas before his tribunal.[b] Pilate, as a cultivated Pagan, looked at these religious matters from the outside; he was without the moral and spiritual perceptions which would enable a man to understand the scene before him. He was like an uneducated peasant examining an engraving of Albert Dürer's, or a person to whom music only represents regulated noise, listening to a sonata of Beethoven. But the Bible supplies us with instances of the same dull insensibility to the solemnity of comparatively simple occasions on the part of men who were by no means without religious interests, and were, in various senses, serving God. Again and again it

[a] St. Mark xi. 3.   [b] St. John xviii. 28-40.

has happened that, like the two disciples, such persons did not understand the meaning of some religious privilege at the time: they only knew its value afterwards, when it had passed, and they were looking back upon it. They saw visions of angels, or they communed with the Lord Himself, without suspecting the greatness of the privilege.[a] God disguises Himself. He comes close to Peter that He may wash his feet; and Peter cannot recognise the meaning of this humiliation of the Infinite and Omnipotent. By and by he will understand the saying, "What I do thou knowest not now, but thou shalt know hereafter."[b] It was true more than once that "these things understood not His disciples at the first: but when Jesus was glorified, then remembered they that these things were written of Him, and that they had done these things unto Him."[c]

This is what happens to us at the present day. We are looking out for the Divine Presence in the great events of life, if we think about God at all. We feel the solemnity of existence, the breath of another world seems to be upon us, on our wedding-day, or at the deathbed of a parent or a wife, or after a very narrow escape, or after some great shock which for the moment overwhelms the spirit and breaks us utterly down. But we do not understand that a quiet conversation with a friend, the perusal of a page in a book, a single prayer, or a good Communion, the train of reflections which are set in motion by an occurrence of very secondary importance, may be seen hereafter to have been of incalculable moment; that what was to us merely ordinary and incidental may have been the turning-point of destiny. Had the two disciples seen our Lord Jesus Christ bursting out from His

[a] Gen. xxviii. 16, 17; Judges vi. 22; xiii. 21.
[b] St. John xiii. 7.   [c] St. John xii. 16.

sepulchre in an effulgence of glory, they would have doubtless fallen prostrate in mingled ecstasy and fear. They met Him walking quietly along a public road, and, although conscious afterwards of a certain glow of the soul in listening to Him, they practically treated Him as if He had been anybody else. It did not occur to them that anything so great could be involved in anything apparently so trivial.

Of course in this world we look at the plan of our lives from below, not from above. We deal with the task of each day, of each hour, as it comes; we have no time or capacity to make a map or theory of the whole and to arrange the several parts in their true proportion and perspective. It is with our conceptions of life as with a landscape painting; some tree in the immediate foreground fills up a third of the canvas, while the towers of a great city, or the outlines of a mountain range, lie far away in the distance.

In another state of existence the relative worth of everything will be clear to us: here we constantly make the wildest mistakes, partly from the narrowness of our outlook, and partly from the false ideals which too often control our judgment. We look out for the sensational, which never comes to us quite as we anticipate it; we walk near Jesus Christ, Who veils His presence, in the ordinary paths of life; perhaps we never get beyond a certain passing glow of emotion, which dies away and leaves us where we were. Our hearts burn within us. But what this has meant we only find out when it is too late.

II.

Another point suggested by the words is the use of religious feeling. "Did not our heart burn within us?"

The disciples ask each other the question in a tone of self-reproach. While our Lord explained to them the true sense of the Hebrew Scriptures with reference to His Person and His work, His sufferings and His triumph, their whole inward being, thought, affection, fancy, had kindled into flame. They were on fire, and yet it all had led to nothing. Ought it not to have led to something? Ought it not, at the least, to have convinced them that, within the range of their experience, One only could have spoken as He did?

In the history of religion, men have formed, at different epochs, very opposite estimates of the value and functions of feeling.

Sometimes it has been distrusted and depreciated. Religion has been held to consist only in the exercise of the understanding on the great and solemn subjects which cannot long be absent from human thought; God, the Future, man's actual place and work in the Universe. These questions, it has been held, should be approached in a temper as dry and passionless as chemistry or astronomy or pure mathematics. Emotion is said to be only a disturbing force; there is no place for emotion, if thought is to be strong, if it is to run clear. According to this view, religion does not differ in temper, nor very greatly in subject-matter, from philosophy. The objects with which it is concerned are indeed already ascertained; but thinking about them—as distinct from feeling about them or acting on them—is said to be the proper function of religion.

At other times religion has been identified no less absolutely with duty. To have a clear conception of what is to be done and avoided in life, and to be practically loyal to it, that, we are told, is the sum and substance of religion. All beyond is surplusage. Thought, even when exercised on the sublimest objects; emotion, even when kindled by the most legitimate considerations, are quite distinct from the true essence of religion. Indeed there is said to be danger lest they should distract attention from that which really has claims upon us, from day to day, from hour to hour, namely, the intrepid and uninterrupted pursuit of duty.

Men never indulge in one-sidedness of this kind with impunity. Every truth that is insulted sooner or later has its revenge; every exaggeration has attached to it the penalty of an exaggeration in the direction opposite to its own.

Accordingly in Germany, during the middle of the last century, and in this country more recently, the reaction from a narrow conception of religion as merely a higher department of intelligence, or merely another name for duty and good conduct, has resulted in religious movements which practically have made religion to consist almost entirely in emotion. Justification by faith has not seldom come practically to mean justification by emotion, roused, from time to time, by discourses or reflections on the atoning work of Christ. Further, this emotion has sometimes seemed to be of greater practical importance than the object which has summoned it into existence, or than the conduct to which it ought to lead. To be in possession of this emotion has appeared enough to enable its possessor to dispense with any accurate ideas about the Being Who has called it forth; until, at last, persons on the edge of extreme unbelief, have congratulated themselves on the possession of religious feeling, though it would have been difficult for them to say exactly about what or whom; and other persons, violating what they knew to be the moral law of God, have satisfied themselves that they have no reason for anxiety, since they have succeeded in retaining warm religious emotions.

Certainly, my brethren, true religion cannot afford to neglect any elements of man's complex nature; and so it finds room for emotion. That glow of the soul with which it should hail the presence of its Maker and Redeemer is as much His handiwork as the thinking power which apprehends His message or the resolve which enterprises to do His will. Yet religious emotion, like natural fire, is a good servant but a bad master. It is the ruin of real religion when it blazes up into a fanaticism that in its exaltation of certain states of feeling, proscribes thought, and makes light of duty, and dispenses with means of grace, and passes through some phase of frantic, although disguised self-assertion, into some further phase of indifference or despair. But, when kept well in hand, emotion is the warmth and lustre of the soul's life. It announces the nearness and the beauty of the King of Truth; it lifts the performance of duty from the level of mechanical obedience to the level of ordered enthusiasm. Often, as in the souls of the two disciples, it is as the brightness of the dawn, which should tell that the Sun of Truth is near;

> "Lift up your eyes, even now His coming glows;
> Where on the skirt of yon heaven-kissing hill
> The trees stand motionless
> Upon the silvery dawn.
>
> Deep ocean treasures all her gems unseen,
> To pave an archway to the Eternal door;
> And earth doth rear her flowers
> To strew the heavenly road."

Yes; the wealth of emotion which muses ere the fire kindles, and the soul, speaking with the tongue of truth, owns its Lord, is a precious gift of God. Only it should always be made to lead to something. It is a means, not an end. And the disciples reproach themselves with having felt this heavenly glow in their hearts without recognising and worshipping the Divine Teacher Who had spoken to them. "Did not our heart burn within us, while He talked to us by the way, and while He opened to us the scriptures?"

III.

A third consideration which the words suggest, is the duty of making an active effort to understand truth as it is presented to us. I say, an active effort; because, as a rule, our minds are apt to be passive. We let truth come to say what it can; we do not go out to meet it, to welcome it, to offer it a lodging in the soul, and, if it may be, to take its measure and understand it. The disciples tacitly reproach themselves with not having done this. Had they seriously endeavoured to make the most of our Lord's instruction, they would have seen at once Who He was.

Everybody who has had experience in teaching knows how much depends upon the teacher's power of rousing the mind of his pupil to take an interest in the subject which is being taught. The information given may be the best to be had, the method of conveying it admirable for its clearness and simplicity, the general capacity of the master beyond dispute, but there is no chance of real success unless a child's mind makes a responsive effort. If it remains passive, the most interesting truths, the most touching narratives, will trickle over the surface of it, and find no place within. The mind of the learner must always co-operate with the teacher in the work of instruction, and the teacher's first duty is to rouse it to do this.

This was well understood in the early Church, and it led to the adoption of the catechetical method of instructing those who were candidates for Baptism. Sermons were not equal to the occasion; because while listening to a sermon the mind may be passive throughout, as were the minds of the two disciples when listening to our Lord. But catechising rouses the mind whether we will or not; it quickens the conscious possession of knowledge, or it creates the healthy sense of ignorance, which, in the absence of knowledge, is always valuable. Far better is it to know that we do not know, than to be really ignorant, especially of an important subject, while we fancy in a vague way that we know something about it. The great Christian school of Alexandria, which was in the first three centuries of the Church's life the chosen home of its ripest and widest thought on the Revelation of God in Christ, was also the great scene, and we may also almost say, the product of the catechetical method.

Every one who is taking pains with his own soul will be careful to catechise himself in private, not only as to questions of conduct, but as to matters of faith and knowledge. What do I believe on this subject? why do I believe it? does it involve my believing anything more? does it oblige me to modify or to re-shape any other opinions that I hold on other subjects? What are its bearings on my conduct? what its demands on my conscience? Surely we may not walk along the road of life, even side by side with the Light of the world, and expect that religious knowledge will come to us as a matter of course, and without our taking trouble to win it. No earthly business or art or science is learnt without the sacrifice of time, without serious and repeated effort; and religious truth is no exception to the rule. And yet how commonly do men think that the most important kind of knowledge will force itself upon them without their making any endeavour to secure and understand it: that some special inspiration or some singular accident will absolve us from the necessity of taking trouble. If we have serious thoughts now and then, and look into our Bibles in a casual way, and attend some of the Church Services, we think we have good reason to be satisfied that we know all that it concerns our soul's health to know; perhaps even that we know enough to discuss religious questions of the day with confidence. We drift through life in this way, some of us; making our feelings and preferences the rule of truth; assuming that what is popular for the passing hour, or what comes readily to us, must be the Will of God. He indeed is near from Whom we might learn the truth; walking by our side, ready and longing to be inquired of if we only will; but we dispense ourselves from the necessity. Religious truth, we say to ourselves, is very simple and easy of acquirement; that which is intended for all must be open to all, and cannot be the monopoly of those who make efforts to know it.

And yet nothing in the Bible is clearer than that it makes the attainment of truth depend upon an earnest search for truth. "Seek," our Lord says, "and ye shall find."[a] "Those that seek Me early shall find Me."[b] "Call upon Me, and I will answer thee, and show thee great and mighty things, which thou knowest not."[c] "If thou criest after knowledge, and liftest up thy voice for understanding; if thou seekest her as silver, and searchest for her as for hid treasures; then shalt thou understand the fear of the Lord, and find the knowledge of God."[d]

In conclusion, let us reflect that our Lord's presence with His disciples during the forty days after His Resurrection was in many ways an anticipation of His presence in His Church to the end of time. His religion wears a

[a] St. Matt. vii. 7.
[b] Prov. viii. 17.
[c] Jer. xxxiii. 3.
[d] Prov. ii. 3-5.

commonplace appearance; its sacred books seem to belong to the same category as the works of human genius; its Sacraments are, St. Augustine said, rites chiefly remarkable for their simplicity; its ministers are ordinary, and often erring and sinful, men. But for all that, the Incarnate Son is here, Who was crucified and rose from death, and ascended and reigns in heaven, He is here; and the trial and duty of faith is what it was eighteen centuries ago, namely, to detect, under the veil of the familiar and the commonplace, the Presence of the Eternal and the Divine. We too walk along the road to Emmaus; and the Divine Teacher appears to us, as St. Mark puts it, " in another form;"* and our hearts, perhaps, glow within us, yet without doing anything for our understandings or our wills.

Surely we should look back on any occasions when He has enabled us to feel something of His nearness, not only with thankfulness but with awe. These occasions do not occur for nothing. We shall be reminded of them one day, and of the use which we have or have not made of them.

"Did not our hearts burn within us?" Before we take leave of Easter—it may be of our last Easter—before its Alleluias have died away upon the air, let us consider how far it has been blessed to us in this way, and whether we have used the blessing to God's glory. It is a main purpose of the great festivals of the Church, to rekindle in Christians a practical devotion to our Divine Redeemer in the leading acts and mysteries of His life. Have we felt any increased love for Him Whose triumph and glory we have been celebrating? Did our heart burn within us, at that early Communion, or during the reading of that familiar Gospel, or when they were singing that anthem, or while we joined in that

* St. Mark xvi. 12.

hymn? Did the associations of some early years, and scenes and faces which have passed away, and modes of feeling which seemed to have been parted with for ever, rise up again, as if from the dead, to be enlarged, enriched, consecrated, by our later experiences, by riper knowledge of our Divine Lord and His redemptive work and grace, and of what life is, and is tending to be? If so it was, let us, while yet we may, try to turn this feeling to good account; to do something that we should not otherwise have done; to forego something that we should otherwise have indulged in; to master some dimly or half-apprehended side of truth; to learn something more of what it most concerns us to know. So will our Emmaus walk be blessed to us; we shall meet our Heavenly Companion again and again in the Breaking of Bread, and we shall know Him one day even more perfectly, when upon recognition He will not vanish from our sight, but will abide with us to be our possession and joy for all eternity.

SERMON XVIII.

JESUS ON THE EVENING OF EASTER DAY.

St. Luke xxiv. 39.

Behold My Hands and My Feet, that it is I Myself: handle Me, and see; for a spirit hath not flesh and bones, as ye see Me have.

IT was on the evening of the day of His Resurrection, and on the occasion described by St. John in to-day's Gospel, that our Lord uttered these words. Of the Eleven, in St. Thomas's absence, only ten were present. They were assembled in a secret chamber for fear of the Jews; and with them were other friends and disciples. They were discussing the report of our Lord's appearance to Peter, when they were joined by the two disciples who had met our Lord, as St. Mark says, in a different form or guise,[a] on the Emmaus road during the afternoon, and who had known Him in the Breaking of Bread. Not to mention what must have reached them from St. Mary Magdalene and the other women, these two reports from the two disciples and from St. Peter, thus combined, may well have made the hearts of those present beat more quickly than they did before. Where was He? Would He show Himself? Would they too see Him? Would

[a] St. Mark xvi. 12.

He most resemble the Jesus of the Transfiguration or the Jesus of Calvary? Would He be as He was before He suffered? or would His visage be still so marred that only a few would know Him? or would He be so changed into an unimagined form of glory and beauty, that the Sacred Face would be hardly recognised, except by very intimate friends, like Simon Peter? Or was all this purely idle speculation? Might not Peter—some may have reasoned thus at that time,—might not Peter have been himself deceived? Might the two disciples have mistaken some one else for their Master; could they have read His well-remembered Features into the countenance of some other Rabbi? It was in the midst of some such a turmoil of hopes and fears, of speculations and doubts, of bold anticipations and despairing conjectures, that Jesus Himself appeared. He gave no sign of His approach. Angels were guarding His empty tomb; but no angel visibly announced Him. There was no sound that rent the air; no blaze of brilliant light, as on the Holy Mount, illumined the chamber; no wall fell, as before the conqueror of Jericho; no door was opened. All had been fastened up for safety's sake against the Jewish enemy: all remained as it had been. But they looked; and behold He was there; He was in the very midst of them. How they knew not, but so it was; the thin air had yielded to their sight that Form, that Countenance Which they could not but recognise. And then, a second sense was summoned to support the evidence of sight. The Form which they beheld spoke; He spoke in a voice with whose every intonation they were so familiar; "Jesus saith unto them, Peace be unto you."*

The Evangelist describes the immediate effect. They were terrified and affrighted. They had seen, as they

* St. Luke xxiv. 36.

thought, an inhabitant of another world. Not an appearance without essence, as some have conjectured; not an angel, since an angel is a specifically distinct being from a man; still less, as it has been imagined, an evil spirit self-changed into a form of light; but the disembodied spirit of their dead Master making itself visible; this was what the disciples supposed that they saw. The language of the Evangelist leaves no real room for question on this head. They thought that the Body of Jesus was still resting in the grave in the rich man's garden; their incredulity, which was proof against the remembered predictions of their Master, was also proof against the report of Peter and the two disciples. But, as they could not mistake either the Form before them or the voice to which they listened, they supposed that Jesus, being dead, had appeared to them as spirit without a body. It was, they believed, His ghost that they saw. My brethren, however we may account for it, man has a secret terror at the thought of contact with pure spirit, unclothed by a bodily form: this dread, I say, is part of our human nature. Perhaps it is due to an apprehension that a disembodied spirit, with its superior freedom and subtlety of movement, may easily take beings such as we are, weighted with a body of sense, at a fearful disadvantage. Perhaps it is to be referred to a dim sense of the truth that our nature is really mutilated, when, during the interval between death and the resurrection, the soul exists for a time apart from the body; it is difficult else to account for the dread of such appearances among those who look forward to a time in which they themselves will be bodiless spirits. St. Paul betrays something of the feeling in question, when he writes to the Corinthians of the spirit after death as "unclothed;"[a] as

[a] 2 Cor. v. 4.

though death inflicted an outrage upon our poor humanity, and the state of the dead until the resurrection had about it inevitably a touch of the unnatural. Certain, at any rate, it is that the feeling expressed by Eliphaz the Temanite holds good for all time:—

> "In the visions of the night,
> When deep sleep falleth on men,
> Fear came upon me, and trembling,
> Which made all my bones to shake.
> Then a spirit passed before my face;
> The hair of my flesh stood up:
> It stood still, but I could not discern the form thereof:
> An image was before mine eyes;
> There was silence. . . ."[a]

This instinct of our nature, which shrinks from contact with the spirits of the dead, is by no means confined to, or chiefly exhibited in, fervent believers in Divine Revelation. On the contrary, doubt as to Revealed Truth is the natural soil for all unreasoning fears: men ever feel that any horror from beneath is possible, when no blessing is certain from above. Saul is naturally drawn towards the witch of Endor;[b] and the spiritualism, so called, of our day, weird and even grotesque as it often is, gains its most distinguished adherents from among the advocates of pure materialism. Had the disciples looked forward to the fulfilment of their Master's word, as a simple matter of course, they would have welcomed Him with reverent love; and this love would have cast out tormenting fear.[c] As it was, they fell back upon the surmise that He was a ghost; and they shivered at perceiving how near this unearthly being was to each of them.

They said nothing. But He, as always, knew what they felt, what they thought.[d] He did not conjecture their

[a] Job iv. 13-16.
[b] 1 Sam. xxviii. 7.
[c] 1 St. John iv. 18.
[d] St. John ii. 24, 25.

thoughts and feelings; He read them with that penetrating inward glance, which makes Him, in time and in eternity, the Master and Judge of souls; and He was ready with His consolations. "Why are ye troubled? and why do reasonings arise in your hearts? Behold My Hands and My Feet, that it is I Myself: handle Me, and see; for a spirit hath not flesh and bones, as ye see Me have."

This scene is suggestive of so many considerations that a choice is difficult. But there are three which, as it appears to me, claim especial attention just at present.

I.

Here we note first of all our Lord's indulgent treatment of mistakes and imperfections in religious belief. We may venture to say that the disciples, seeing our Lord in the midst of them, ought to have recognised Him at once. They knew, from long companionship with Him, that there were no discoverable limits to His power over life and nature. They knew that He had been transfigured on the mountain,[a] and had walked upon the sea.[b] They knew that He had formally claimed to be Messiah, by assuming the distinctive title of Messiahship,—the "Son of Man."[c] They knew that He had shown to them from the Old Testament that the Messiah must suffer, and rise again the third day, in virtue of a prophetic necessity.[d] They knew indeed that to remove all doubt He had, on more occasions than one, and very solemnly, stated that this would happen to Himself;[e] so that, when they saw Him led forth to death, and expiring in agony,

---

[a] St. Matt. xvii. 1-8.   [b] St. Mark vi. 48.
[c] St. Matt. xvi. 13.
[d] St. Luke xviii. 31-33; St. Mark ix. 12.
[e] St. Matt. xvi. 21; xvii. 22, 23.

and laid in a tomb, they might have known what would follow. The earlier part of His prediction had been fulfilled to the letter; were they not sure enough of His power to be certain that what remained would be fulfilled as well?

That our Lord held His disciples responsible for such knowledge as this is plain from the words which He had used, earlier in the afternoon, when addressing the two on the Emmaus road: " O fools, and slow of heart to believe all that the prophets have spoken: ought not the Christ to have suffered these things, and to enter into His glory?"[a] And then, continues the Evangelist, " beginning at Moses and all the prophets, He expounded unto them in all the scriptures the things concerning Himself."[b] The reproach addressed to the two disciples seems to imply that, in their case, the responsibility may have been enhanced by the enjoyment of certain opportunities which we cannot accurately measure. But St. Mark refers to the very scene we are now considering by saying that Jesus appeared to the Eleven as they sat at meat, and upbraided them for their unbelief and hardness of heart, because they believed not them that had seen Him after He rose from the dead.[c] Yet, looking to St. Luke's report, what tender censure it is! Here certainly is no expression which betrays grief or anger. He meets their excitement with the mildest rebuke; if it be a rebuke. " Why are ye disquieted? and why do critical reasonings arise in your hearts?"[d] He traces their trouble of heart to its true source; the delusion which possessed their understandings, about His being only a "spirit." In His tenderness He terms their unworthy dread a mere disquietude of the heart; they are on a false track, and He will set them right. They

[a] St. Luke xxiv. 25, 26. [b] St. Luke xxiv. 27.
[c] St. Mark xvi. 14. [d] St. Luke xxiv. 38.

doubt whether what seems to be the Body which hung upon the Cross is really before them; let them look hard at His Hands and at His Feet which had been pierced by the nails. They doubt their sense of sight; very well, let them handle Him; they will find that it is not an ethereal form, which melts away at the experiment of actual contact. He does not peremptorily condemn their notion that a bodiless spirit had appeared to them, as if it were a mere superstition; He even seems to sanction it, when He observes that such spirits have not flesh and bones which answer to the sense of touch. He appeals, let us observe, not merely to hearing and to sight, but to touch. "Handle Me," He says, "and discern."[a] Remember St. John's language at the beginning of his First Epistle; "That Which we have heard, That Which we have seen with our eyes, Which we have looked upon, and our hands have handled, of the Word of Life;"[b] it may well show that they took Him at His word. Touch indeed is the least intellectual, the bluntest, the most material of the five senses. In the order of spiritual precedence, it is below taste and smell, just as sight, and still more hearing, are above them. Touch may be deceived at least as easily as sight. But in certain depressed mental states touch affords a sense of confidence which sight cannot command; it supplies a kind of evidence which, united with other and higher testimony, removes a last obstacle to faith.

Our Lord knows that all this might have been, that it ought to have been unnecessary. But He also measures human weakness. He knows how the tyranny of sense, and of the mental habits which are governed by the senses, holds down the aspirations of faith and love. He, the True Parent and Deliverer of men, "knoweth of what we are made; He remembereth that we are but dust."[c]

[a] St. Luke xxiv. 39.   [b] 1 St. John i. 1.   [c] Ps. ciii. 14.

What a lesson is here for all who, whether as fathers and mothers, or teachers, or clergymen, have upon their hands the immense responsibility of imparting religious truth to others! The first condition of successful teaching is patient sympathy with the difficulties of the learner. To be able to remember that others may have difficulties of their own which we have never had; that they may have been denied opportunities which have been freely granted to us; that they are possibly weighed down by incumbrances of which we have known nothing; that they perhaps need assistance, which for us may have been unnecessary; this is a first requisite for successful teaching. It is easy to upbraid; it is not always easy to explain or to convince. To be patient with misapprehension, even with folly; to condescend to explanations where they might be deemed superfluous; to make the best of all that is admitted in the direction of truth, and the least of all that obscures and contradicts it; to make truth easy of acceptance, by appealing to the lower as well as to the higher powers of the learner, to the senses as well as to the reason;—this is to imitate our Lord. Very often indeed it depends upon a teacher, whether the learner is to be satisfied that he is face to face with the substance, and not merely with the ghost of a religion; whether he really beholds the hands and feet; whether he is convinced of the reality of the flesh and bones.

A great master was once asked, "What is the first condition of successful teaching?" "Patience," he said. "What is the second?" "Patience." "What is the third?" He paused, then said; "Sympathy." And what a rebuke is here on the want of considerateness, of courtesy, of generosity, which so often disfigures our modern treatment of real or supposed religious error! Is it not the case, brethren, that instead of making a return to reason or a return to faith easy for a straying sheep, modern Christians often set themselves to making it impossible? Do they not exaggerate mistakes? Do they not exasperate misunderstandings? Do they not imagine that, in order to be faithful to known truth, a man must needs display a certain measure of official ferocity towards those who misapprehend it? Do they not sometimes assume that to be tender and considerate implies a certain lack of straightforwardness? Are arguments never valued less for their intrinsic worth than for the language which enforces them in terms calculated to convey pain or insult? Who can wonder at our failures to convince, when our methods are so unlike that of the Great Teacher!

II.

Here, too, we see our Lord's sanction of the principle of inquiry into the foundations of our religious belief. Certainly He said to St. Thomas a week afterwards, that they were blessed who had not seen His open Wounds, and yet had believed His Resurrection.[a] But in St. Thomas's case, as a week earlier in that of the Ten and their friends, He sanctions, nay He invites, inquiry, observation, reflection. He does not say, 'If after the testimony of My prophets, after My Own assurances, after the report of My disciples, you cannot believe that I am risen from My grave, and that you see Me before you; then continue in your unbelief; be gone.' He does say, 'Use the means of inquiry which God has given you: behold My pierced Hands and Feet; see for yourselves that I am He Who hung upon the Cross: nay, touch Me, if thus only you can escape from your illusion, and can discover for yourselves that a Body of flesh and bones

[a] St. John xx. 29.

is before you, endowed indeed with new and glorious properties, but with Its substantial identity unimpaired.'

Certainly, my brethren, inquiry into the grounds of faith is not the noblest department of religious activity. Our highest duty towards religious truth is to act on it; to expend the strongest and choicest forces of our souls in paying the rightful tribute of love, adoration, obedience, joyful and constant devotion to Him Whose glory and beauty, and mercy and strength, are thus made known to us. And undoubtedly there are souls who, from childhood until death, thus offer to God a continuous service of the affections and of the will. They see truth intuitively as did St. John; they sit and gaze on it as did Mary of Bethany; to them one prayer beyond all others is dear: "Behold, my delight is in Thy commandments; O quicken me in Thy righteousness."[a] And thus, though they live in an age of cold indifference to, or of insolent rebellion against, Revealed Truth, they are "not afraid for any terror by night, nor for the arrow that flieth by day; for the pestilence that walketh in darkness, nor for the sickness that destroyeth at the noonday."[b] Happy and privileged souls! some of whom are to be recognised in every generation, and not least in our own; happy souls whose eyes are ever directed upwards, whose feet are ever pressing forwards, upon whom the burning fiery furnace of human struggle and passion has had no power; as though they had been all along "hidden privily in God's Own presence from the provoking of all men, and kept secretly in His Tabernacle from the strife of tongues."[c] Some such there were in that upper room. They needed not to gaze curiously at the glorious Wounds, or reverently to handle the very Limbs of the Redeemer; they knew that He

[a] Ps. cxix. 40.   [b] Ps. xci. 5, 6.   [c] Ps. xxxi. 22.

was there; that He had risen indeed; that He had appeared unto Simon.

With most of us, it is different; God knows how different. We are of our age; acting perhaps feebly upon it; acted upon by it, we may be sure, most powerfully; sharing its great privileges, its inspiriting hopes and efforts; sharing too its prejudices, its errors, its illusions. On most of us it leaves many a scar; if it does no worse. We, after our fashion, meet Stoics and Epicureans at Athens;[a] we, too, after the manner of men, fight, or ought to fight with beasts at Ephesus.[b] And this means that the life of affection and obedience is necessarily traversed by another life; the life of the critical understanding. If in our day the understanding cannot but survey religious truth, seriously, eagerly, keenly; it need not forget the duties of reverence; it may enable us the better to do the Apostle's bidding, and "be ready to give to every man a reason of the hope that is in us."[c]

Undoubtedly the understanding has great and exacting duties towards Revealed Truth. If God speaks, the least that His rational creatures can do is to try to understand Him. And therefore, as the powers of the mind gradually unfold themselves, the truths of religion ought to engage an increasing share of each of them, and not least of the understanding. What too often happens is, that while a young man's intelligence is interesting itself more and more in a widening circle of subjects, it takes no account of religion. The old childish thoughts about religion lie shrivelled up in some out-of-the-way corner of a powerful and accomplished mind, the living and governing powers of which are engaged in other matters. Then, the man for the first time in his life meets with some sceptical book; and he brings to bear on it the

[a] Acts xvii. 18-20. [b] 1 Cor. xv. 32. [c] 1 St. Pet. iii. 15.

habits of thought and judgment which have been trained in the study of widely different matters. He forms, he can form, no true estimate of a subject, so unlike any he has really taken in hand before: he is at the mercy of his new instructor, since he knows nothing that will enable him to weigh the worth or the worthlessness of startling assertions. He makes up his mind that science has at length spoken on the subject of religion; and he turns his back, with a mingled feeling of irritation and contempt, on the truths which he learned at his mother's knee.

This is no imaginary case; and among the reasons which go to explain so sad a catastrophe, this, I say, is one; that the understanding has not been properly developed in the boy and the young man, with relation to religious truth. What is the law of that development? It is this; that as the mind grows, it learns to reinforce the teaching of authority by the inquiries of reverent reason. When we learn religious truths as children, we necessarily take them all as our mother teaches them. She offers us no explanations, and we could not understand her if she did. And, mark you well, to the end of the longest life, and in the case of the strongest and most cultivated minds, there must always be much in God's Revelation of Himself which stretches away high into the heights of heaven, and deep into the depths beneath, out of the reach and ken of any human faculty; much which must be received, if at all, on God's authority, without possibility of verification. But this does not apply to the whole of the Christian Creed. In respect of many districts of a Christian's faith, if the mental and moral growth be healthy and symmetrical, there should be a constant invigoration of what is learnt from authority through what is observed, thought out, handled by the mind for itself. Authority does not disappear. The collective Christian society gradually takes the place of the single parent. But authority is no longer the sole support of faith. Faith finds its support increasingly in that which is suggested by reason from within, as well as in that which is imposed from without. According to the Apostle's rule, to faith is added, first virtue; then to virtue, knowledge;[a] and knowledge, which, in other circumstances, and later, might be a foe to sincere belief, is in early life the secret of its vigour.

Depend on it, a time comes to many thoughtful young men and women, when they are tempted to think that what they have learnt in childhood about life and death, and God and Jesus Christ, and all that bears on our place in the eternal world, is uncertain; the shadow of an old creed which still haunts the earth; the echo of voices which ought wholly to have died away at the close of the Middle Ages. To many a young man, the first visit to his mind of this terrible suspicion, has brought real and keen agony, in this our own day and country. But in every such trial, to every sincere soul, there is, I dare to say, a voice to be heard which still whispers, "Behold My Hands and My Feet, that it is I Myself: handle Me, and see; for a spirit hath not flesh and bones, as ye see Me have." You think, young man, that it is the ghost of a religion which confronts you; handle it, and you will see for yourself that it rests on a basis, at least as sure as any of the ordinary forms of human knowledge. It rests on history. The Life, and Death, and Resurrection of Jesus Christ is not a work of the sanctified imagination of a later age; it is, at least, as much a part of the story of our race as are the life, the victories, the assassination of Julius Cæsar. Handle it, searchingly but reverently, and you will discern this for yourself: you will see that there is in it an intrinsic consistency, a solidity, a power of resist-

[a] 2 St. Pet. i. 5.

ance to critical solvents, which you have not suspected. But do not suppose that, because it condescends to be thus tested by your understanding, as regards its reality, it is therefore within the compass of your understanding, as regards its scope. It begins with that which you can appraise; it ends in that which is beyond you: because while you are finite and bounded in your range of vision, it is an unveiling of the Infinite, of the Incomprehensible. Yes; Christianity plants its feet firmly on the soil of earth; its hands are seen again and again working in the stirring agencies of human history; but it rears its head towards the sky; it loses itself amidst the clouds of heaven. We see the very feet, the hands, the utter reality of the One Incomparable Life; but we only see enough to know assuredly that there is much more which is necessarily and utterly above us, since it is lost, as the Apostle would say, in the majestic "depths of the riches both of the wisdom and of the knowledge of God."[a]

III.

Once more, note here the direction which our Lord purposely gave to the thoughts of His perplexed disciples. He does not turn them in upon themselves; He does not take their trouble, so to speak, sympathetically to pieces, and deal with its separate elements: He does not refute one by one the false reasonings which arise within them. He does not say to them: 'These disquietudes, these doubts, are mere mental disorders, or interesting experiences, and the mind itself can cure diseases which the mind has produced.' He would, on the contrary, have them escape from themselves; from the thick jungle of their doubts and fears and hopes and surmises; and come

[a] Rom. xi. 33.

to Him. Whatever they may think, or feel; He is there, seated on a throne which enthusiasm did not raise, and which doubt cannot undermine; in His Own calm, assured, unassailable Life. "Behold My Hands and My Feet, that it is I Myself: handle Me, and see; for a mere spirit hath not flesh and bones, as ye see Me have."

Religious men, speaking broadly, may be divided into two classes: those who are mainly occupied with themselves, and those who are mainly occupied with God. In modern language, we should call the religion of the first class, subjective; that of the second, objective. Subjective religion makes self the centre of all else; the soul's feelings, thoughts, experiences, are of first account; while Almighty God, His Truth and Grace, are interesting as ministering to or illustrating the varying experiences and moods of the thinking subject, of self. Thus self is the centre of the circle; God is only a point on the circumference. Objective religion, on the contrary, makes God the Being around Whom all else, the soul included, revolves. God, the Perfect and Self-existing, His Almightiness, His Intelligence, His Mercy, His Justice, His matchless Beauty, His unruffled and everlasting Peace; and then, His self-manifestation in the Eternal Son, Incarnate and Crucified, with the resulting Gifts of Grace, ministered by His Spirit, through His Sacraments; all this is of first account. When contemplating this splendid vision of the Truth the soul forgets itself. It forgets the relative, the shifting, the transitory, when it gazes on the Absolute, the Unchanging, the Eternal; it forgets its own petty, narrow, uncertain moods, when it looks out in good earnest on the awful and entrancing magnificence of God. Of objective religion, then, God is the centre; and self, with all its fitful experiences, is a mere point on the circumference.

Not that any religion, to be adequate, can be wholly of the one or of the other description. Objective religion, if unaccompanied by earnest care of the conscience, may easily degenerate into the sort of interest which an intelligent man cannot but take in the highest of all subjects, without its practically changing, moulding, invigorating his life. Doubtless to know God truly we must feel our personal need of Him; the fear of the Lord is the beginning of wisdom. To commune with our own hearts and search out our spirits, till we can say with David, "My sin is ever before me;"[a] to study self in order to be self-distrustful and humble, and for no other purpose whatever;—this is beyond doubt of vital import to our eternal peace. It is in the feebleness of his own resolutions, in the history of his own failures, often in the profound degradations of his own life, that the Christian learns the folly of "going about to establish his own righteousness" instead of submitting himself to the righteousness given by God in Jesus Christ.[b] Not to know self, is to be only a speculative divine, or a heartless formalist.

But the danger of our day lies mainly in the opposite direction. Of modern religion, the greater part is subjective. It is not our Lord Jesus Christ, but our faith in Him, our affections towards Him, our experiences, our assurances, our convictions, about which many of us think chiefly. If it is healthy to dwell on our sins, it is very far from healthy to dwell on our emotions. Man himself, not Christ, is the object of this sort of religious enthusiasm. There is in it no forgetfulness of self, for a single moment; there is nothing of the spirit of St. Paul's saying, "To me to live is Christ;"[c] since self is exalted at the very feet of the Redeemer. We even hear faith spoken of as a creative faculty. It is said by some to create whatever God

[a] Ps. li. 3. [b] Rom. x. 3. [c] Phil. i. 21.

gives us through His Sacraments. Others, with fatal consistency, go further, and speak as though faith could create the righteousness which justifies the sinner, or even the Attributes of the Eternal Being. And thus, as the human mind is represented, not as simply receiving, but as originating the strength which is to save it and the objects upon which it dwells, it soon finds out that it can change these objects at will. Idols may be made by the mind just as easily as with the hands; and so it comes to pass that, side by side with the Christ of the Gospels, there are false and imaginary Christs in Christendom, who approve of all that their votaries desire, who condemn only what their votaries dislike, who are crowned, not with thorns, but with roses, and who smile tolerance or recognition upon errors and excesses which the true Christ of Christendom has for ever condemned. And thus is realised the stern irony of the Psalmist: "With the holy Thou shalt be holy: and with a perfect man Thou shalt be perfect. With the clean Thou shalt be clean: and with the froward Thou shalt learn frowardness."[a] This is the ripe product of the subjective spirit in its exaggeration; and you will observe how closely allied it is to the conclusion of a Pantheistic thinker, that the whole object-matter of religion is really reflected into the heavens by the real or supposed necessities of the human soul. The only safeguard against it lies in clinging firmly to the objective character of real Christianity, as based upon assured historical facts. Let us remind ourselves that whether we believe them or not, the facts of the Christian Creed are true; and that faith only receives, but that it cannot possibly create or modify Christ and His gifts. Whether men believe or not in His Eternal Person, in the atoning virtue of His Death, in the sanctifying influences of His Spirit, in the invigorating

[a] Ps. xviii. 25, 26.

grace of His Sacraments;—these are certain truths. They are utterly independent of the hesitations and vacillations of our understandings about them. To ourselves, indeed, it is of great moment whether we have faith or not: to Him, to His truth, to His gifts, it matters not at all. "The Lord sitteth above this waterflood" of our changing and inconstant mental impressions; "the Lord remaineth a King for ever."[a] "If we believe not, yet He abideth faithful; He cannot deny Himself."[b]

Let this, then, be our Easter work; to forget ourselves, if we can; to gaze on the Wounds, to clasp the Feet of our Redeemer. Water cannot rise above its level; and if the soul of man is to be restored, it must be from without. It cannot be from within. Left to itself, the soul lacks the light, the strength, the impetus which it needs; it finds them in the Eternal Christ. It can, by faith, gaze on Him even now. It can, by faith, handle Him and discern that He is Man as well as God, God as well as Man, even now. Let us associate ourselves with that company in the upper chamber. Many of us share their trouble; why should we be denied their consolations? To our weakness, to our fears, to our indolent despair, to our barren self-complacency, He says, "Behold My Hands and My Feet, that it is I Myself: handle Me, and discern." Away, brethren, with the illusions which may have kept us from Him! Let us arise, and live.

[a] Ps. xxix. 10.   [b] 2 Tim. ii. 13.

END OF VOL. I.